BAKING RECIPES
FROM
THE WIVES & MOTHERS
OF
CIVIL WAR HEROES, HEROINES
&
OTHER NOTABLES

Authentic Baking Recipes of, and Trivia About,

Men and Women Involved in the

War Between the States

ISBN 0-7414-2589-0

Published by:

PUBLISHING.COM

1094 New De Haven Street, Suite 100
West Conshohocken, PA 19428-2713
Info@buybooksontheweb.com
www.buybooksontheweb.com
Toll-free (877) BUY BOOK
Local Phone (610) 941-9999
Fax (610) 941-9959

Printed in the United States of America

Printed on Recycled Paper

Published December 2005

"When we weren't killing each other

"We were the best of friends."

Unknown Union soldier

Foreword

My heartfelt gratitude and thanks goes to my good friends, Richard and Donna Bauman, for their help to me in completing this book in exactly the manner in which I had always intended it to be, or hoped it would be.

For without their combined computer expertise, unselfish assistance, and dedicated hard work, my book, because of an unbelievably horrific mess by a not to be named typist, would have in all probability been consigned to the junk heap of writer's dreams.

I must say that I had all but given up on the seemingly insurmountable task when they both stepped up and agreed to take on a most difficult task of repairing what I believed to be an irreparable mess of a book length manuscript. And I do not say this lightly as I have written and published more than 75 books without anyone's aid.

My words of gratitude should not be mistaken as a forward written just to have a forward, or to simply courteously thank some obscure typist, an illustrator, an editor or a multitude of friends and family members, spell checker, grammatical or who ever else an author usually appears to graciously thank for their assistance. Instead, this is meant to be a very special forward, one designed to honor two very special friends, Richard and Donna – two individuals without whose generous time and effort was graciously given to this book project.

Part of the Pelton Historical Cookbook Series

Includes the Following Titles

Baking Recipes of Our Founding Fathers

Historical Thanksgiving Cookery

Historical Christmas Cookery

Civil War Period Cookery

Revolutionary War Period Cookery

Categories Covered Include:

Confederate Military Leaders

Union Military Leaders

Heroes of the Blue and the Gray

Famous Women of the Civil War Era

Political Leaders of the Period

Includes the Favorite Recipes of:

Robert E. Lee

Ulysses S. Grant

Nathan Bedford Forrest

Jefferson Davis

Abraham Lincoln

John Mosby

Mary Edwards Walker

George Armstrong Custer

Stonewall Jackson

William Sherman

Jeb Stuart

Dedication

To my early ancestors, Barnabus Horton of Leichestershire, England, who sailed to America on the *Swallow* some time between 1633 and 1638 with his wife Mary and their two sons, Joseph and Benjamin. They landed at Hampton, Massachusetts, and were Puritans.

And also to General Nathan Bedford Forrest, a man whose name became so famous during the Civil War, that it symbolized the entire Confederate cause. During his phenomenal military career, Forrest was unquestionably the finest cavalry leader on either side of the conflict. So feared was this warrior on horseback that Union General Sherman swore to stop him even *"if it costs ten thousand lives and bankrupts the federal treasury."* But even Sherman had little success in this regard.

And lastly, to Stan Dalton, a highly dedicated man who most accurately portrays this great military leader, Nathan Bedford Forrest, at Civil War reenactments all over the country.

Contents

Preface – to Set the Tone

The *Civil War, War Between the States, the War for Southern Independence,* or as Generals Robert E. Lee and Nathan Bedford Forrest referred to this ungodly American travesty as *the "War of Northern Aggression"* still captures the imagination of Americans as does no other war in our history. How a war fought well over a century ago can still hold such power over the thinking, and stir the hearts of many Americans today, is astounding to say the very least.

The Confederate Republic, better known as the Confederate States of America, was invaded and ultimately overwhelmed by the sheer numbers of their Northern counterparts. This war was as controversial then as was the Vietnam War in modern day politics.

Read what famed New York Tribune journalist, Horace Greeley (1811-72) had to say:

"The right to secede may be a revolting one, but it exists nevertheless. … We hope to never live in a Republic where one section is pinned to the other section by bayonets. If the Declaration of Independence justified the secession of 3,000,000 colonists in 1776, I do not see why the Constitution ratified by the same men would not justify the secession of 5,000,000 Southerners from the Federal Union in 1861."

Dates Southern States Seceded from the Union

South Carolina	Dec. 20,	1860
Mississippi	Jan. 8,	1861
Florida	Jan. 10,	1861
Alabama	Jan. 11,	1861
Georgia	Jan. 19,	1861
Louisiana	Jan. 26,	1861
Texas	Feb. 1,	1861
Virginia	Apr. 17,	1861
Arkansas	May 6,	1861
North Carolina	May 20,	1861
Tennessee	June 8,	1861

*11 States belonged to the Confederate States
Kentucky and Missouri
were admitted to the Confederacy;
that accounts for the 13 stars on the
Confederate Battle Flag.*

Approximately 620,000 people died in the War for Southern Independence. This is the equivalent of five million deaths by standardizing this figure to match the population in the United States today. This would be 100 times the number of Americans losing their lives in the Vietnam War—and 17 times the number of our men and women killed in World War II.

Almost one-fifth of the Americans who served, died during this war.

Approximately 600,000 American soldiers were killed (in close to four years).

This figure includes more than 258,000 Confederate troops and more than 360,000 Union troops.

The death rate in the Civil war was higher than in any other war in American history.

In fact, the death rate claimed more American lives than *all* of our other wars combined!

Fighting during the Revolutionary War resulted in about 4,500 American battle deaths (in about five and one-half years).

More than 116,500 Americans died in World War I!

More than 450,000 Americans were killed in World War II (in three and one-half years).

Close to 53,650 Americans died during the time the Korean War was fought (in little more than three years).

At least 58,150 Americans met their maker during the Vietnam conflict (approximately eight and one-half years).

Yes, all of this and more took place in a war that really didn't have to happen in the first place.

Consider this astounding figure—one out of every four Confederate boys and men aging from 14 to 40, were killed in this reprehensible war. Unknown numbers in the hundreds of thousands on both sides in were wounded, lost limbs, or were otherwise maimed.

New York Times correspondent Samuel Williamson's son, Bayard, was killed in the War on July 2, 1863. As a result of this tragedy, the boy's father wrote this touching memorial to the memory of his only son. It pretty well sums up the horror and the hope or the entire Civil War:

"My pen is heavy, O, you dead, who at Gettysburg have baptized with your blood the second birth of Freedom in America, how you are to be envied! I rise from a grave whose wet clay I have passionately kissed, and I look up and see Christ spanning the battle-field with his feet, and reaching fraternal and loving up to Heaven, His right hand opens the gates of Paradise, --with his left he sweetly beckons to these mutilated, bloody, swollen forms to ascend."

1

Introducing Baking Recipes From the Wives & Mothers of Civil War Heroes, Heroines & Other Notables

Baking Recipes From the Wives & Mothers of Civil War Heroes, Heroines & Other Notables is a unique collection of special recipes dating from the Civil War period of our history. It's a practical baking book as well as the modern person's guide to authentic baking recipes from the Civil War period. These recipes were popular, or at least regularly used before, during and just after the Civil War or War Between the States. Many come from women who so expertly made bread and other baked goods for the legendary fighting men with the Union. These would include Generals Ulysses S. Grant, Abner Doubleday of later baseball fame, as well as the renowned George Armstrong Custer. And they are the  recipes used by mothers, wives and daughters of the Confederacy when they baked for their heroic leaders—men such as Generals Jonathan "Stonewall" Jackson and James Longstreet as well as others including Lieutenant Harry Buford (Loreta Janeta Velazquez) and the illustrious President of the Confederacy, Jefferson Davis.

Despite everything, the Civil War almost didn't happen. Brigadier General Robert Augustus Toombs (1810 to 1885) was Georgia's turbulent Congressman from 1845 to 1853 and U.S. Senator from 1853 to 1861. A successful planter and lawyer, Toombs led the Army of Northern Virginia at Peninsula, Second Bull Run and Antietam. He served briefly as Confederate Secretary of State under Jefferson Davis from March to July of 1861. Had President Davis listened to Toombs, the War Between the States might never have taken place. This man warned the Confederate President against an attack on Fort Sumter.

Toombs told Davis this: *"The firing upon that fort will inaugurate a civil war greater than and the world has yet seen. You will wantonly strike a hornet's nest which extends from mountains to ocean, and legions now quiet will swarm out and sting us to death. It is unnecessary; it puts us in the wrong; it is fatal."*

Despite this warning, Davis sent orders to General Beauregard, the man in command at Charleston, to demand the evacuation of Fort Sumter. In case of refusal, he was ordered "to reduce it." The Union officer in command, Major Robert Anderson, refused to surrender. A bombardment was begun on the morning of Friday, April 12, and continued until the following Sunday afternoon. The little garrison finally surrendered. All the military men were allowed to march out flying their colors. Not a man was killed on either side, but the War was begun.

Here's a marvelous recipe for **Graham Biscuits**. The Toombs' family handed it down over a period of years. His mother and grandmother prepared often for the family table, and especially when guests were visiting:

3 tsp baking powder   *Pinch of salt*
3 cups graham flour   *1-1/2 tbls sugar*
1 cup regular flour   *2 tbls shortening (melted)*
                    3 cups milk

Blend baking powder with both kinds of flour. Sift these ingredients together into a large wooden mixing bowl. Then stir in salt and sugar. Blend in melted shortening quickly and lightly. Slowly pour in milk last. Lightly stir until everything is smoothly blended. Knead dough only enough to prepare for rolling out. Use as few strokes as possible because too much kneading will ruin the biscuits. The dough should be extremely soft and pliable. If too stiff, simply add a little more milk. Then roll dough out into ½ to ¾ inch biscuit. Using an upside down drinking glass of the appropriate size, cut into small biscuits. Put biscuits in rows on floured baking tin. Place in quick oven (425 degrees) and bake for 10 to 15 minutes. Test for doneness by sticking toothpick in center of one or more muffins. They are done if toothpick comes out clean. **Note:** *Mrs. Toombs said: "This biscuit is very light and sweet. They are excellent eaten cold as well as hot."*

Baking during the Civil War period was far from an easy task. The women of the house made an art out of making tasty loaves of bread, biscuits, pastry, pies, cakes, cookies, and all of their other homemade goodies. In those days, homemakers couldn't always purchase good flour. Every sack or barrel or bag might present new baking problems. Flour always had to be tested for quality before using it for baking.

In 1761, Miss Mary Chew became the bride of William Paca (1740-1799) of Maryland. Her husband would later affix his signature to the *Declaration of Independence* on August 2, 1776. Here's how she wrote down her flour testing instructions in a 1765 recipe ledger:

> *"As good a test of flour as can be had at sight, is to take up a handful and squeeze it tight; if good, when the hand is unclasped, the lines on the palm of the hand will be plainly defined on the ball of flour. Throw a little lump of dried flour against a smooth surface, if it falls like powder, it is bad."*

The identical method of flour testing was still used by homemakers around 100 years later during the time the Civil War was raging around them. Many shady millers used unwanted additives in order to make a less expensive product in order to obtain more profit. My Great-great grandmother Huldah Horton developed a *"reliable"* method of determining the ingredients in her flour: It reads as follows:

> *"A solution of ammonia turns pure wheat flour yellow. If any corn has been ground with it, however, a pale brown. If peas or beans have been ground with it, a still dark brown."*

In the South, corn meal muffins, pound cake, rolls, cookies, pies, etc., were all baked in the oven of her wood stove. Good baking was simply a matter of experience. Women were able to satisfactorily prepare and bake these favorites with no reliable temperature gage. A good homemaker relied on how hot her oven *"felt"* when she was ready to bake. She simply stuck an arm in while counting 1001, 1002, 1003, etc. How hot her arm felt in a given number of seconds (or how long it took to scorch the hair on her arm) would determine whether or not her oven was at the correct temperature for whatever it was she wanted to bake. Homemakers of today, with all the modern conveniences in their kitchens, can hardly surpass the finished breads and cakes and pies baked so many years ago.

 Housewives of the mid-1800s baked, cooked, sewed, cleaned house and cut everyone's hair. She was the resident doctor of the house. And she was in charge of settling arguments by popping her kid's bottoms with the flat side of a cast iron skillet when a wooden paddle wasn't handy

.

Hot corn bread represented a Southern homemaker's hospitality. If cold corn bread was served, it was a sign that the particular guest was not welcome. This was her method of letting them know. Lieutenant Colonel John Pelham's mother made the following **Corn Bread** for her son:

3 cups white corn meal	*3 tbls baking powder*
1 cup flour	*1 tbls shortening*
1 tbls sugar	*3 eggs, well beaten*
1 tsp salt	*3 cups milk*

Sift the following into a large wooden mixing bowl: corn meal, flour, sugar, salt and baking powder. Thoroughly rub in cold shortening. Then blend in beaten eggs. Lastly, stir milk in gradually. Mix until a smooth, moderately stiff batter is attained. Pour into well-buttered, shallow baking pans (round pie tins are suitable. Place in rather quick oven (400-425 degrees) and bake for 30 to 40 minutes. Test for doneness by sticking toothpick in center of corn bread. It is done if toothpick comes out clean.

John Pelham (1836-1863) was, according to General Robert E. Lee, *"gallant and courageous"* at Fredericksburg. Born in Alabama, this idealistic young man resigned his U.S. Army_commission and left West Point in 1861. He offered his services to the Confederate cause. Pelham, a dedicated Christian, was willing to fight and, if necessary, to die for his beloved Confederacy. This dashing young officer firmly believed that he was *"fighting a holy war with the unconditional blessing of God Almighty.*" When this handsome young man was killed at Kelley's Ford, at least three lovely Southern Belles were said to have gone into mourning.

Who can possibly resist trying to make **Lady Cakes,** as Jefferson Davis liked to have placed before him on the dinner table? How about baking a few loaves of **Salt Rising Bread** as it was made by the mother of General Nathan Bedford Forrest? Or would you rather make a batch of **Potato Rolls** exactly the way Julia made them for her husband, General Ulysses S. Grant?

Most of these baked items are not difficult to make. Each recipe has been updated for the convenience of today's homemaker. The end result will be exactly as it was for our Civil War ancestors. For example, it would be quite a task to make President Lincoln's favorite **Almond Layer Cake** if the original recipe in paragraph form was the only one available to use. Here it is:

Cream one cup of butter and two cups of sugar lightly. Sift three cups of flour and two teaspoons full of baking powder together; then alternate with one cup of milk to the creamed mixture. Beat six egg whites until they form a stiff froth. To the first mixture add one cup of well-floured chopped blanched almonds and then one teaspoonful of vanilla. Now fold in the frothy egg whites to which has been added one-quarter teaspoonful of salt. Pour the batter in three pans about eight or nine inches across, and bake in a moderate oven. Cover each layer with boiled icing to which has been added a half-cup of blanched almonds.

Now look over the modern adaptation of this same Lincoln recipe with a list of ingredients followed by a paragraph of easy-to-follow instructions. This is exactly how every old historical recipe in this cookbook has been updated and made applicable for baking today:

Lincoln's boyhood home

9

3 cups flour	2 cups sugar
2 tsp baking powder	1 tsp vanilla
1 cup almonds, blanched	1 cups milk
chopped fine	6 eggs, whites only
1 cup butter	¼ tsp salt

Blend together the flour and baking powder in a large mixing bowl. Sift three times. Then stir in the chopped almonds and set aside temporarily. Beat butter and sugar together in a smaller bowl until it is creamy. Blend vanilla into this. Alternately stir in the flour mixture and milk until; it's all used. Set aside momentarily and beat together the egg whites and salt in another bowl. Continue until the egg whites are stiff and fluffy. Carefully fold stiff egg whites into your batter. Now grease and coat with flour three round nine-inch cake pans. Divide batter equally when pouring into each pan. Bake at 350 degrees for about 20 minutes. Test for doneness by sticking each cake with a toothpick. The cake is done when toothpick comes out clean when withdrawn. Set cake layers aside to thoroughly cool before frosting them.

While the above cake layers are cooling, go ahead and prepare a batch of Lincoln's favorite **Boiled Icing** as follows:

½ cup hot water	1/8 tsp cream of tartar
2 cups sugar	2 egg whites
1 tsp lemon juice	
½ cup almonds, blanched and chopped	

Boil the water in a clean saucepan. Stir in the sugar. Continue boiling until it strings, but **do not** stir. Drop the egg whites into a clean wooden mixing bowl and beat until stiff. Slowly stir the sugar-water mixture into the stiffly beaten egg whites. Blend mixture well. Now stir in the cream of tartar and finely chopped almonds. Lastly, add lemon juice. Beat thoroughly until mixture is thick and smooth. Immediately spread icing between each layer as well as on the top and sides of cake.

NOTE OF HISTORICAL INTEREST:
When cakes like the above were made in the Old South, many a housewife would stir a coin into the dough before baking. The family member finding the

coin in his or her piece of cake was believed to be going to have some sort of unexpected good luck of a financial nature. If the cake was served at a wedding, any single young woman finding the coin in her piece of cake was believed destined to be the next one married.

This old recipe for **Billy Goat Cookies** was found inscribed by Mary Boykin Miller Chesnut in an old family ledger. It was no more than a list of ingredients. However, Mrs. Chesnut knew exactly what to do with these ingredients as did most other homemakers of the day:

> *3 cups of flour*
> *1 cup of butter*
> *1-1/2 cups of brown sugar*
> *3 eggs*
> *1 cup of chopped raisins*
> *1 cup chopped walnuts*
> *1 scant teaspoon of soda sifted in flour*
> *1/4 scant cup of water*

Brigadier General James Chesnut, Jr. (1815-1885) was a fiery orator, an ardent secessionist and a staunch defender of slavery. This fourth generation South Carolina planter was a Princeton graduate and a devout Christian. He was an aide-de-camp to General P.G.T. Beauregard during the battles at Fort Sumter and First Bull Run. Chesnut was later a trusted advisor to the President of the Confederacy, Jefferson Davis, and his aide-de-camp from 1862 to 1864.

Captain John Ericsson (1803-89) was a brilliant engineer who had immigrated to the United States from Sweden in 1839. Ericsson designed the *USS Princeton* in 1844. It was the first warship ever built with underwater propellers invented by this man. Ericsson later designed, and supervised the building of, the Union's iron clad *USS Monitor*, the world's first turret ship. Construction was finished in a mere 100 days and the vessel was launched in January of 1862. She was a small flat craft, presenting very little surface for an adversary's cannon balls to strike. Amidships there was an iron cylinder made to revolve by machinery.

This revolving cylinder, or turret, carried two enormous guns that could shoot much heavier cannon balls than had ever been used before. This was the world's first revolving gun turret. After the Confederate ironclad frigate, the *CSS Merrimac,* had sunk the *USS Cumberland,* it had to withdraw from battle when going up against the *USS Monitor* on March 9, 1862. Here is a recipe favorite of the Ericsson family. It was one of his mother's many baking specialties:

Rice Muffins

2 eggs	*1 tsp sale*
1 cup boiled rice(cold)	*1 tbls butter*
4 cups milk	*2 cups flour*

Beat eggs in large wooden mixing bowl. Add cold rice, milk and salt. Blend well. Melt butter and stir it in with other ingredients in bowl. Lastly add flour and beat batter very hard. When smooth and lump free, pour into buttered muffin tins. Bake in quick oven (425 degrees) for about 20 minutes.. Test for doneness by sticking toothpick in center of one or more muffins. They are done if toothpick comes out clean. Send to table as soon as taken from oven. **Note:** *Ericsson's mother always made these treats on Sunday mornings, as they were her son John's favorite kind of muffin. She sometimes substituted whole-wheat flour in place of regular flour.*

One very special traditional cake recipe handed down from the Civil War era is this favorite from the family of Confederate Brigadier General Roger Atkinson Pryor (1828-1919). Mrs. Pryor made this wonderful sponge cake for her family each Christmas season in three distinct steps as follows:

Christmas Sponge Cake

Step 1:

5 egg whites	*5 egg yolks*
1 cup sugar, sifted 4 times	*½ lemon, rind only (grated)*
1 tbls lemon juice	*1 cup flour, sifted 4 times*
¼ tsp salt	

Beat egg whites until stiff. Gradually beat in 5 tbls of the sugar and set aside. Add lemon juice to egg yolks and beat until lemon colored and so thick that beater turns with difficulty. Add grated lemon rind and beat in remaining sugar. Combine egg yolks with egg whites and fold together with a spoon until mixture is blended evenly, Mix and sift together flour and salt in separate bowl. Fold this into egg mixture. Do not beat after adding flour to avoid breaking air bubbles. Pour

into an unbuttered 9-inch tube pan. Cut through mixture several times to break air bubbles. Bake at 350 degrees for 1 hour or more. When cake is done, loosen with spatula or knife and remove from tube pan. Turn out on wire rack and let stand until cool.

Custard

Step 2:

4 cups milk	*½ cup sugar*
2 eggs, beaten slightly	*¼ tsp salt*

1 tsp vanilla extract

Scald milk in covered saucepan. In a separate saucepan, combine beaten eggs with sugar and salt. Blend well. Stir scalded milk into egg mixture and stir constantly. Let cook until mixture coats spoon. Set aside and chill. Then stir in vanilla. If custard should curdle, beat until smooth.

Cake Assembly

Step 3:

3 cups split almonds, blanched   1-1/2 cups sherry wine
½ pint heavy cream

Carefully slice cake into three layers. Stick 1 cup of split almonds into each layer, dividing them as evenly as possible. Pour ½ cup of the sherry wine over each layer as it is reassembled. An hour before serving, pour the soft custard over the cake. Make occasional deep gashes with a knife so custard will seep all the way through cake. Whip the cream and place on cake in large tablespoonfuls.

General Roger Atkinson Pryor (1828-1919) was an influential Christian newspaper publisher in Virginia and a firebrand secessionist. He resigned from his first term in Congress in 1861 to join the Confederate Army and fought heroically at Seven Pines and Williamsburg. An impatient man who was disillusioned with the political machinations of the Confederate War Department, he resigned his commission and went on to fight as a mere private in August of 1863 with General Fitzhugh Lee's cavalry brigade. Pryor was taken prisoner by Union troops near Petersburg in November of 1864, but was given his freedom in a prisoner exchange a few months later.

Pearlash was a requisite for many cakes as a leavening agent prior to the breakout of the Civil War. Mrs. Leslie had a recipe for **Dover Cake** in her 1827 cookbook titled **SEVENTY-FIVE RECEIPTS.** In this she dissolved a *"half-teaspoon of pearlash in a little vinegar."* She warns the reader of its use for cakes:p*earlash will give it a dark color."* Approximately 30 years later, her book

was updated and she substituted *"sub-carbonate of soda"* as a leavening agent.

In her 1833 **AMERICAN FRUGAL HOUSEWIFE,** Lydia Marie Child also used pearlash for her cakes and other baked goods. Saleratus (sodium bicarbonate or baking soda) followed pearlash as a leavening. But for use only with sour milk in baking recipes. Many homemakers didn't like to use saleratus as it made their cakes yellow and coarse.

Hannah Widdifield's **PRACTICAL RECIPES FOR THE HOUSEWIFE** was published in 1856. Included in her book was this recipe:

"TO PREPARE SALERATUS FOR CAKE
    "Take one-quarter pound of saleratus, put it in a pint bottle, which fill with water; shake it well, and after remaining a sufficient length of time to settle, it will be fit for use. "If tightly corked, this will keep a long time, and when more than half is used, the bottle may be refilled with water."

Commercial baking powder wasn't available to homemakers of the past. They had to improvise and create up their own concoctions. Here are a couple of recipes from an old handwritten ledger of my Great great grandmother Huldah Radicke Horton:

"Baking Powder
"1 ounce sub-carbonate soda
"7 drachms tartaric acid
"Roll smoothly and mix thoroughly. Keep in a tight glass jar or bottle. Use one teaspoonful to a quart of flour."
                    or
"12 teaspoonfuls carb. Soda
"24 teaspoonfuls cream of tartar
"Put as above, and use in like proportion."

In 1855, *"a portable yeast"* was recommended in the **PRACTICAL AMERICAN COOKBOOK.** This consisted of blending baking soda with cream of tartar for bread making. The author said: *"This bread is easily made, requires little labor, no kneading or time for dough to rise."*

A recipe for one of the more popular kinds of potato yeast made and used during the Civil War comes from the mother of Confederate General "Jeb" Stuart. Here is how she prepared her yeast:

"6 large potatoes   *½ tablespoon of ginger*
"1 handful of hops   *2 tablespoons of salt*
"flour to suit   *¾ cup of yeast*
           "½ cup of sugar

"Boil the large potatoes in 6 cups water. Tie the hops in a small muslin bag and boil in with the potatoes. When thoroughly cooked, drain the water on enough flour to make a thin batter. Set this on the stove and scald it enough to cook the flour. This makes the yeast keep longer. Remove from the fire and let cool. Mash the potatoes and add them along with the sugar, ginger, salt and yeast. Blend well and let stand in a warm place until it has thoroughly risen. Then put the yeast in a large-mouthed jug and tightly cork. Store in a cool place." **Note:** *Mrs. Stuart said this "Be sure to scald the jug before putting in yeast. 2/3 cup of this yeast will make 4 nice loaves of homemade bread."*

Mrs. Stuart goes on to tell how she was able to make **Dry Yeast Cakes** from the above potato yeast recipe. Follow these simple instructions:

"Make a pan of yeast the same as that given above. Blend with it corn meal that has been sifted and dried. Knead well until it is thick enough to roll out. Then roll it out and cut into cakes or crumble up. Spread out and dry thoroughly in the shade. Store in a cool place."

James Ewell Brown Stuart (1833-1864) was born on Laurel Hill Plantation in Patrick County, Virginia. He graduated from West Point in 1854. Stuart wrote to Jefferson Davis in January of 1861 and requested a commission in the *"Army of the South."* He fast gained a reputation as a brilliant military strategist and fearless leader. His daring wartime exploits made him a legendary hero of the Confederacy. He was mortally wounded on May 11, 1864, during a fierce battle at Yellow Tavern, Virginia, just North of Richmond. Major Stuart's death was a devastating blow to the Confederacy. This dashing young Christian officer was but 31 years old when he died. He never doubted that he was fighting for what he called ***The will of the Almighty.***

"Ordinary yeast may be kept for several months," declares Julia Ward Howe (1819-1910), American writer, poet and reformer, *"by placing it in a close canvas bag, and gently squeezing out the moisture in a screw press, till the remaining matter becomes stiff as clay. It must be preserved in close stone vessels."*

In 1850, a patent was issued to Gail Borden (1801-75) of Brooklyn, New York for his *"Portable Soup Bread."* Mr. Borden baked a blend of vegetable flour and animal extracts in a flat, brittle cake. We know this today as the bouillon cube.

A patent was issued for Borden's condensed milk in 1851. Less than a decade later, America's first milk condensing plant was built in New Jersey. The Union Army purchased most of Borden's milk for use as field rations. Mr. Borden faced a unique problem during the war. His son Lee joined the Confederate Army and rode with the Texas cavalry. John Gail, his older son, decided to go in the other direction and fought for the Union.

An interesting sidelight during the time of the Civil War took place on May 19 and 20, 1856. Charles Sumner (1811-1874) was an uncompromising abolitionist and fervent anti-South Radical Republican Senator from Massachusetts. He made a fiery speech on the floor of the Senate that contained personal and tasteless allusions to Senator Butler of South Carolina. Two days later Butler's nephew Preston Brooks, Representative from South Carolina, walked up to Sumner. The unsuspecting man was absorbed in work at his desk in the Senate

Chamber. Without warning, Brooks began beating Sumner on the head with his cane until he nearly killed him. For three years, while Sumner was incapacitated and undergoing medical treatment, his chair in the Senate remained vacant. A motion was made to expel Brooks from Congress, but it failed to secure the necessary two-thirds vote. On July 14, Brooks finally resigned his seat and returned to South Carolina where he was given a heroes welcome. Three weeks later, Preston Brooks was overwhelmingly reelected to Congress.

Here are a couple of baking recipes from the families of these two men:

Mrs. Sumner's "Coconut Cookies"

"1 cup milk	*2 cups sugar*
"1/2 tsp baking soda	*1 cup coconut, grated*
"2/3 cup butter, melted	*1 tsp cream of tartar*
"flour to suit	

"Put milk into large wooden mixing bowl. Dissolve baking soda in milk. Stir in melted butter, sugar and grated coconut. Sift cream of tartar with a little flour. Beat this into mixture. Add sufficient flour to make soft dough. Put dough on floured board and roll out to ¼ inch thick sheet. Using an upside down drinking glass, cut into small round cookies. Place cookies on shallow buttered baking pan. Bake in quick oven (425 degrees) until lightly browned."

Mrs. Brooks' "Quick Graham Bread"

"½ cup brown sugar	*1 cup flour*
"¾ cup cold water	*1-1/3 tsp salt*
"½ cup shortening, melted	*1 tsp baking powder*
"¾ cup milk	*2 cups graham flour*

"Put brown sugar and cold water in wooden mixing bowl and stir until sugar is completely dissolved. Then stir in melted shortening and milk. Sift together into this mixture flour, salt and baking soda. Gradually add graham flour. Blend thoroughly. Grease one loaf pan. Pour batter into pan and bake in a moderately quick oven (375 degrees) for about one hour. Test for doneness by sticking toothpick in center of one or more muffins. They are done if toothpick comes out clean."

THE AMERICAN KITCHEN DIRECTORY AND HOUSEWIFE, of 1864, gave homemaker's advice on properly using her oven and how to take care of cast iron baking pans: *"New ovens, previous to being used, should have a fire kept in them for half a day. When the fire is removed, the mouth of the oven should be closed. It should not be baked* *in till heated the second time. If not treated in this manner, it will not retain their (sic) heat well.*

A recipe emerging from the Civil War era for *"Soda and Cream of Tartar Biscuits"* can be found in Mary Henderson's 1876, **PRACTICAL COOKING AND DINNER GIVING:**

"Ingredients: One quart of flour, one teaspoonful of soda, two teaspoonfuls cream of tartar, one even teaspoonful of salt, lard or butter the size of a small egg, and milk.

"Put the soda, cream of tartar and salt on the table; mash them smoothly with a knife; and mix well together; mix them as evenly in the flour as possible; then pass it all through a sieve two or three times. The success of the biscuits depends upon the equal distribution of these ingredients. Mix in the lard or butter (melted) as evenly as possible, taking time to rub it between the open hands to break any little lumps. Now pour in enough milk to make the dough consistent enough to roll out, mixing it lightly with the ends of the fingers. The quicker it is rolled out, cut and baked, the better will be the biscuits."

Yes, every recipe in **BAKING RECIPES FROM THE WIVES & MOTHERS OF CIVIL WAR HEROES, HEROINES & OTHER NOTABLES** is a classic in the historical sense. Each is known to have been a favorite of, or invention of, some family or individual that lived and loved and prayed while the Civil War raged on around them. Many were coveted treasures within a family, some famous, some not so famous, and handed down through the years or lost with the passage of time. Each delightful recipe is followed by often forgotten facts about the heroes and heroines of the as well as a few not so well known individuals. Also included are interesting biographical highlights about the person or family to whom the recipe is attributed.

Each recipe was among the best used in the North and the South during the time the Civil War was raging. Here they are presented for the first time for today's American families to enjoy and experience the pleasure of preparing, baking and serving—just as it was done in the past.

Here's a quick baking poem to end this chapter. An unknown early American authored it. It nicely sums up the art of good baking:

"With weights and measures just and true,

"Oven of even heat,

"Well buttered tins and quit nerves,

Success will be complete."

2

Bread Baking Recipes
to be Fondly Remembered

Potato Bread—
James Longstreet's Most Enjoyable

4 cups milk and water   2/3-cup yeast
2 potatoes, medium size   flour to suit

Prepare this mixture about bedtime. Boil potatoes and mash fine in a wooden mixing bowl. Blend in 4 cups warm milk and water (or just plain water), 2/3-cup yeast and mashed potatoes. Add sufficient flour to make thin batter. Carefully wrap and cover with woolen blanket in cold weather. Do not set where a draft will blow on it during rising process.

In the morning, knead the rising with sufficient flour until it becomes quite stiff. Place back in bowl, cover, and allow to rise again. Then knead into 5 loaves and put each loaf into greased bread pan. Again cover and set in warm place until the loaves rise to double in size. Bake in moderately quick oven (375 degrees) 20 to 35 minutes or until done. Test for doneness by sticking toothpick in center of each loaf. Toothpick will come out clean if bread is done.

James Longstreet (1821-1904)

HERITAGE: Born in South Carolina. Raised in Georgia and Alabama. Son of a farmer.

RANK: General.

FOUGHT FOR: Confederacy.

RELIGION: Christian. See quote below.

MARRIAGE: Unknown.

CHILDREN: Unknown.

EDUCATION: West Point graduate – class of 1842.
> Graduated near the bottom of his class.

CAREER HIGHLIGHTS & TIDBITS: Considered by General Lee to be one of his most reliable commanders.
> Dubbed him as his "Old War Horse".
> Seriously wounded during a counterattack at the Battle of the of the Wilderness in 1864. Unable to return to fighting for six months.
> Had earlier fought in the Mexican War under the command of Zachary Taylor, who would later become President of the United States.

QUOTABLE QUOTE: Once said this: *"I am pleased to say: I believe in God, the Father, and his only begotten Son, Jesus Christ, our Lord. It is my custom to read one or more chapters of my bible daily for comfort, guidance, and instruction."*

SAW ACTION AT: First Battle of Bull Run, Second Bull Run, Williamsburg, Seven Pines, Fredericksburg, Antietam, Manassas, Chickamauga, The Wilderness, Petersburg, Richmond, Knoxville, etc.

LITTLE KNOWN FACT: He and General Grant, and their wives, had developed a close, lasting friendship when they had served together at Jefferson barracks during the 1840's.

Turnip Bread—
As Made by Mrs. Butler on Thanksgiving

3 turnips, mashed   3 cups flour
1 yeast cake

Peel skin from a few turnips and discard. Put turnips in kettle and cover with water. Bring to boil and cook until they become soft and mushy. Drain all water from kettle. Squeeze turnips dry as possible. Then mash them. Measure out 3 cups of flour. Blend mashed turnips with the flour and crumbled yeast cake. Add sufficient warm water to make a smooth, soft dough. Knead thoroughly. Form into 2 nice loaves. Put into greased bread pans. Again cover and set aside in warm place to rise. Then put in moderate oven (350 degrees) and bake for about 30 minutes or until done. Test for doneness by sticking toothpick in center of each loaf. Toothpick will come out clean if bread is done. The loaves should be nicely browned on top.

Note*: Any left over mashed turnips after making the bread can be used to make more loaves, or as a vegetable dish at dinner time.

Benjamin Franklin Butler (1818-1893)

HERITAGE: Born and raised in Deerfield, New Hampshire.

RANK: General.

FOUGHT FOR: Union.

EDUCATION: Schooling unknown. Became a nationally known and influential criminal lawyer in Massachusetts.

MARRIAGE: Unknown.

CHILDREN: Unknown.

CAREER HIGHLIGHTS & TIDBITS: Gave strong support to Jefferson Davis as President of the Confederate States of America.
  A typical politically appointed General with few, if any qualifications to be a military leader.
  Made no contribution to the success of the Union during the War Between the States.
  His first major military disaster occurred at Fredericksburg.
  His incompetence at Fort Fisher and Petersburg finally cost him his command position.
  Became military governor of New Orleans in May of 1862.
  Was dictatorial, corrupt and power-mad.
  Issued his notorious *"Woman Order."*
  Per this controversial order, any woman caught insulting a Union military man would be punished as a prostitute.

QUOTABLE QUOTE: *"I hold the rebellion is treason, and that treason, if persisted in, is death."* *(December 24, 1862)*

SAW ACTION AT: Big Bethel, Petersburg, Fort Fisher, Fort Hatteras, Fort Clark, New Orleans, Fredericksburg, etc.

LITTLE KNOWN FACT: Hanged a man in New Orleans for merely tearing down a Union flag.

White Bread—
As Eaten by Stonewall Jackson

1 yeast cake	5 tsp salt
1 tbls flour	1 cup condensed milk (warm)
1 tbls sugar	3 cups water (warm)
½ cup water (lukewarm)	or
6 cups flour	2 cups milk (scalded)
½ cup sugar	2 cups water (warm)

4 tbls shortening (melted)

Crumble yeast cake in small wooden bowl. Add 1 tbls flour, 1 tbls sugar and 1/2 cup lukewarm water. Blend these ingredients. Cover with towel and set aside in warm place. Let yeast get bubbly and thick. Meanwhile, put 6 cups flour in large wooden mixing bowl. Add the sugar and salt. Blend melted shortening with the warm milk-water mixture. Add this to the flour mixture in wooden mixing bowl. Stir lightly – not very much (only until flour is dampened). Lastly, add bubbly yeast mixture to the flour in other bowl. Stir well. Turn dough out on floured board and knead thoroughly. Kneading must be continued until dough is no longer sticky. This is the minimum amount of kneading. For best results, keep on beating the dough with the hands for at least 10 minutes. Sprinkle flour on board very gradually as required while kneading. Be careful not to use abundant flour as it will add too much to the dough and make the bread coarse. After kneading, put dough ball into a large greased bowl. Cover with towel or blanket. Set aside in warm place. Leave until dough has doubled in size (for about 1 to 2 hours). When dough has risen, punch it down to get air out. Cut into 4 loaves and place in greased bread pans. When all loaves are cut, take one at a time out of its pan. Place back in greased bowl and knead into shape. Then put back into baking pans. Again cover. Set aside to rise (about 1 hour). Put in a moderately quick oven (375 degrees). Bake 20 to 30 minutes, or until bread is hollow sounding when tapped on. Test for doneness by sticking toothpick in center of each loaf. Toothpick will come out clean if bread is done. The loaves should be nicely browned on top. When done, empty bread pans onto a clean towel. Butter the top of each loaf

"Stonewall" Jackson (1824-1863)

HERITAGE: Parents died in poverty when he was a child.
Grew up as orphan in Clarksburg, Virginia. An uncle raised him.

RANK: General.

FOUGHT FOR: Confederacy.

RELIGION: Christian – Never wrote or sent a letter on Sunday.
Not only did he preach, but he also lived his faith (See below).

EDUCATION: Little formal education.
West Point graduate – class of 1846. Graduated 17th in class of 59.
Class included future leaders such as Confederate General A.P. Hill and Union General McClellan

MARRIAGE: First wife, Eleanor Junkin, died in 1854. Married Mary Anna Morrison three years later.
Both wives were daughters of Presbyterian ministers.

CAREER HIGHLIGHTS & TIDBITS: Accidentally shot by one of his own men while on a reconnaissance mission at dusk.
He was General Daniel Harvey Hill's brother-in-law.
His arm is buried in Elwood, Virginia.

QUOTABLE QUOTE(S): *"Nobody seems to understand him,"* said a member of his staff. *"...When we ordinary mortals can't comprehend a genius, we get even with him by calling him crabby."*

SAW ACTION AT: First Bull Run, Manassas, Winchester, Port Republic, Fredericksburg, Antietam, Sharpsburg, etc.

LITTLE KNOWN FACT: In a letter to his pastor, Jackson said: *"My Dear Pastor, In my tent last evening, after a fatiguing day's service, I remembered that I failed to send you my contribution for our colored Sunday School. Enclosed you will find a check for that object, which please acknowledge at your earliest convenience."*

Whole Wheat Bread—
General Miles Favorite

1 yeast cake	1-1/2 cups milk,
3 tbls brown sugar	scalded and cooled
1-1/2 cups water,	3 tbls butter, melted
lukewarm	7-1/2 cups whole wheat flour
	1 tsp salt

Put yeast and brown sugar in a wooden mixing bowl. Add lukewarm water and let it dissolve. Then stir in milk and melted butter. Gradually blend in the whole-wheat flour. Lastly add salt. Knead thoroughly, being sure to keep dough soft and pliable. Then place dough ball in well-greased bowl. Cover and set aside in warm place for about 2 hours. When doubled in bulk, turn dough out lightly floured kneading board. Cut dough into 4 equal pieces and form into loaves. Place each loaf in a well-greased bread pan. Cover and again set aside to rise for about 1 hour or until light and fluffy. Bake in moderate oven (350 degrees) for 20 to 25 minutes. Test for doneness by sticking toothpick in center of each loaf. Toothpick will come out clean if bread is done. The loaves should be nicely browned on top. When done, empty bread pans onto a clean towel. Butter the top of each loaf.

Nelson Appleton Miles(1839-1925)

HERITAGE: Born and raised in Boston, Massachusetts.

RANK: General.

FOUGHT FOR: Union.

RELIGION: Christian. Prayed constantly while a mere store clerk for a chance at military greatness.

EDUCATION: Unknown.

MARRIAGE: Unknown.

CHILDREN: Unknown.

CAREER HIGHLIGHTS & TIDBITS: Started out as a clerk in a Boston store.

     Dreamed of attaining military glory in his life.

     A brilliant and natural military tactician.

     Led his men into battle heroically during the Battle of Antietam in September of 1862.

     Immediately promoted to the rank of Colonel of the New York 61st after this impressive showing of leadership qualities.

     Later became a famous Indian fighter on the Western frontier.

     Commanded the detachment that captured Geronimo in 1886.

     In charge of the detachment assigned the duty of guarding the President of the Confederacy while he was incarcerated in Fortress Monroe, Virginia.

     Went on to become Commander-in-Chief of the United States Army from 1895 to 1903.

SAW ACTION AT: Chancellorsville, The Wilderness, Spotsylvania, Petersburg, Antietam, etc.

LITTLE KNOWN FACT: Shot in the hip during the fighting at Glendale. This wound would bother him for the rest of his life.

Wholesome Buttermilk Bread—
a Davis Family Favorite

2 cups buttermilk	1 tsp baking powder
flour to suit	pinch of salt
¼ cup yeast	2 tbls butter, melted

Heat buttermilk until scalding. Pour into large wooden mixing bowl. Stir in enough flour to make a tolerably thick batter. Add yeast and stir well. Cover bowl with heavy towel. Set aside in warm place to rise (about 5 hours). When dough is light (has risen) dissolve baking powder in a little hot water. Blend it, the salt, melted butter, and enough flour to make the dough comfortable to handle. Turn dough out on floured board. Knead well for at least 15 minutes. Form into 2 or 3 loaves. Put into well-greased bread pan. Cover with towel and set aside in warm place. Let rise again until loaves are light and fluffy feeling. Bake in moderately quick oven (375 degrees). When done, empty bread pans onto a clean towel. Butter the top of each loaf.

Note: This makes a very white and wholesome bread. Test for doneness by sticking toothpick in center of each loaf. Toothpick will come out clean if bread is done. The loaves should be nicely browned on top. When done, empty bread pans onto a clean towel. Butter the top of each loaf.

Jefferson Davis (1808-1889)

HERITAGE: Born in Kentucky.

Tenth child of a settler who fought during the Revolutionary war.

POSITION: President of the Confederate States of America.

FOUGHT FOR: Confederacy.

RELIGION: Christian – Studied at a Roman Catholic seminary in Kentucky. Came very close to renouncing his family's Baptist faith.

EDUCATION: West Point graduate – class of 1828. Graduated one year ahead of Robert E. Lee. Also attended Transylvania University.

MARRIAGE: First married in 1835 to the daughter of Zachary Taylor. She died three months later.

Remarried in 1845 to Varina Howell, the daughter of a prominent Mississippi planter.

CAREER HIGHLIGHTS & TIDBITS: Suffered greatly from a painful eye disease in the late 1850's.

Afflicted with other ailments including neuralgia.

Hot-tempered and inflexible.

Described by wife, Varina, as a "mere mass of throbbing nerves."

Quite often gave his support to mediocre Generals such as Braxton Bragg at the expense of more capable military leaders.

Departed swiftly from Richmond on April 3, 1865, just ahead of Union occupation and troops.

Captured near Irwindale, Georgia on May 10, 1865.

Held prisoner in Fortress Monroe for two years.

Treated harshly like a common criminal.

Finally released in 1877.

LITTLE KNOWN FACTS: Wrote his two volume *The Rise and Fall of the Confederate Government* from 1878 to 1881.

Died in New Orleans approximately three weeks before Christmas on December 6, 1889.

Milk Yeast Bread—
As Made by Albert Sidney Johnston's Mother

½ cup corn meal
1 tsp baking soda
1 tsp salt

flour to suit
3 cups warm milk

At noon the day before baking, take corn meal and put it in a wooden mixing bowl. Pour in enough boiling hot milk to make a mixture the thickness of battercakes. Cover with heavy cloth or towel and place where it will keep warm.

 Before breakfast the next morning pour 2 cups boiling water into a pitcher. Add 1 tsp baking soda and 1 tsp salt. Stir and allow mixture to cool enough so it won't scald the flour. Then add enough flour to make a rather stiff batter. Now add the cup of meal and milk that was set aside the day before. This mixture will be full of tiny bubbles. Mix this all together and place pitcher in kettle of warm water. Carefully cover top with folded towel. Put it where it will keep warm. You will be surprised to see how soon the yeast batter will be at the top of the pitcher. After it has risen, pour batter into large wooden mixing bowl. Add 3 cups warm milk (or ½ milk and ½ water). Add flour enough to knead it into 5 loaves. Knead a little harder than for biscuits. Place each loaf in a greased bread pan. Cover, set in warm place and allow to rise to top of baking pan. Then put into moderately quick oven (375 degrees) and bake for 25 to 35 minutes. Test for doneness by sticking toothpick in center of each loaf. Toothpick will come out clean if bread is done. The loaves should be nicely browned on top. When done, empty bread pans onto a clean towel. Butter the top of each loaf.

Albert Sidney Johnston (1803-1862)

HERITAGE: Born in Washington, Kentucky.

RANK: General.

FOUGHT FOR: Confederacy.

RELIGION: Christian. Attended Sunday School and church regularly as a child.

EDUCATION: West Point graduate – class of 1826.

MARRIAGE: Unknown.

CHILDREN: Unknown.

CAREER HIGHLIGHTS & TIDBITS: Secretary of war for the Republic of Texas from 1838 to 1840.
    Wounded in leg on first day of fighting at Shiloh on April 6, 1862.
    Subsequently died from this injury.
    Loss was called *"irreparable"* by Jefferson Davis.
    Davis once called him *"the greatest soldier…then living."*
    Turned down offer by Lincoln to be General Winfield Scott's second-in-command.
    Instead chose to become a full General in the Confederate cause.
    Oversaw the retreat of Confederate forces from Nashville.

QUOTABLE QUOTE: Said Jefferson Davis in 1861: *"I hoped and expected that I had others who would prove Generals, but I knew I had one, and that was Sidney Johnston,"*

SAW ACTION AT: Shiloh.

LITTLE KNOWN FACT: Appointed to be the commander of the Texas Army. Resulted in a duel with another officer who believed that he should have been given the promotion instead of Johnston.

German White Bread—
A Barksdale Specialty

2 cups milk (boiled)   ½ cup yeast
¾ cup sugar   2 tbls butter or lard
                              flour to suit

 Blend well-boiled milk, yeast and enough flour to make a batter (rising) about the consistency of griddlecakes. Cover bowl with towel. Set in warm place to rise. This should take no longer than 1/2 hour. When light and foamy, mix in the sugar and butter (or lard). Add enough flour to make as soft a dough as can be handled. Flour pastry board well. Place dough ball on board and proceed to roll out to about ½ inch thick sheet. Cut dough sheet in half. Lay each sheet in large baking tin. Make about 12 indentures on top of each loaf. Use fingers for this. Put a small piece of butter in each. Let stand for second rising. When perfectly light, put in moderately quick oven (375 degrees) for 15 to 20 minutes. Test for doneness by sticking toothpick in center of each loaf. Toothpick will come out clean if bread is done. The loaves should be nicely browned on top. When done, empty bread pans onto a clean towel. Butter the top of each loaf.

Note: To add a different touch, sift a mixture of 1 tbls sugar and 1 tsp cinnamon over the loaves prior to placing in oven.

William Barksdale (1821-1863)

HERITAGE: Born in Tennessee.

RANK: General.

FOUGHT FOR: Confederacy.

RELIGION: Christian.

EDUCATION: Unknown.

MARRIAGE: Unknown.

CHILDREN: Unknown.

CAREER HIGHLIGHTS & TIDBITS: Fought in Mexican War.
Served as a congressman in 1861 as a Democrat.
Resigned from Congress in January of 1861 and joined the Confederate Army.
His unit became known as "Barksdale's Mississippi Brigade."
Attached to Lafayette McLaw's Division of General James Longstreet's corps.
Commanded a brigade that was involved in especially heavy fighting.
One of the better Confederate fighting units in the Civil War.
Publisher of a popular pro-slavery newspaper.
Very distinguished-looking lawyer.
Wounded at Peach Orchard, Virginia.
Died the next day.

SAW ACTION AT: First Bull Run, Peach Orchard, Peninsular Campaign, Antietam, Fredericksburg, Chancellorsville, Gettysburg, etc.

LITTLE KNOWN FACT: Wounded at Peach Orchard, Gettysburg, Pennsylvania, on July 2, 1863. Died the next day. Just before Barksdale died, he said: *"Tell my wife I am shot, but that we fought like hell."*

Whole Wheat Bread—
As Enjoyed by General Sherman

14 cups whole wheat flour   ½ cup butter (optional)
1 tsp salt   ¾ cup yeast
2 cups milk (optional)

Sift flour into large bread pan or wooden mixing bowl. Make a hole in the middle. Pour in the yeast. Stir slightly. Then pour in milk (or water) to act as the "wetting." Use warm milk in the winter and cold milk in the summer. If water is used for the "wetting" dissolve in it the butter. If milk is used then no butter is necessary. Stir in the "wetting very lightly. Do not mix all the flour in it. Cover bowl or pan with thick blanket or towel. Set aside in warm place to. Rise. This called *putting the bread in sponge*. This should not be set overnight during the summer months.

In the morning add salt and proceed to mix all flour in pan with the sponge. Add milk or water as required to gain the proper consistency. Knead thoroughly. Let stand 2 or more hours until it has risen and become quite light and fluffy. Remove dough and place on floured board. Proceed to knead a long time. Cut dough into small pieces and mold then together again and again. Do this until dough is elastic under the pressure of the hands. Use as little flour as possible while accomplishing this segment of the process.

When dough is ready, break into 6 chunks and shape each loaf. Put loaves in greased bread pans. Cover once again and set aside to rise until bulk is doubled. When ready to put in oven, the oven should be ready to receive them. It should be hot enough to brown a teaspoon of flour in 5 minutes. Allow loaves to stand another 10 to 15 minutes. Then prick each loaf 3 or 4 times with a fork. Place loaves in moderate oven (350 degrees) for from 45 to 60 minutes. Test for doneness by sticking toothpick in center of each loaf. Toothpick will come out clean if bread is done. The loaves should be nicely browned on top.

When bread has finished baking, remove from oven and turn each loaf out of the pan. Wrap loaves while still hot, in a towel or thick cloth. Stand loaves up against pans until they have cooled. Remove towel and store loaves in well-covered tin box or stone crock.

William Tecumseh Sherman (1820-1891)

HERITAGE: Born in Lancaster, Ohio. Son of an Ohio Supreme Court Justice. Orphaned at nine years of age.

RANK: General.

FOUGHT FOR: Union.

RELIGION: Christian – Both he and wife were Roman Catholics.

EDUCATION: Early education at local academy.
West Point graduate – sixth in his class of 1840.

CAREER HIGHLIGHTS & TIDBITS: Fought with distinction in the Mexican War.
Resigned from the army in 1853 to become a banker.
The bank failed as a result of mismanagement..
Started practicing law.
Lost his one and only case.
Led his troops to victory in Charleston, South Carolina, on February 18, 1865., by soundly thrashing General Beauregard.
Among the greatest of all Union Generals in the Civil War.
He started his famous *"March to the Sea"* on November 15, 1864.
Told General Grant that he would *"make Georgia howl!"*
Marched his 60,000 man army though the interior of Georgia. Cut a 60-mile swath of indescribable devastation and destruction.

QUOTABLE QUOTE(S): *"The skill of the men in collecting forage [pillaging and looting] was one of the features of this march; often was I amused at their strange collections."*
In June of 1864 he stated, *"There will be no peace in Tennessee until [Nathan Bedford] Forrest is dead!"*
SAW ACTION AT: Chattanooga, Vicksburg, First Battle of Bull Run, Shiloh, his famous *"march to the Sea."*

LITTLE KNOWN FACT: General Joseph Johnston, an old Confederate adversary during the war, was a pallbearer at his funeral

Graham Bread—
E. Kirby Smith Often Ate This

¾ cup wheat flour   1 tsp salt
½ cup yeast   2 cups water (warm
½ cup molasses   graham flour to suit
　　　　　tsp baking soda

This recipe should be started at night. Blend wheat flour, yeast, molasses, salt and warm water in a large wooden mixing bowl. Add sufficient graham flour to make batter as stiff as can be stirred with large wooden spoon. Cover bowl with thick towel and set aside overnight in warm place to rise. In the morning, add the baking soda dissolved in a little warm water. Blend everything well. Put mixture in 2 well-greased, medium-sized bread pans. Each pan should be about half full. Cover and let stand in warm place until batter rises to top of pans. Bake for 1 hour in a moderately quick oven (375 degrees). Test for doneness by sticking toothpick in center of each loaf. Toothpick will come out clean if bread is done.

Note: Pans should be covered for about 20 minutes when first placed in oven. Use thick brown paper or an old tin cover for this. It will prevent upper crust from hardening before loaves have risen enough. If these directions are correctly followed, the bread will not be heavy or sodden. It never fails!

Edmond Kirby Smith (1824-1893)

HERITAGE: Born in Florida.
Son of Connecticut attorney.
Father was War of 1812 veteran.

RANK: General.

FOUGHT FOR: Confederacy.

RELIGION: Christian
Once seriously considered becoming an Episcopal minister.

EDUCATION: West Point graduate – class of 1845.

CHILDREN: Raised 11 children.

CAREER HIGHLIGHTS & TIDBITS: Decided to become a soldier at the age of 12 years.
Once fought Indians in Texas.
Fought in the 5th infantry during the Mexican War.
Taught mathematics at the University of the South.
Also taught mathematics at West Point for three years.
Helped organize the army of Shenandoah in early 1861.
Led a division under General Beauregard.
Chief of Staff under General Joseph's Johnston at Harper's Ferry.
Badly wounded during the Battle of First Bull Run in 1863.
President of the University of Nashville from 1870-1875.
Once headed the Atlantic Pacific Telegraph Company.
Went into exile in Mexico for a time after the war ended.

SAW ACTION AT: Harper's Ferry, First Bull Run, Cumberland Gap, Kentucky, Perryville, etc.

LITTLE KNOWN FACT: Surrendered the last Confederate Army in Galveston, Texas on June 2, 1865

Unfermented Graham Bread— Mrs. Toombs Very Best

3 cups graham flour   1-1/2 tsp salt
1 cup wheat flour   4 tsp baking powder
½ cup sugar   milk to suit

Blend graham flour and wheat flour in large wooden mixing bowl. Stir in sugar, salt and baking powder. Add sufficient milk to make as stiff a batter as can be stirred with a large wooden spoon. When everything has been thoroughly blended, turn batter out into 2 well-buttered bread pans. Place in moderate oven (350 degrees) and bake for about 45 minutes or less. Test for doneness by sticking toothpick in center of each loaf. . Toothpick will come out clean if bread is done.

Note: Water may used in place of milk. In such cases a lump of butter the size of a walnut must be, melted and stirred into the batter.

Robert Augustus Toombs (1810-1885)

HERITAGE: Native of Georgia.

RANK: General.

FOUGHT FOR: Confederacy.

RELIGION: Christian.

EDUCATION: Studied law at the University of Virginia.

CAREER HIGHLIGHTS & TIDBITS: A turbulent Georgia Congressman from 1845 to 1885.
> Totally against secession initially.
> Turned secessionist after the 1860 failure of the Crittenden Compromise.
> Served in the United States Congress (1845-1853).
> United States Senator from 1853 to 1861.
> Successful planter and lawyer.
> Briefly and unhappily served as Secretary of State under Jefferson Davis from March to July in 1861.
> Led the Army of Northern Virginia for a time in various battles.
> His brigade fought with distinction while fighting at Antietam.
> Was wounded in the hand while fighting at Antietam.
> Ran against Jefferson Davis for the President of the Confederate States of America.
> Lost this hard fought election.
> Strongly opposed the Southern defensive strategy.
> Resigned his army commission in March of 1863.
> Was upset after being denied a promotion.
> Suffered from blindness in his later years.
> Became an alcoholic as an old man.

SAW ACTION AT: Second Bull Run, Antietam, Malvern Hill, and during the Atlanta Campaign.

LITTLE KNOWN FACT: Bitter when he lost his Presidential bid against Jefferson Davis.

Pumpernickel Bread—
Mrs. Polk's Prize Recipe

1-1/2 cups water (warm)
3 packs dry yeast
½ cup molasses
 3-1/2 tsp salt
3-3/4 cups flour, sifted

3 tbls caraway seeds
2-3/4 cups rye flour.
2 tbls butter, softened

Put warm water in large wooden mixing bowl. Add yeast and stir until it dissolves. Blend in molasses, salt and caraway seeds. Put in rye flour and soft butter. Blend well with large wooden spoon. When smooth add regular flour and thoroughly mix with hands. Turn dough out on floured board. Knead hard for at least 10 minutes. Cover with heavy towel or cloth. Set aside to rise in warm place. Should double in size within 2 hours. Test by pressing fingers into dough. Indentations will be left if the dough has risen enough. Then punch dough down hard. Cover and allow to again rise. It should almost double in size within 40 minutes. When risen, cut dough in half and shape into 2 round, slightly flattened loaves. Butter a shallow baking sheet and liberally sprinkle with corn meal. Place rye loaves on opposite corners of pan.. Cover with damp towel and set aside to rise for 1 hour. Then remove towel and put loaves into moderate oven ((350 degrees). Bake for about 35 minutes, or until loaves are nicely browned. Test for doneness by sticking toothpick in center of each loaf. . Toothpick will come out clean if bread is done.

Leonidas Polk(1806-1869)

HERITAGE: Father assisted in the founding of the University of North Carolina.

Father fought in the Revolutionary War.

RANK: General.

FOUGHT FOR: Confederacy.

RELIGION: Christian. Organized a "praying squad" during his senior year at West Point.

Had been converted while in West Point by the new chaplain.

EDUCATION: West Point graduate.

Also studied for four years at the University of North Carolina.

CAREER HIGHLIGHTS & TIDBITS: Resigned his army commission in order to attend the Virginia Theological Seminary.

Ordained as a priest in the Episcopal Church in May of 1831.

Served in the Confederate military while retaining his position in the Episcopal church.

Owned 400 slaves through an inheritance of his wife.

Established Sunday School for his slaves.

His sugar plantation was a financial failure.

Became Bishop of Louisiana in 1841.

Accepted a commission of Major General at the request of President of the Confederate States of America, Jefferson Davis.

His men fondly referred to him as *"Bishop Polk"*.

He and Jefferson Davis were lifelong friends.

Killed at Marietta, Georgia during Sherman's Atlanta campaign.

A sharpshooter (sniper) shot him from his saddle.

SAW ACTION AT: Shiloh, Perryville, Stone's River, Chickamauga, The Atlanta Campaign, etc.

LITTLE KNOWN FACTS: He and Jefferson Davis had been cadets at the same time while attending West Point.

Kinsman of James Knox Polk – 11th President of the United States.

Hominy Bread—
A Reynolds Family Special

1 cup hominy   1 cup milk
1 tbls shortening, melted   ½ cup corn meal
2 eggs, well beaten   ½ tsp salt
                1 tsp baking powder

Blend hominy, melted shortening, beaten eggs and milk in a large wooden mixing bowl. Stir in corn meal, salt and baking powder. Set aside while greasing a large baking pan. Now pour batter into pan. Bake in quick oven (425 degrees) for 35 minutes or until rich golden brown. Test for doneness by sticking toothpick in center of each loaf. Toothpick will come out clean if bread is done.

John Fulton Reynolds (1820-1863)

HERITAGE: Born and raised in Lancaster, Pennsylvania.

RANK: General.

FOUGHT FOR: Union.

RELIGION: Christian. Once wrote a letter to his mother just before going into battle: *"Never deny the truth of the Bible. Never show disrespect to the Lord."*

EDUCATION: West Point graduate – class of 1841. Was 26th in a class of 52.

MARRIAGE: Never married.

CHILDREN: None.

CAREER HIGHLIGHTS & TIDBITS: Extremely highly regarded for his bravery and his leadership qualities.
> Commandant of West Point when the Civil War broke out.
> Fought with distinction during the Mexican War.
> Captured in July of 1862 at Glendale (White Oak Swamp) during the Seven Days Battle.

QUOTABLE QUOTE(S): At Gettysburg on July 1, 1863 he said this: *"The enemy is advancing in strong force. I will fight him inch by inch, and if driven into the town I will barricade the streets and hold him back as long as possible."*

SAW ACTION AT: Mechanicsville, Gaine's Mill, Seven Days Battle, Second Bull Run, Fredericksburg, Chancellorsville, etc.

LITTLE KNOWN FACTS: Killed by a sniper on the first day of the Battle of Gettysburg.
Mortally wounded on July 1, 1863 he yelled to the men under his command: *"Forward! For God's sake, forward."*

Special Laxative Bread— From the Family Ulysses Simpson Grant

2 cups whole wheat flour   2 cups oatmeal
2 cups flour   1 yeast cake
                     warm water to suit

Put all of the above ingredients in a large wooden bowl or pan and blend thoroughly. Add sufficient warm water to work into a smooth dough. Cover with towel or cloth. Set aside to rise in warm place. When dough has risen, divide into 2 equal pieces. Mold into loaves smoothly and quickly. Place both loaves in well-greased bread pans. Bake immediately in moderate oven (350 degrees) for about 25 minutes. Test for doneness by sticking toothpick in center of each loaf. . Toothpick will come out clean if bread is done.

Note: General Grant's wife, Julia, insisted that her husband eat a portion of this laxative bread at least once or twice a day

Ulysses Simpson Grant (1822-1885)

HERITAGE: Born in Mt. Pleasant, Ohio. Father a man of modest means, a tanner.

RANK: General.

FOUGHT FOR: Union.

RELIGION: Christian (See quotes below).

EDUCATION: West Point graduate – class of 1843.
   Didn't especially stand out as a cadet.

MARRIAGE: Julie Dent in 1848.

CAREER HIGHLIGHTS & TIDBITS: Man of quiet determination and calm resolution.
   He once declared : *"I believe in the Holy Scriptures, and who lives by them will benefit thereby. Men may differ as to the interpretation, which is human, but the Scriptures are man's best guide."*
   Became President of the United States in 1868.
   General Grant refused to consider an exchange of prisoners with General Lee, saying: *"If we commence a system of exchange we will have to fight until the whole South is exterminated..."*

QUOTABLE QUOTE: This is what Grant said when Robert E. Lee surrendered at Appomattox: *"I felt like anything rather than rejoicing at the downfall of a foe that had fought for so long and valiantly and had suffered so much for a cause, though the cause was, I believe, one of the worst for which people had ever fought."*

SAW ACTION AT: Vicksburg, Chattanooga (Missionary Ridge), Cold Harbor, Shiloh, The Wilderness, Spotsylvania, Petersburg, Five Forks, Richmond, Fort Henry, Fort Donelson, etc.

LITTLE KNOWN FACTS: Very shy and quiet. Liked to spend a lot of time to himself. Totally unpretentious.

Salt-Rising Bread—
as Made by General Forrest's Mother

12 cups flour	1 tsp salt
pinch brown sugar	4 cups salted milk

This delicious bread is best started while getting breakfast in the morning. As soon as the teakettle has boiled, take a quart tin cup or an earthen quart milk pitcher and carefully scald it. Then fill 1/3 full of water about as warm as the finger can be held in. To this water add brown sugar, salt and coarse (unsifted) flour enough to make batter of about the right consistency for griddlecakes. Set cup or pitcher of batter, with spoon in it, in closed vessel (large pot) half filled with moderately hot but not scalding water. Keep the temperature as nearly even as possible. Blend in 1 tsp flour once or twice during process of fermentation. This yeast batter should rise fully to top of cup or pitcher in about 5 hours.

When above batter has risen, sift 12 cups flour into large wooden mixing bowl. Make opening in center and pour in yeast batter. Have ready a quart pitcher of warm salted milk, or use combination of milk and water in equal quantities. Do not have milk too hot or it will scald the yeast. Stir rapidly into pulpy mass with large wooden spoon. Cover this sponge with folded towel or piece of heavy table linen. Keep in warm place for 1 hour. Then dump on floured board and knead into loaves. Add as little flour as is required to make dough the proper consistency. Place in war, well-greased bread pans. Cover again with folded towel and leave until light and fluffy. Bake in steady moderately quick oven (375 degrees). Test for doneness by sticking toothpick in center of each loaf. Toothpick will come out clean if bread is done. When bread is done, take each loaf out of the pan. Stand loaves tilted up against pans until cooled somewhat. This allows all the hot steam to escape. Wrap while still warm in damp towels. When cold, remove towels and place loaves in closed tin box or stone jar. Keep container tightly covered until bread is wanted for use.

Nathan Bedford Forrest (1821-1877)

HERITAGE: Born on the Tennessee frontier.
Father a blacksmith who settled on the frontier in 1806.

RANK: General.

FOUGHT FOR: Confederacy.

RELIGION: Christian.
Raised in a fundamental Christian home.
The Bible was read nightly to him by his mother.

EDUCATION: Little, if any, formal education.

CAREER HIGHLIGHTS & TIDBITS: The most outstanding cavalry leader on either side of the Civil War.
Seriously wounded in 1862.
In April of 1864, his command is said to have participated in the brutal and massacre of Negro troops at Fort Billow, Tennessee.
Forrest emphatically denied ordering the killings.
Faced enemy fire more than 100 times.
Had from 27 to 39 horses shot out from under him.
General Joseph E. Johnston was asked who he believed was the war's preeminent leader. He responded: *"Forrest, who, had he had the advantages of a thorough military education and training, would have been the great central figure of the Civil War."*

QUOTABLE QUOTE: *"Follow Forest to the death if it costs 10,000 lives and breaks the federal] treasury,"* exclaimed General Sherman. *"There will be no peace in Tennessee until Forrest is dead!"* Sherman didn't get his wish.

SAW ACTION AT: Fort Donelson; Murfreesboro, Parker's Crossroad, Tennessee; Chickamauga, Bryer's Crossroads, Selma; etc.

LITTLE KNOWN FACT: Once threatened General Bragg: *"You are a coward. I say to you that if ever you again. interfere with me or cross my path again it will be at the point of your life."*

3

Homemade Sweet Breads as Made During the Civil War

Rolled Oat Banana Bread
As Made For the Hood Family

1 cup sugar	½ tsp baking powder
½ cup butter	1-1/2 tsp baking soda
1 tsp vanilla	½ tsp salt
3 eggs, well beaten	½ cup buttermilk
1-1/4 cups flour	1-1/4 cups rolled oats

1-1/4 cups banana, mashed

Put sugar, butter and vanilla into a large wooden mixing bowl. Beat until a light creamy mixture is obtained. Whip in frothy beaten eggs, one at a time. Then sift together the flour, baking powder, baking soda and salt. Add these to the bowl, alternately with buttermilk. Beat hard for each part put in bowl. Then stir in rolled oats and lastly bananas. Pour batter into 2 round 9-inch well-buttered and floured cake pans. Bake in moderate oven (350 degrees) for 25 to 30 minutes. Test for doneness by sticking toothpick in center of each loaf. Toothpick will come out clean if bread is done. When finished baking take cakes from oven and set on wire racks to cool for 10 minutes. Then turn out cakes and set-aside until cold. When cold, spread each layer with chocolate frosting. Set one layer upon the other and cover sides with same frosting.

John Bell Hood (1831-1878)

HERITAGE: Born and raised in Owensville, Kentucky.

RANK: General.

FOUGHT FOR: Confederacy.

RELIGION: Christian – baptized into Episcopal Church by General Leonidas Polk (see below for details).

EDUCATION: West Point graduate – class of 1853. Near the bottom of his class. He was 52nd in a class of 54.

CAREER HIGHLIGHTS & TIDBITS: A favorite of his commander, General Lee, another well-known Christian leader.

Outstanding military leader.

Initially saw some service in the frontier in California and Texas. Joined the Confederate Cavalry in April of 1801.

Fast became known as the "fighting General".

Lost right leg during the battle of Chickamauga.

Had previously lost the use of his right arm during the Battle of Gettysburg.

So badly maimed was this man that he had to be strapped to his horse with a special leather harness.

Known to be an aggressive warrior and was called "The Gallant Hood" by Jefferson Davis, President of the Confederate States of America.

Wasn't thought very bright by his contemporaries, but he did graduate from West Point and this was no easy task.

Severely wounded both times while riding borrowed horses.

Surrendered in Mississippi in May of 1865.

LITTLE KNOWN FACT: Confided in General Leonidas Polk that he wished to be baptized just before the Battle of Resaca. Polk, known as *"the fighting bishop"* performed the baptismal service. The crippled Hood leaned on his crutch while a horse bucket was used for the consecrated water.

Graham Brown Bread
As Enjoyed by General Lee

2 cups corn meal   1 cup molasses
2 cups white bread sponge   graham flour to suit

Put corn meal into large wooden mixing bowl. Pour enough boiling water over cornmeal to thoroughly scald it. Set aside and allow to cool. When lukewarm, add the light white bread sponge and blend everything together. Then add molasses and enough graham flour to make soft, pliable dough. Mold into 2 loaves. Place each in greased bread pan. Cover with thick cloth or towel and set aside in warm place to rise. When loaves are light (have risen), put in moderate oven (350 degrees). Bake for 1-1/2 hours. Test for doneness by sticking toothpick in center of each loaf. Toothpick will come out clean if bread is done. When finished baking take loaves from oven and set on wire racks to cool for 10 minutes.

Robert Edward Lee (1807-1870)

HERITAGE: Born in Virginia, raised in Alexandria.
Fourth son of Revolutionary War hero, Lighthouse Harry Lee.

RANK: General.

FOUGHT FOR: Confederacy.

RELIGION: Christian – Professed to have a *"personal relationship with the Lord Jesus Christ."* (See quote below).

EDUCATION: West Point graduate – class of 1829. Brilliant student. Graduated second in his class.

MARRIAGE: Married Mary Anne Randolph Custis, great-granddaughter of Martha Dandridge Custis Washington.

CAREER HIGHLIGHTS & TIDBITS: A deeply religious man with no formal church affiliation.
Did not join the Episcopal church until 1854.
One of two of the Civil War's greatest Christian Generals.
The other was Jonathan "Stonewall" Jackson.
Offered field command of the Union Army by Lincoln.
Rejected Lincoln's offer.
Resigned his military commission when Virginia seceded.
Prayed reverently before each battle.

QUOTABLE QUOTE: *"God's will ought to be our aim ... His design should be accomplished and not mine."*

SAW ACTION AT: Commanded the Seven Days Battles, Manassas, Antietam, Sharpsburg, Chancellorsville, Gettysburg, Battle of Bull Run, The Wilderness, Spotsylvania, Cold Harbor, Petersburg, etc.

LITTLE KNOWN FACT: Indicted for treason in June of 1865 by a U.S. Grand Jury in Norfolk, Virginia.Never brought to trial.

Tin Can Raisin-Nut Bread—
Mrs. Wilson's Thanksgiving Receipt

1/3 cup butter, melted	3 cups raisins
2 cups water	2 eggs
2 tbls baking soda	1 tbls salt
2 cups sugar	4 cups flour
2 cups hickory nuts, chopped	

Put raisins and water in small pot. Bring to boil. Then set aside to cool. When cooled, stir in baking soda, sugar, melted butter, eggs and salt. Then add flour, a little at a time. Blend well so there are no lumps. Fill well-greased tin cans about ½ full. Bake in moderately slow oven (325 degrees) for 1 hour. . Test for doneness by sticking toothpick in center of each loaf. Toothpick will come out clean if bread is done. Let cool before taking bread from cans.

Note: Bread was sometimes baked over campfires in this manner by soldiers during the Civil War.

James Harrison Wilson (1837-1925)

HERITAGE: Born and raised in Illinois.

RANK: General.

FOUGHT FOR: Union.

RELIGION: Christian.

EDUCATION: West Point graduate – class of 1860.

CAREER HIGHLIGHTS & TIDBITS: One of the Union's outstanding Christian leaders.
> Quite a distinguished looking man.
> A brilliant commander and daring officer.
> A no nonsense leader.
> An instigator of many spectacular raids when Petersburg was under siege.
> Led a cavalry corps in 1864 and 1865.
> Capped off his career with an especially brilliant raid in Selma, Alabama.
> Served under General George McClellan, General David Hunter, and General W.T. Sherman.
> Highly thought of for his outstanding courage while under fire.
> An outstanding military tactician.
> Assisted mightily in stopping the Boxer Rebellion.
> Responsible for destroying untold miles of vital railroad track throughout the South during the Civil War.
> Authored many official military manuals in later life.
> Re-enlisted to fight in the Spanish-American War.
> Helped suppress the Boxer Rebellion.

SAW ACTION AT: Petersburg, Selma, Siege of Atlanta, Sherman's "March to the Sea", etc.

LITTLE KNOWN FACT: The sensational finale to his military career was the capture of Confederate President Jefferson Davis.

Gingerbread—
Mrs. Quantrill's Best

1 cup butter	1 cup buttermilk
1 cup molasses	1 tsp baking soda (dissolved
1 cup sugar	in boiling water)
1 tbls ginger	2 egg whites, beaten
1 tsp cinnamon	2 egg yolks, beaten

4 cups flour

Stir butter, molasses, sugar and spices together in saucepan. Blend until they make soft creamy mixture. Then set on stove to warm slightly. When warmed sufficiently, stir in buttermilk. Add beaten egg whites and yolks, baking soda and lastly flour. Put in additional flour as needed to make thick batter. Beat very hard for 10 minutes. Pour batter into buttered bread pans. Bake in moderate oven (350 degrees). Test for doneness by sticking toothpick in center of each loaf. Toothpick will come out clean if bread is done.

Note: 1-1/2 cups raisins, cut in half, greatly improves this kind of gingerbread. Dredge raisins in flour and stir in last if this is to be tried.

William Clark Quantrill (1837-1865)

HERITAGE: Born and raised in Canal Dover, Ohio.

RANK: None. Commanded group of Confederate irregulars.

FOUGHT FOR: Confederacy with his guerrilla band.

EDUCATION: Unknown.
   Taught school in Illinois and Ohio.

CAREER HIGHLIGHTS & TIDBITS: Initially a law abiding Kansas homesteader.
   Initiated a life of crime in Kansas.
   Started out with petty thievery.
   Quickly became well known for his numerous surprise bloody border skirmishes.
   Instrumental in the murder of five abolitionists in 1862.
   Killed them because for plotting to free a number of slaves owned by a Missouri farmer.
   Operated as a guerilla leader despite a ban on such activities by Union authorities.
   Robbed and committed wholesale murder while conducting raids and sacking pro-Union communities.
   Was no more than a hardened psychopathic killer hiding behind a handsome, clean-cut exterior.
   Burned most of Lawrence, Kansas.
   Murdered 150 people late in 1863.
   Early in 1865, just before the Civil War ended, took 33 of his men and rode into Kansas.
   Conducted a series of fresh killings, robberies and wanton wholesale destruction throughout the territory.
   Killed by Union troops in Taylorsville, Kentucky in May of 1865.

SAW ACTION AT: Independence, Missouri; Kentucky; throughout the territory of Kansas

LITTLE KNOWN FACT: Worked as a professional gambler in Utah under the name of Charlie Hart.

Unfermented Brown Bread— as Mrs. DuPont Baked It

1 cup rye flour	½ cup molasses
1 cup wheat flour	or
2 cups corn meal	½ cup brown sugar

1 tsp salt

Blend all of the above ingredients in large wooden mixing bowl. Use sour milk for wetting. Stir into as stiff a batter as can be mixed with a large wooden mixing spoon. Then add 1 tsp baking soda dissolved in 1 tbls warm water. Beat this thoroughly before pouring batter into well-greased baking pans. Bake in moderate oven (350 degrees) until done. Test for doneness by sticking toothpick in center of each loaf. Toothpick will come out clean if bread is done.

Note: This delicious unfermented bread can also be made with sweet milk instead of sour milk as called for above. If sweet milk is used, merely substitute baking powder for baking soda.

Samuel Francis DuPont (1823-1865)

HERITAGE: Born and raised in Bergenpoint, New Jersey.

RANK: Admiral.

FOUGHT FOR: Union.

RELIGION: Christian.

CAREER HIGHLIGHTS & TIDBITS: Began his 50-year career in the United States Navy in1815.

Fought heroically in the Mexican War while in command of the sloop-of-war *Cyane*.

Drove the Mexican Navy out of the Gulf of California.

Recommended in 1851 that the U.S. Navy use steam to power their ships.

Appointed in 1861 as the first man to command the South Atlantic Blockading Squadron.

The squadron then consisted of 75 ships.

In command, at this point, of the largest fleet of vessels ever to be under the one officer.

Ordered, against his advice by Department of the Navy, to attack Charleston, South Carolina.

His fleet of ships (ironclads) was either destroyed or damaged.

Blamed Secretary of the Navy, Gideon Welles, for the defeat.

Relieved of any further command.

Spent the rest of his military career in Washington on various commissions and war boards.

Dupont Circle in Washington, D.C. was named after him.

SAW ACTION AT: Set up and enforced a blockade and seized Port Royal in 1861.

Captured St. Augustine and Jacksonville, Florida.

LITTLE KNOWN FACTS: Washington D.C.'s Dupont Circle was named after him.

Assisted greatly in establishing the U.S. Naval Academy in Annapolis, Maryland in 1850.

Pumpkin Bread—
As Prepared For the Gray Ghost

4 cups pumpkin,
   stewed and strained
1/3 cup sugar
1 tsp salt

½ cup butter, melted
1 cup milk, scalded
½ yeast cake
5 cups flour

Put stewed and strained pumpkin in a wooden mixing bowl. Add sugar, salt, melted butter and scalded milk. Blend everything thoroughly. Crumble yeast cake in a little warm water and let it dissolve. When mixture in bowl is lukewarm, stir in dissolved yeast and flour. Knead well. Cover bowl with towel or heavy cloth. Leave overnight in warm place to rise. In the morning, turn dough out on lightly floured board. Shape into 1 large loaf. Lay loaf on a greased baking tin. Place in moderately quick oven (375 degrees) and let bake for 20 minutes. Then reduce heat in oven to moderate (350 degrees) and let bake for 40 more minutes. Test for doneness by sticking toothpick in center of each loaf. Toothpick will come out clean if bread is done.

John Singlton Mosby (1833-1916)

HERITAGE: Born and raised in Virginia.

RANK: Captain.

FOUGHT FOR: Confederacy.

RELIGION: Christian.

EDUCATION: Attended University of Virginia. Arrested and jailed for shooting another student.
>Released when it was found that the other student had "provoked" him. Studied law while in jail with the help of his attorney.

CAREER HIGHLIGHTS & TIDBITS: On March 9,1863 Mosby's Rangers pulled off a daring exploit.
>Raided a Union camp at the Fairfax County Courthouse.
>Captured Brigadier General Edwin Stoughton as he lay in bed soundly sleeping.
>Mosby awoke Stoughton with a slap and shouted: *"Get up General and come with me!"*
>Stoughton jumped from bed and bellowed: *"What is this? Don't you know who I am, sir?"*
>*"I reckon I do, General. You ever heard of Mosby?"*
>*"Yes, have you caught him?"*
>*"No, but he's caught you!"*

QUOTABLE QUOTE(S): *"My men had no camps...They would scatter for safety and gather at my call like Children of the Mist."*

SAW ACTION AT: First Bull Run, and many other places. Primarily undertook raids all over Virginia with "irregulars."

LITTLE KNOWN FACTS: Also captured in his famous raid at the Fairfax County Courthouse were two captains, 38 privates, and 58 horses.
>Not one of his cavalrymen was either killed or wounded in this famous and heroic escapade!

Steamed Brown Bread—
A Favorite of the Sheridan Family

1 cup flour	pinch of salt
2 cups graham flour	2 cups corn meal
1 cup molasses	1 tsp baking soda

3-1/2 cups sour milk

Blend all of the above ingredients in a large wooden mixing bowl. When thoroughly beaten together and mixed, pour batter into well-greased baking pan. Set this pan into a larger pan of water. Place in slow oven (300 degrees) and let steam for at least 4 hours. When steaming is completed, remove from oven. Slip brown bread from baking pan. Set bread back in rather quick oven (400-425 degrees) for another 15 minutes. This improves the bread's flavor. It should always be eaten with plenty of butter while still warm.

Note: When sweet milk is used in place of sour milk, substitute 1 tsp baking powder for the 1 tsp baking soda

Philip H. Sheridan (1831-1888)

HERITAGE: Born in Albany, New York; Boston; or Somerset, Ohio. Son of Irish immigrants who came to America in 1831 from County Cavan, Ireland.

RANK: General.

FOUGHT FOR: Union.

RELIGION: Christian.

EDUCATION: West Point graduate – class of 1853.
    Ranked 34th in his class of 39.
    Also attended village (public) schools in Somerset, Ohio.

CAREER HIGHLIGHTS & TIDBITS: Succeeded General Grant as Commander-in-Chief of the U.S. Army in 1884.
    Back in 1864, Grant had ordered him to destroy General Jubal Early's small army unit.
    He was ordered to confiscate all livestock and burn the crops.
    Grant, with Lincoln's approval, ordered him to conduct a *"scorched earth"* policy in order to *"make the area unfit for any Confederate operations."*
    One of his reports to General Grant told of his capturing almost 4,000 horses, 10,000 beef cattle, more than 400,000 bushels of grain.
    Became commander-in-chief of a 10,000 man cavalry force in March of 1864.

QUOTABLE QUOTES: *"The people must be left nothing but their eyes to weep with over the war."*
"Mosby has angered me considerably."

SAW ACTION AT: Boonville, Perryville, Stones River, Chickamauga, Missionary Ridge, The Wilderness, Spotsylvania, Richmond, Winchester, Five Forks, etc.

LITTLE KNOWN FACT: Graduated near the bottom of his class at West Point for assaulting another cadet with a bayonet.

4

Not to be Forgotten Civil War Era Cornbread Recipes

Brown Sugar Corn Bread—
As Made by Clara Barton

1 cup flour   1 cup cornmeal
¾ tsp baking soda   2 tbls brown sugar
1 tsp salt   ¼ cup shortening, melted
1 tsp baking powder   2 eggs, well beaten
                1-1/2 cups sour milk

Sift some flour and measure out 1 cup. Then sift together in a wooden mixing bowl the sifted flour, baking soda, salt and baking powder. Blend in corn meal. In separate bowl, combine brown sugar, melted shortening and beaten eggs. Lastly add sour milk. Stir this mixture into dry ingredients in first bowl. Beat everything together until batter is smooth and lump free. Grease a shallow baking pan. Fill 2/3 with batter. Bake in quick oven (425 degrees) for 25 to 30 minutes, or until lightly browned. Serve while hot with butter. Makes enough to feed 8 people.

Clara Barton (1821-1902)

HERITAGE: Farmer's daughter. Born near Oxford, Massachusetts. Father was a veteran of General Anthony Wayne's Indian campaigns.

POSITION: Nurse, philanthropist.

RELIGION: Christian.

EDUCATION: Home-schooled by older brothers and sisters as well as her mother, Sarah.
     Studied at the Liberal Arts Institute in Clinton, New York in 1851.

CAREER HIGHLIGHTS & TIDBITS: Became one of the first women to volunteer her services to nurse the sick and wounded when the Civil War broke out in April of 1861.
     Had previously nursed her brother, David, through a two year illness, by staying by his side day and night.
     The Surgeon General, because of her valuable contribution to the war effort, granted her permission to expand her work to the frontlines in July of 1862.
     Fast became known as the *"Angel of the Battlefield"*.
     After the war ended, President Lincoln asked this great Christian lady to organize a search for soldiers who had been listed as missing in action.
     Founder of the American Red Cross Society in 1881.
     First director of the Red Cross.
     Headed the Red Cross for 23 years.
     Worked as a schoolteacher at the age of only 15 years.
     Taught school without a salary in Bordentown, New Jersey.

QUOTABLE QUOTE: *"If it must be, let it come, and when there is no longer a soldier's arm to raise the stars and stripes above our capitol, may God give me strength to use mine."*

LITTLE KNOWN FACTS: Only 5 feet tall and rather frail.
After the battle of Antietam, Dr. James Dunn wrote, "General McClellan, with all his laurels, sinks into insignificance behind the heroine of the age, the Angel of the Battlefield."

Spider Corn Cake—
Something Abe Loved as a Boy

1-1/4 cups yellow corn meal   1 tsp baking soda
¾ cup flour   2 cups sour milk
¼ cup sugar   2 eggs, well beaten
1 tsp salt   1-1/2 tbls butter

1 cup milk

Sift together in a wooden mixing bowl the yellow corn meal, flour, sugar and salt. Dissolve baking soda in sour milk. Stir beaten eggs in with this. Add to dry ingredients in mixing bowl and beat together. Melt butter in square cast iron skillet that has been thoroughly heated. Make certain sides of skillet are also nicely greased. Pour batter into skillet. Holding cup of milk about 6 inches above skillet, slowly pour it back and forth over the batter. Be careful not to jiggle skillet as it is placed in oven. Bake in moderate oven (350 degrees) for 50 minutes. When done, corn cake will have a delicious custard streak running throughout. Serve while of with lots of butter.

Abraham Lincoln (1809-1865)
His Thoughts on Race

EQUALITY: *"Negro equality! Fudge! How long in the government of a God, great enough to make and maintain this Universe, shall there continue knaves to vend, and fools to gulp, so low a piece of demagoguism as this."*

SLAVERY: *"My paramount object in this struggle is to save the Union, and is not either to save or to destroy slavery. If I could save the Union without freeing any slave, I would do it; and if I could save it by freeing all the slaves, I would also do that. What I do about slavery and the colored race, I do because...it helps to save the Union."*

THE PROBLEM: *"But what shall we do with the Negroes after they are free? I can hardly believe that the South and North can live in peace, unless we can get rid of the Negroes."*

EXPORTING BLACKS: *"I believe that it would be better to export them all to some fertile country with a good climate, which they could have to themselves...Now, we shall have no use for our very large navy; what, then, are our difficulties in sending all the blacks away?"*

LINCOLN-DOUGLAS DEBATE – 9/18, 1858: Voting rights: *"I will say then that I am not, nor ever have been in favor of making voters or jurors of Negroes, nor of qualifying them to hold office, nor to intermarry with white people..."*

LINCOLN-DOUGLAS DEBATE – 10/13, 1858: *"I have no purpose directly or indirectly to interfere with the institution [of slavery] in the States where it exists. I believe I have no right to do so. I have no inclination to do so. I as well as Judge Douglas am in favor of the race to which I belong having the superior position."*

DURING LINCOLN'S PRESIDENTIAL CAMPAIGN: Don Piatt, while stumping Illinois, said this in one of his speeches: *... he hated the Negro and the Negro hated him, and he was no more concerned for that wretched race than he was concerned for the horse he worked or the hog he killed."*

Southern Johnny Cake—
Stonewall Jackson Enjoyed This

2 tbls bacon grease	1 cup sugar
2 cups corn meal	1 tsp salt
1 cup flour	2 tsp baking soda
2 eggs, well-beaten	2 cups sour milk

Put bacon grease, corn meal and flour in a wooden mixing bowl. Blend thoroughly. Stir in beaten eggs, sugar and salt. Dissolve baking soda in sour milk. Add this to rest of ingredients in mixing bowl. Grease a small shallow baking pan. Pour batter into baking pan. Bake in quick oven (425 degrees) for 20 to 25 minutes. Serve while hot with plenty of butter. Make enough to serve 8 people.

Thomas "Stonewall" Jackson (1824-1863)

HERITAGE: Parents died in poverty when he was a child. Grew up as an orphan in Clarksburg, Virginia. Raised by an uncle.

RANK: General.

FOUGHT FOR: Confederacy.

RELIGION: Christian. On his deathbed, he said to his wife, *"Please remember me in your prayers, but never forget to use the petition, 'thy will be done'."* (Also see quote below).

EDUCATION: Little formal education. West Point graduate – class of 1846.

CAREER HIGHLIGHTS & TIDBITS: One of the South's greatest Christian Generals. The other was Robert E. Lee.

> Stopped to say this prayer on the battlefield at Manassas: *"Oh God, let this horrible war quickly come to an end that we may all return home and engage in the only work that is worthwhile – and that is the salvation of men."*
> Was only 39 when he died.
> Described the war as *"the sum of all evils."*
> After going off to fight in what he called *"The War of Northern Aggression,"* Jackson sent money each month to support a Sunday School class for the Negro children of slaves.

QUOTABLE QUOTE: *"I cannot think of anything more glorious than being a preacher."*

SAW ACTION AT: Manassas, Shenandoah Valley Campaign, Bull Run, Front Royal, Winchester, The Wilderness, Fredericksburg, etc.

LITTLE KNOWN FACT: Only Told cadets at VMI:: *"...time for war has not yet come, but it will come and when it does come, my advice is to draw the sword and throw away the scabbard."*

Skillet Baked Corn Bread—
A Favorite of the Welles Family

2 cups corn meal
2 cups flour
4 tsp baking powder
1 tsp salt

1 tsp sugar
2 tbls butter, melted
2 eggs
6 tbls heavy cream

1-1/2 cups water

Sift together in a large wooden mixing bowl the corn meal, flour, baking powder, salt and sugar. In a separate bowl blend melted butter, eggs, heavy cream and water. Combine the two mixtures and blend thoroughly. Beat to a creamy batter. Then carefully pour batter into large, well-greased cast iron skillet. Bake in very slow oven (275 degrees). Be sure to loosen corn bread from sides of skillet as soon as crust forms. Then turn over and bake on other side as well. Makes enough corn bread to serve 8 to 10 people.

Gideon Welles (1802-1878)

HERITAGE: Born and raised in Connecticut.

POSITION: Lincoln's Secretary of the Navy.

RELIGION: Christian.

CAREER HIGHLIGHTS & TIDBITS: Started out writing copy for the *Hartford Times. Became part-owner and editor of the newspaper* before the Civil War from 1826 to 1836.

- Brought his vast public service experience to Washington.
- Became President Lincoln's Secretary of the Navy in 1861.
- A hard driving no-nonsense leader.
- Served ably throughout the Civil War from 1861 to 1869.
- One of Lincoln's most influential advisors.
- Solely responsible for developing a successful federal (Union) shipbuilding program.
- Increased the Union naval fleet from 90 to 670 ships.
- Increased the number of naval personnel from 9,000 to more than 57,000 men.
- Enforced the successful blockade of all Confederate ports during the Civil War.
- The Presidents most trusted cabinet member.
- Promoted new naval technology.
- Pushed for the which the development of ironclad ships.
- His three-volume diary was published in 1911.
- One of the most important records pertaining to the Civil War.
- Founded the *Hartford Evening Press* in the early 1900's.
- His publication was New England's first Republican oriented newspaper.
- Unsuccessful Republican candidate for Governor of Connecticut in 1856.

LITTLE KNOWN FACT: In his diary he asserted that President Lincoln had *"thought it essential to provide an asylum for a race which we had emancipated, but which could never be recognized or admitted to be our equals."*

Molasses-Sour Milk Corn Bread—
Mrs. Surratt's Favorite

1 cup milk	2/3 cup molasses
2 cups sour milk	1 cup flour
4 cups corn meal	1 tsp baking soda

Mix all of the above ingredients in a large wooden mixing bowl. When thoroughly blended, pour into buttered baking pan. Set his pan in a larger pan of hot water and place in moderate oven (350 degrees). Allow to steam for at least 3 hours. When steaming in completed, remove pan from oven. Slip corn bread out of its pan. Place loaf back in very quick oven (425 degrees) and allow to brown a few minutes.

Note: This corn bread can be made using regular milk if desired. In such cases, merely substitute 1 tsp baking powder in place of the 1 tsp baking soda called for in the recipe.

Mary Surratt (?-?)

HERITAGE: Born near Waterloo, Maryland.

POSITION: Confederate conspirator of questionable guilt.

MARRIAGE: Wed to 28-year old John Surratt.

CHILDREN: Three children – Isaac, Anna and John jr.

CAREER HIGHLIGHTS & TIDBITS: Ran a boarding house in Washington, D.C. during the Civil War.

One son was a Confederate dispatch rider during the early part of the Civil War.

Son was also a spy for the Confederacy.

Her boardinghouse was believed to have been the rendezvous place for the conspirators who planned Lincoln's assassination.

On April 17, the occupants of the Surratt house were arrested: Those arrested were Mrs. Surratt, her daughter, Anna, a Mrs. Fitzpatrick, and Miss Holaham.

Surratt and the others were believed to have been aware of Booth's intentions some hours before his assassination.

Tried by a special military commission in Washington, D.C.

Mrs. Surratt and a number of others received a death sentence by the jury on July 6, 1865..

The jury then officially recommended mercy for her because of her *"sex and age."*

President Andrew Johnson ignored the plea.

He later lied and claimed to have never been given the jury's recommendation to read and consider.

Mary was hanged on July 7, 1865.

Son, John, fled to Canada immediately after Lincoln's assassination.

He returned from Canada in 1867.

Tried, but his trial ended in a hung jury.

LITTLE KNOWN FACT: Only Current research has uncovered information that Mary may have been innocent of any involvement in the plot to assassin President Lincoln.

Spoon Batter Bread—
A Booth Family Favorite

6 egg yolks	2 tsp baking powder
2 tsp sugar	3 cups milk
1 tsp salt	1 cup buttermilk
½ cup grits, boiled	6 egg whites, stiffly beaten
1 cup yellow corn meal	3 tbls butter

Put egg yolks in a large wooden mixing bowl. Stir in sugar and salt. Beat until it is a custard-like consistency. Then blend in boiled grits. Sift together yellow corn meal and baking powder in separate bowl. Add this, milk and buttermilk to beaten egg mixture in first bowl. Lastly fold in stiffly beaten egg whites. Now melt butter in bottom of baking pan. Turn pan so as to butter sides well. Pour in creamy batter mixture. Bake in moderate oven (350 degrees) for about 30 minutes. This is a deliciously different old-time spoon bread. It bakes to the consistency of a soufflé. Serve by scooping with large spoon from baking pan. Makes enough to serve 6 people.

Note: This is the spoon batter bread that the mother of infamous John Wilkes Booth (1839-1865) made for her sons when they were children. The Booth boys were reared on a farm near Bel Air, Maryland, under the guidance of a strict Christian mother. Despite his early Christian home life, as we all now know, John Wilkes grew up to become the notorious assassin of President Abraham Lincoln at Ford's Theater on April 14, 1865.

John Wilkes Booth (1838-1865)

HERITAGE: Born and raised in a large family on a small farm near Bel Aire, Maryland.

POSITION: Actor, assassin.

RELIGION: Christian – see quote below.

EDUCATION: Little, if any, formal education. School bored him. Interested only in becoming a famous actor.

CAREER HIGHLIGHTS & TIDBITS: Started acting at age 17 in Baltimore's St. Charles Theater.
> Strikingly handsome and adventurous.
> Quite athletic as a youngster.
> Played minor roles in 1857-1858 at Philadelphia's Arch Street Theater.
> Became a prominent actor at Ford's Theater.
> Unpopular with audiences because he failed to properly memorize his lines.
> A fanatical Southern sympathizer yet failed to enlist in the Confederate army.
> Strongly in favor of slavery.
> Had initially planned only to kidnap President Lincoln and carry him to Richmond.
> The President was to be held hostage in hopes of forcing an end to the Civil War.
> Saw the Civil War as a struggle between tyranny and freedom.
> Believed himself to be fulfilling the wishes of God by murdering the President.

QUOTABLE QUOTE: An entry in his diary dated April 13-19, 1865, reads: *"Our country owed all her troubles to him [Lincoln], and God simply made me the instrument of His punishment."*

LITTLE KNOWN FACTS: His last words before dying were: *"Tell mother I die for my country."*
> His brother called him "one of America's greatest stage talents among the youthful actors in America."

Bacon Ham Corn Bread—
A Favorite of General Matthew Maury

1 slice country ham	2 cups flour
6 slices bacon	6 tsp baking powder
2 eggs, well beaten	1 tsp salt
2 cups milk or cream	1 cup white corn meal

Fry ham slice and bacon strips in cast iron skillet. Fry until crisp. Chop into small pieces and set aside to cool. When cool, combine ham and bacon pieces, beaten eggs and milk in a large wooden mixing bowl. Sift together flour, baking powder and salt into same bowl. Lastly stir in corn meal. Blend everything thoroughly. Grease a muffin tin. Pour in batter. Fill each cup about 2/3 full. Bake in very quick oven (450 degrees) for about 15 minutes. Makes 10 servings.

Note: In the old South, especially Virginia, corn breads were made only with white stone ground corn meal. And sugar was seldom, if ever, used in corn bread recipes.

Matthew Fontaine Maury (1806-1873)

HERITAGE: Born near Fredericksburg, Virginia.
Raised on a frontier farm in Tennessee.

RANK: Naval Commander.

FOUGHT FOR: Confederacy.

RELIGION: Christian.

EDUCATION: Unknown.

MARRIAGE: Wed Anne Hull Herindon and settled in Fredericksburg, Virginia.

CHILDREN: Unknown.

CAREER HIGHLIGHTS & TIDBITS: Dreamed since childhood of the joining the navy, emulating his older brother who was a naval officer.
Joined the navy in 1825.
Soon thereafter wrote *A New Theoretical and Practical Treatise on Navigation* in 1836.
Crippling accident in 1839 ended his career at sea.
Devoted the rest of his naval career to research and writing.
Established oceanography as a major science with the publication of his *Physical Geography of the Sea* in 1855.
Chief of Naval Operations from 1862 to 1865.
Arranged to purchase ships from England for the Confederacy.
Invented the electric mine laying system.
Went into exile to Mexico and Europe when the Civil War ended. Returned to America in 1818.
Became a member of the Virginia Military Institute Faculty. Taught meteorology at VMI. .

LITTLE KNOWN FACT: Compiled his classic study in 1847 called Wind and Current Charts of the North Atlantic.

Steamed corn bread—
A Favorite of Mary Edwards Walker

2 cups corn meal 2-1/4 cups buttermilk
1 cup flour   1 tsp baking soda
2 tbls sugar   1 tsp salt
   1-1/2 tbls shortening, melted

Put all of the above ingredients into a large wooden mixing bowl. Beat hard and long. Pour batter into well-buttered baking pan. Tie coarse cloth over pan. Set pan in larger pan of boiling water. Take care that the pan of batter does not touch boiling water. Lay a tight fitting cover over the cloth tied around the pan in order to keep in all the heat. Let steam for 1-1/2 hours. Then slip bread out of pan onto baking tin. Put in very quick oven (450 degrees). Bake for about 10 minutes.

Note: Mary Edwards Walker sometimes served this steamed bread as a desert dish. She merely had her guests eat it with some pudding sauce.

Mary Edwards Walker (1832-1919)

HERITAGE: Born in Oswego, New York. Father a brilliant, self-taught and exceptionally talented physician.

POSITION: Union doctor, nurse, surgeon.

RELIGION: Devout Christian.

EDUCATION: Graduated from the Syracuse Medical College– the nations first medical school.

MARRIAGE: Wed another physician, Dr. Albert Miller, who had been her classmate in medical school.
>Divorced 13-years later.

CAREER HIGHLIGHTS & TIDBITS: Opened a medical practice with her husband prior to her militate service.
>Only woman and only civilian to be awarded the *Medal of Honor* during the Civil War.
>Her *Medal of Honor* cites her work at First Manassas.
>Began her medical work during the Battle of Chickamauga on September 19, 1863.
>Served in the Union Army Hospital in Chattanooga, Tennessee.
>Tirelessly worked as a volunteer surgeon.
>Often crossed enemy lines to assist soldiers in need of help.   Helped as a surgeon during the Battle of Atlanta.
>General W.T. Sherman recommended her for a *Medal of Honor*. *Medal of Honor* was awarded to her in 1866.
>She proudly wore her medal every day until she died.

SAW ACTION AT: Chickamauga, Battle of Atlanta, First Manassas, Chattanooga, etc.

LITTLE KNOWN FACTS: Captured by Confederate troops on April 10, 1864. Sent to prison as a "spy".
>Exchanged after four months, along with two dozen other Union doctors for 17 Confederate surgeons.

Corn Rolls—
A Favorite of George McClellan

4 cups corn meal   1 tbls shortening or
1 tsp salt   butter, melted

Sift corn meal into large wooden mixing bowl. Then add salt and melted shortening or butter. Blend everything with sufficient cold water to make a soft pliable dough. When dough is ready, break into small chunks. Mold with your hands into thin oblong cakes. Lay these cakes in well-buttered baking tins. Place in rather quick oven (400 to 425 degrees). Bake until crust is nice and brown. Corn rolls are always broken, never cut, and eaten with plenty of butter while still very hot.

George Brinton McClellan (1826-1885)

HERITAGE: Born in Philadelphia, Pennsylvania. Son of a distinguished surgeon.

RANK: General.

FOUGHT FOR: Union.

RELIGION: Christian. Raised in strict Christian atmosphere as a child and young adult.

EDUCATION: Attended the University of Pennsylvania before enrolling in West Point in 1842.
West Point graduate – class of 1846. Second in his class.

MARRIAGE: Married Ellen Maray. She had been courted by himself and General Ambrose Powell Hill

CAREER HIGHLIGHTS & TIDBITS: Outspoken, he once declared: *"The President is an idiot! I only wish to save my country and find the incapables around me will not permit it!"*
> One of the Union's top military leaders during the Civil War.
> Soundly defeated the Confederate forces under the command of General Robert E. Lee at Antietam, Maryland on September 16, 1862.
> Lee said that McClellan was the best Union commander he had faced during the war.
> Governor of New Jersey (1878-1881).

QUOTABLE QUOTE: June 2, 1862: *"I am tired of the battlefield, with its mangled corpses and poor wounded. Victory has no charms for me when purchased at such as cost."*

SAW ACTION AT: Rich Mountain, Richmond, the Peninsular Campaign, Fain Oaks, Seven Days' Battles, Antietam, etc.

LITTLE KNOWN FACT: On June 28, 1862 he told Secretary of War, Edwin M. Stanton: "If I save the army now, I tell you plainly that I owe no thanks to you or any other persons in Washington."

Spider Corn Bread—
A Favorite of Fightin' Joe Wheeler

2 eggs
2 tbls sugar
3 cups milk
1 tsp salt

1-1/3 cups corn meal
1/3 cup flour
1 tsp baking powder
2 tbls butter

Harshly beat eggs and sugar together in wooden mixing bowl. Lightly stir in 2 cups of the milk and salt. Lightly stir in 2 cups of milk and salt. Gradually stir in cornmeal, flour and baking powder. Make certain everything is thoroughly blended. Now melt butter in cast iron skillet. Turn skillet so as to grease sides. Pour creamy batter from mixing bowl into skillet. Smooth over the top. Hold other cup of milk about six inches above skillet. Slowly pour over top of batter in circular motion. Do not stir! Carefully place skillet in rather quick oven (400 degrees). Bake for 30 minutes. When spider cake is done it will have a streak of tasty custard running throughout. Serve with plenty of butter.

Joseph Wheeler (1836-1906)

HERITAGE: Born and raised in Georgia.

RANK: General.

FOUGHT FOR: Confederacy.

RELIGION: Christian.

EDUCATION: Attended West Point.
Graduated near the bottom of his class.

CAREER HIGHLIGHTS & TIDBITS: Fought on the frontier prior to the Civil War.
Had at least 16 horses shot out from under him while engaging the enemy during the Civil War.
Called *"Fighting Joe"* because of his *"dogged aggressiveness"*.
Wrote *Cavalry Tactics* in 1863.
Alabama congressman (1880 to 1882) (1884 to 1899).
Famous for his assaults against Union supply lines.
One such series of raids ran October 1 through October 9 in Chattanooga, Tennessee.
Able to force the Union military to evacuate Chattanooga.
Reorganized and commanded the cavalry for the Army of Mississippi.
Proceeded to lead raids against Union communications.
Became the senior cavalry officer in the Confederacy by 1864.
Fought unsuccessfully against General Sherman during his *"March to the Sea."*
Captured in May of 1865.
Was the only Confederate force to actively oppose Sherman's legions at this time.

SAW ACTION AT: Perryville, Stones River, Knoxville, Shiloh, the Atlanta Campaign, etc.

LITTLE KNOWN FACT: Fought in at least 1,000 skirmishes and engagements throughout the Civil War.

5

Civil War Era Coffeecakes
and Sweet Rolls

Old-Time Cinnamon Rolls—
A Favorite of the Custer Family

2/3 cup yeast   1/2 tsp salt
2 tbls sugar   2 1/2 cups flour
1/4 cup shortening   brown sugar to suit
1 egg, well beaten   1 1/2 tsp cinnamon

Put the yeast in a large wooden mixing bowl. Stir the sugar into this and let it stand for 10 minutes. While waiting, melt the shortening. Then add the shortening, beaten egg, salt and 3/4 cup of lukewarm water. Gradually stir in the flour. Beat the entire mixture well. Place the dough in a lightly buttered bowl, cover with a towel, and set in a warm place to rise. When the dough has doubled its original size, lay it on a floured board (or counter top) and roll our in a 1/2 inch think sheet. Brush over the entire sheet with melted butter. Then sprinkle with brown sugar and cinnamon. Roll the sheet up tightly like a jellyroll. Cut in 1-inch slices. Place each slice flat in a buttered baking pan. Again set aside to rise. When doubled in bulk, place in rather quick oven (400 to 425 degrees) until nicely browned.

George Armstrong Custer (1839-1876)

HERITAGE: Grandfather was Hessian mercenary named Kuster. Settled in Pennsylvania after the Revolutionary War.

Father a farmer, later migrated to Ohio.

RANK: General.

FOUGHT FOR: Union.

RELIGION: Christian.

EDUCATION: West Point graduate – class of 1861.

Ranked last in his class – 34th of 34.

CAREER HIGHLIGHTS & TIDBITS: Had 11 horses shot out from under him while in combat situations during the Civil War.

Wounded only once during the Civil War.

A tall, handsome, *Bible*-believing cavalry man

Had since childhood dreamed only of being a soldier.

No man was braver under fire.

Best known for his curly, blond, flowing locks.

Was unbelievably courageous.

Served on the staff of General's Kearney, Smith and McClellan.

Few people realize that he was only 37 when he died.

Gained lasting fame in what history calls *"Custer's Last Stand."* This is where he and his army were meticulously slaughtered by Sitting Bull's warriors at Little Big Horn on July 23, 1876.

QUOTABLE QUOTE: At Cedar Creek, Virginia, on September 19, 1864, he was in charge of the 1st cavalry. He declared: *"This is the bulliest day since Christ was born."*

SAW ACTION AT: Bull Run, Peninsular Campaign, Gettysburg, Winchester, Fisher's Hill, Cedar Creek, Dinwiddle Courthouse, Five Forks, Appomattox, etc.

LITTLE KNOWN FACT: More than 10,000 Confederate prisoners were captured under his command.

Southern Breakfast Break—
Mrs. Johnston'sThanksgiving Treat

3/4 cup sugar
3 tbls butter
1 egg, beaten
3/4 cup milk

2 cups flour
2 tsp baking powder
1/4 tsp salt
1/2 cup brown sugar

cinnamon to suit

Cream the sugar and 1 teaspoon of butter in a wooden mixing bowl. Stir in the beaten egg and milk. Sift together in a separate bowl the flour, baking powder, and salt. Blend these dry ingredients with those in first bowl. Grease a large baking pan. Pour batter into pan. Sprinkle over top of batter with brown sugar and cinnamon. Don't top with the rest of the butter. Bake in quick oven (425 degrees) for 25 minutes. Makes 6 generous servings.

Albert Sidney Johnston (1803-1862)

HERITAGE: Born in Washington, Kentucky.

RANK: General.

FOUGHT FOR: Confederacy.

RELIGION: Christian – Mother and father made him attend both Sunday School and church when he was a child.

EDUCATION: West Point graduate – class of 1826

CAREER HIGHLIGHTS & TIDBITS: Appointed to be commander of the Texas Army in 1837.
> Resulted in a duel with another officer who believed he should have been given the promotion instead of Johnston.
> Secretary of War for the Republic of Texas from 1838 to 1840.
> Fought in the Black Hawk War.
> Fought in the Mexican War.
> Led the famous "Utah Expedition" against the cultist Mormons from 1838 to 1860.
> Believed by Jefferson Davis, President of the Confederacy, to be *"the greatest soldier…then living."*
> Suffered serious leg wound at Shiloh on April 6, 1862 on the first day of fighting.
> Subsequently died as a result of this injury.
> Oversaw the retreat of Confederate forces from Nashville.

QUOTABLE QUOTE: Jefferson Davis, President of the Confederate States of America, had this to say in September of 1861: *"I hoped and expected that I had others who would prove Generals, but I knew I had one, and that was Sidney Johnston."*

SAW ACTION AT: Shiloh.

LITTLE KNOWN FACT: Never owned a slave, as did General Grant, General Winfield Scott, and numerous others.

Pumpkin Coffeecake—
As Made for Admiral Farragut

1/2 cup olive oil	1/4 tsp salt
2 eggs	1 tsp baking soda
1/3 cup water, warm	1/2 tsp nutmeg
1 cup pumpkin, mashed	1 tsp cinnamon
1 2/3 cups flour, sifted	1 cup nuts, chopped
1 1/4 cups sugar	1/2 cup cherries, chopped

Blend the olive oil, eggs, water, and pumpkin in a large wooden mixing bowl. Beat hard together. Then sift together the flour, sugar, salt, baking soda, and spices. Gradually add these dry ingredients to those in the mixing bowl. Beat hard until it is smooth and creamy. Lastly stir in the nuts and cherries. Pour the batter into a well-buttered and floured shallow baking pan. Sprinkle the top with finely chopped nutmeats. Bake in moderate oven (350 degrees) for 1 hour. When done take the coffee cake from the oven and sprinkle over the top with powdered sugar. Serve while hot or when cold.

David Glasgow Farragut (1801-1870)

HERITAGE: Born in Tennessee. Orphaned as a youngster.

RANK: Admiral.

FOUGHT FOR: Union.

RELIGION: Christian (see quote below).

EDUCATION: Home schooled as a child by only the best of tutors in Washington, D.C. and Pennsylvania.

>Attended lectures at Yale while living in New Haven, Connecticut during the 1820's.

>Attended lectures at the Smithsonian Institution while on a tour of duty in Washington, D.C.

CAREER HIGHLIGHTS & TIDBITS: First joined the Union Navy in 1810 when only nine years old.

>Went to sea in 1811 on the frigate *U.S.S. Essex.*

>Only 10 years old, he stayed under the watchful eye of his guardian, Commodore David Porter.

>Given his first command of a ship when only 12-years old.

>Captain Porter gave this 12-year old midshipman his first shipboard command.

>The ship was a war prize captured in the Pacific Ocean.

>Farragut sailed the vessel safely across the Pacific.

>Docked in Valparaiz, a Chilean seaport.

>Served in the War of 1812 while 11 years old.

>Became the Civil War's first admiral.

>Destroyed the Confederate fleet in Mobile Bay on April 5, 1864.

QUOTABLE QUOTE: His son Lowell wrote this of his revered Christian father : *"He never felt so near his Master as he did in a storm, knowing that on his skill depended the safety of so many lives."*

LITTLE KNOWN FACT: Gideon Welles, Lincoln's Secretary of the Navy, had this to say: *"He would more willingly take great risks to obtain great results than any officer in either the Army or the Navy."*

Cranberry-Apple Coffeecake—
A Favorite of Captain Henry Wirz

1/2 cup butter	1 tsp cinnamon
1 cup sugar	1/2 tsp mace
1 egg	1/2 tsp nutmeg
2 cups flour, sifted	1/3 cup orange juice
2 tsp baking powder	1 1/2 tbls orange rind, grated
1/2 tsp baking soda	1 cup fresh cranberries, chopped
1/2 tsp salt	1 cup apples, grated

Cream the butter and sugar in a large wooden mixing bowl. When it is light and fluffy add the egg and beat thoroughly. In a separate bowl combine the flour, baking powder, baking soda, salt, and spices. Sift these ingredients into the mixture in the first bowl, alternately with the orange juice. Lastly blend in the orange rind, cranberries, and apples. Pour the batter into a well-buttered and lightly floured shallow baking pan. When done, the center of the coffeecake should spring back to the touch. Let it cool for 10 minutes before taking from the pan.

Henry Wirz (1822-1865)

HERITAGE: Born in Switzerland. Immigrated to America in 1849.

RANK: Captain – Commandant of Andersonville Prison in Georgia.

RELIGION: Christian (see quote below).

EDUCATION: A Swiss-educated physician.

CAREER HIGHLIGHTS & TIDBITS: First settled in Louisiana as a medical doctor.

> Assigned to be Commandant of the Andersonville Prison.
> Wounds previously received at Seven Pines became infected.
> He suffered with this for the rest of his life.
> His arm was useless either in a sling or hanging limply at his side.
> Accused of war crimes because of the horrible conditions in the prison camp – overcrowding, poor sanitation, starvation and brutality of the guards.
> 13,000 prisoners died at Andersonville.
> Wirz was unfairly blamed.
> *Harper's Weekly* deliberately distorted the truth against him.
> Public wrath was incited.
> Quickly arrested when the Civil War ended.
> Unfairly tried and convicted for *"murder in violation of the laws and customs of war."*

QUOTABLE QUOTE(S): The last words of Henry Wirz were: *"I go before my God, an Almighty God, who will judge between us. I am innocent and I will die like a man."* A black hood was then placed over his head and the noose around his neck.

SAW ACTION AT: Seven Pines where he was wounded in the shoulder and right arm on June 2, 1862.

LITTLE KNOWN FACTS: Only person to be executed for so-called *"war crimes"* after the Civil War ended.

> Hanged in November of 1865 for *"conspiracy to murder prisoners."*

Coffeecake—
Julia Grant's Best

1/2 cake yeast	1/2 tsp salt
1 cup milk, scalded and cooled	2 cups flour
1 tbls sugar	1/4 cup butter, soft
	1/2 cup sugar
1 egg, well beaten	

Crumble the yeast in 1/4 cup lukewarm water and let it dissolve. Meanwhile put the milk into a large wooden bowl. Add the sugar, salt, and flour. Stir well and blend in the yeast. Cover the bowl with a thick towel and set it in a warm place to rise overnight. In the morning blend in the soft butter, sugar, and egg. Work in enough flour to make a very soft and pliable dough. Break the dough into 2 equal pieces. Place each in a buttered shallow pan. Cover again and let rise until very light. Then uncover and rub the cake tops with sugar dissolved in milk. Sprinkle with dry sugar and cinnamon. Bake in moderate oven (350) degrees for about 25 minutes. The coffee cake should be about 1 1/2 inches thick when finished. Serve while either warm or cold.

Ulysses Simpson Grant (1822-1885)

HERITAGE: Born in Mt. Pleasant, Ohio. His father, a man of modest means, was a tanner.

RANK: General.

FOUGHT FOR: Union.

RELIGION: Christian – see quote below.

EDUCATION: West Point graduate – class of 1843. Didn't especially stand out as a cadet.

MARRIAGE: Wed Julia Dent in 1848.

CAREER HIGHLIGHTS & TIDBITS: Brilliant military tactician.
Relentless warrior. Constantly hammered away at the enemy.
Earned a citation for bravery in the Mexican War (1846-1847).
His son, Frederick Dent, born in St. Louis, Missouri in 1800 accompanied him often during the Civil War.
Grant declared in 1861: *"I have but one sentiment now. That is we have a government and a flag and they must be sustained. There are but two parties now—treasons and patriots, and I want hereafter to be ranked with the latter..."*
Became the 18th President of the United States (1869-1873).

QUOTABLE QUOTE: *"I believe in the Holy Scriptures, and who lives by them will be benefited thereby. Men may differ as to the interpretation ... but the Scriptures are man's best guide."*

SAW ACTION AT: Five Forks, Cold harbor, Petersburg, Shiloh, Vicksburg, Missionary Ridge (Chattanooga), The Wilderness, etc.

LITTLE KNOWN FACT: He and General James Longstreet – as well as their two wives- had all developed a close friendship when they served together at Jefferson Barracks during the 1840's. Julia Dent Grant was a cousin of General Longstreet.

Holiday Sweet Rolls—
Mrs. Porter's Finest

2 cups flour	2 tbls sugar
4 tsp baking powder	1/3 tsp cinnamon
1/2 tsp salt	1/2 lemon rind, grated
2 tbls butter	1/2 cup raisins, cut fine
2/3 cup milk	2 tbls citron, finely chopped

Sift the flour, baking powder and salt together in a large wooden mixing bowl. Rub in the butter. Add the milk and blend thoroughly. Roll the dough out into a 1/4-inch thick sheet (or thinner if you can). Brush over the top with melted butter. Then sprinkle with the sugar, cinnamon, lemon rind, raisins and citron. Tightly roll the dough up like a jellyroll. Cut into 1/2 to 1-inch slices. Place each slice flat on a buttered pan. Bake in a hot oven (425 to 450 degrees).

David Dixon Porter (1813-1891)

HERITAGE: Born and raised in Chester, Pennsylvania.

RANK: Admiral.

FOUGHT FOR: Union.

RELIGION: Christian.

EDUCATION: High school graduate.

CAREER HIGHLIGHTS & TIDBITS: Joined the Mexican Navy at the age of 13 years in 1826.
> Entered the United States Navy in 1829 as a midshipman.
> Saw action in the Mexican War.
> Took part in an unsuccessful assault on Vera Cruz.
> Commanded landing party that stormed a coastal fort at Tabasco.
> First command was the *Spitfire*, a steam vessel.
> Later served in the Mediterranean aboard the *United States* and the *Constellation.*
> Ready to leave the navy out of boredom but the Civil War started.
> Given command of the *U.S.S. Powhattan.*
> Commodore David Porter was David Glasgow Farragut's guardian.
> Worked on coastal surveying for a period of six years.
> Appointed to be superintendent of the United States Naval Academy in Annapolis, Maryland in 1865.
> President Grant appointed him to be an advisor to the Secretary of the Navy in 1869.
> Uncle of Union General Fitz-John Porter.

SAW ACTION AT: New Orleans, Blockade of Pensacola, Mobile, and the Southwest pass of the Mississippi River in 1861.

LITTLE KNOWN FACTS: Taken prisoner after doing battle with a Spanish frigate off the coast of Cuba.
> Spent time in a jail in Havana, Cuba before being repatriated.

6

Biscuit Making and Baking
as the War Raged On

Minute Biscuits—
A Favorite of Sue Rose Powell Hill

2 tsp butter   2 cups buttermilk
1 tsp baking soda   flour to suit

 Melt the butter and blend it with the baking soda and buttermilk. Add enough flour to make a very soft dough—just stiff enough to barely handle. *Do not knead* this dough or you will ruin the biscuits. Roll our lightly into a sheet about 3/4 inch thick. Rapidly cut into small round cakes and place them on a floured baking pan. Handle as little as possible. Bake in a quick to very quick oven (425 to 450) degrees).

NOTE: Sour milk may be used in place of the buttermilk called for above. The biscuits will be equally as good made either way.

Ambrose Powell Hill (1825-1865)

HERITAGE: Born and raised in Culpepper, Virginia.
  Son of a soldier.

RANK: General.

FOUGHT FOR: Confederacy.

RELIGION: Christian.

EDUCATION: West Point graduate – class of 1848. He was 15th in his class of 48. Struggled mightily to get through the Academy.

MARRIAGE: Courted Ellen Maury, but lost out to George McClellan.
  Married a sister of John Hunt Morgan, later to become famous as a prominent General in the Confederate Army.

CAREER HIGHLIGHTS & TIDBITS: Fought in the Mexican War in 1847.
  Fought in Seminole War from 1849-1850 and 1853-1855.
  Later against General Grant as he launched his final assault on Petersburg.
  Wounded at Chancellorsville.
  Shot and killed as he fearlessly rode to the front lines to rally his men. This was in all probability best. He had earlier remarked that he did not want to be alive to witness the end of the Confederacy.

QUOTABLE QUOTE: *"Damn you, if you will not follow men, then I'll die alone!" Thrilled, his men charged and overcame a Union attack.*

SAW ACTION AT: First Bull Run, Second Bull Run, The Peninsular Campaign, Williamsburg, Mechanicsville, Gaine's Mill, Cedar Mountain, Antietam, Petersburg, Gettysburg, etc.

LITTLE KNOWN FACT: Roommate at West Point with the to become famous General George McClellan.

Yam Biscuits—
John Wilkes Booth's Favorite

1 1/2 cup yams, mashed   2 1/2 cups flour
1 1/3 cup milk   8 tsp baking powder
8 tbls butter, melted   2 tbls sugar

2 tsp salt

Put mashed yams, milk, and melted butter in wooden mixing bowl. Sift together flour, baking powder, sugar, and salt in same bowl. Mix thoroughly to make soft dough. Turn out on floured board. Toss lightly until outside of dough appears smooth. Roll out to ½ inch thick sheet. Cut with floured biscuit cutter or upside down drinking glass. Bake on greased baking tin in very quick oven (450 degrees) for about 15 minutes.

John Wilkes Booth (1838-1865)

HERITAGE: Born and raised on small farm near Bel Aire, Maryland.   One child in a large family.

POSITION: Actor, assassin.

RELIGION: Christian – see quote below.

EDUCATION: Little, if any, formal education. School bored him. Interested only in becoming a famous actor.

CAREER HIGHLIGHTS & TIDBITS: Started acting at age 17 in Baltimore's St. Charles Theater.

    Extremely handsome young man.

    Adventurous and athletic as a youngster.

    Played minor roles in 1857and 1858 at Philadelphia's popular Arch Street Theater.

    Unpopular with audiences because he failed to properly memorize his lines.

    Eventually became acknowledged Shakespearean star throughout while on tour throughout the country.

    A fanatical Southern sympathizer yet he failed to enlist in the Confederate army.

    Strongly in favor of slavery.

    Had planned initially to kidnap President Lincoln and carry him to Richmond.

    The President was to be held hostage in hopes of forcing an end to the Civil War.

    He saw the Civil War as a struggle between tyranny and freedom.

QUOTABLE QUOTE: An entry in his diary dated April 13-19, 1865 reads: *"Our country owed all her troubles to him [Lincoln], and God simply made me the instrument of His punishment."*

LITTLE KNOWN FACTS: Last words before dying were: *"Tell mother I die for my country."*

    His brother called him *"one of America's greatest stage talents among the youthful actors in America."*

Christmas Drop Biscuits—
Abner Doubleday's Favorite

2 3/4 cups flour   1 tsp salt
4 tsp baking powder   6 tbls butter
1 1/4 cup milk

Sift together in a wooden mixing bowl the flour, baking powder, and salt. Rub in butter with fingers until mixture resembles corn meal. Add milk. Stir sufficiently to blend everything thoroughly. Set aside momentarily. Grease a large baking sheet. Drop batter by tablespoonfuls onto baking sheet. Bake in hot oven (425 degrees) for 10 to 15 minutes. Serve while hot with butter.

Abner Doubleday (1819-1893)

HERITAGE: Born and raised in New York State.

RANK: General.

FOUGHT FOR: Union.

RELIGION: Christian. Raised in a stalwart Christian home.

EDUCATION: West Point graduate.
Trained as a civil engineer. Brilliant student.

CAREER HIGHLIGHTS & TIDBITS: Fought heroically in the Seminole War .
Received much battlefield experience during the Mexican War.
Fought gallantly in the Shenandoah Valley Campaign in 1862. Won regular promotions.
Given temporary command of I Corps when General John Reynolds was killed.
This took place during the Battle of Gettysburg in 1863.
Not considered much of a military leader by his peers..
Later denied permanent command of I Corps.
Served out his time in the military in administrative posts.
Retired from the Union Army in 1837.
Later became famous as the founder of America's national past-time – baseball.
Widely credited with inventing the game in 1839, although some sports authorities and historians dispute this.
Commenting on Major Robert Anderson, Commander of Fort Sumter: *"He desired not only to save the Union, but to save slavery with it. He could not read the signs of the times and see that the conscience of the nation and the progress of civilization had already doomed slavery to destruction."*

SAW ACTION AT: Second Bull Run, Antietam, Fredericksburg, Shenandoah Valley Campaign, South Mountain, Gettysburg, etc.

LITTLE KNOWN FACT: Was the man who, while on garrison duty, is said to have fired the first shot from Fort Sumter.

Bacon Biscuits—
Thanksgiving Favorite of the Wirz Family

4 cups flour	1 cup bacon, fried,
5 tsp baking powder	finely chopped
1 tsp salt	1/2 cup bacon grease
1/4 tsp pepper	1 1/2 cup milk

Sift together in a wooden mixing bowl the flour, baking powder, salt and pepper. Blend in crispy chopped bacon bits. Pour in cooled bacon grease and stir until mixture looks like coarse corn meal. Make a hole in center of the mixture. Pour in milk and thoroughly blend. The mixture should be soft but not sticky. Turn out onto a floured board. Knead lightly about 10 to 15 strokes. Then roll out to a 1/4 inch thick sheet for crusty biscuits. Cut with lightly floured biscuit cutter or an overturned drinking glass. Place on an ungreased baking sheet. Bake in very quick oven (450 degrees) for 12 to 15 minutes or until golden brown. Makes about 16 large biscuits.

Henry Wirz (1822-1865)

HERITAGE: Born in Switzerland.
  Immigrated to the United States in 1849.

RANK: Commandant of the infamous Andersonville Prison.

RELIGION: Christian (see quote below).

EDUCATION: A Swiss-born physician.

CAREER HIGHLIGHTS & TIDBITS: First settled in Louisiana as doctor of medicine.
  Worked as a mere clerk in the Libby Prison.
  Assigned to be Commandant of the Andersonville Prison in Georgia.
  His wounds received at Seven Points became infected.
  He suffered with this for the rest of his life.
  His arm was useless and was either always held in a sling or seen dangling limply at his side.
  13,000 prisoners died at Andersonville.
  Wirz was wrongly blamed for this situation by Northern radicals.
  Quickly arrested when the Civil War ended.
  Unfairly tried and convicted for *"murder in violation of the laws and customs of war."*

QUOTABLE QUOTE: The last words of Henry Wirz were: *"I go before my God, an Almighty God, who will judge between us. I am innocent and I will die like a man."*
  A black hood was then placed over his head and the noose around his neck.

SAW ACTION AT: Seven Pines. Wounded in the shoulder and right arm on June 2, 1862.

LITTLE KNOWN FACTS: Captain Henry Wirz was the only person to be executed for so-called *"war crimes"* after the War ended.
  He was hanged in November of 1865 for *"conspiracy to murder prisoners."*

Wholewheat Biscuits—
J.E.B. Stuart's Favorite

1 1/2 cup whole wheat flour   1 tsp salt
3 cups flour, sifted   1/2 cup butter
5 tsp baking powder   1 1/2 cup cream

Sift together in a wooden mixing bowl the whole-wheat flour, sifted flour, baking powder and salt. Using a fork, cut butter into these dry ingredients until mixture looks like coarse corn meal. Make a hole in the center. Pour cream in hole and blend by stirring quickly and lightly until everything is nicely blended. The mixture should be soft but not sticky. Turn it out onto a lightly floured board. Knead about 15 strokes. Pat or roll out to a 1/2 inch thick sheet. Cut with lightly floured biscuit cutter or an overturned drinking glass. Place on ungreased baking sheet. Bake in very quick oven (450 degrees) for 12 to 15 minutes or until golden brown. Makes about 16 soft and fluffy biscuits.

James Ewell Brown Stuart (1833-1864)

HERITAGE: Born on Laurel Hill Plantation, Patrick County, Virginia. Seventh of ten children.   Family was wealthy.

RANK: General.

FOUGHT FOR: Confederacy.

RELIGION: Christian.
      Quiet and not vocal about his religious beliefs. (see quote below)

EDUCATION: West Point graduate – class of 1854. He was 13th in a class of 46.
      Home-schooled as a child. Attended Emory and Henry College before entering West Point in 1850.

CAREER HIGHLIGHTS & TIDBITS: Never doubted that he was fighting for what he called the *"will of the Almighty."*
      Had a crush on General Lee's daughter.
      One of Lee's favorite cadets.
      Wanted to ask General Lee if he could "court" his daughter, but never did because a cadet simply did not ask the man in charge of West Point a question of this nature.
      Mortally wounded and his command defeated on May 11, 1864 during a fierce battle at Yellow Tavern, just north of Richmond.
      His death was a devastating blow to the Confederacy.
      A dashing young officer, and brilliant military strategist.

QUOTABLE QUOTE: Stuart's last words: *"If it were God's will I should like to live longer and serve my country. If I must die, I should like to see my wife first, but if it is His will that I die now I am ready and willing to go if God and my country think that I have fulfilled by destiny and done my duty."*

SAW ACTION AT: Harper's Ferry, Bull Run, Chambersburg, Dumfries Raid, Chancellorsville, Gettysburg, Yellow Tavern, etc.

LITTLE KNOWN FACT: His father-in-law was Virginia-born, Union General Philip St. George Cooke, also a Cavalry leader.

Squash Biscuits—
Made for the Rosecrans Family

1 yeast cake	1 cup sugar
1 cup water, lukewarm	2 tbls butter, softened
2 cups squash	1/2 tsp salt
flour to suit	

This is to be started before going to bed. Crumble yeast cake in lukewarm water and stir until completely dissolved. Set aside momentarily. Now rub squash through a sieve and put in wooden mixing bowl. Add sugar, softened butter and salt. Beat together until all are well blended. Add yeast and beat once again to blend. Sift flour. Add just enough flour to mixture in bowl to make stiff batter. Cover and leave in warm place over night. In the morning put into greased biscuit tins. Bake in rather quick oven (400 to 425 degrees) for 15 minutes.

William Starke Rosecrans (1819-1898)

HERITAGE: Born in Delaware County, Ohio.

RANK: General.

FOUGHT FOR: Union.

RELIGION: Christian.

EDUCATION: West Point graduate. Class of 1842.

MARRIAGE: Unknown.

CHILDREN: Unknown.

CAREER HIGHLIGHTS & TIDBITS: Great-grandson of a well-known Christian leader in early America – Stephen Hopkins, Colonial Governor of Rhode Island.

> Great-grandfather was also a signer of the *Declaration of Independence*.
> Respected battlefield strategist.
> Became commanding officer of the 23rd Ohio Volunteer infantry.
> Other members of the Ohio 23rd were two future Presidents – Rutherford Hayes and William McKinley.
> Fondly nicknamed "Old Rosie."
> Highly regarded as a military strategist.
> Served as U.S. minister to Mexico in 1868 and 1869.
> Taught natural and experimental philosophy and engineering at West Point.

SAW ACTION AT: Rich Mountain, Corinth, Stones River Campaign, Chickamauga, etc.

LITTLE KNOWN FACT: Graduated from West Point with such later-to-become-famous military men as James Longstreet and Abner Doubleday who would years later to be credited with the founding of America's favorite pastime – baseball.

Rye Biscuits—
Stonewall Jackson's Favorite

2 cups rye meal   1 tsp baking powder
1 tbls shortening   1/2 cup molasses
pinch of salt   1 cup milk
                flour to suit

Put the rye meal into a large wooden mixing bowl. Rub in the shortening and salt. Then stir in the baking powder, molasses, and milk. Blend thoroughly and add sufficient flour to make a very soft dough. Roll the dough out into a 1/2 thick sheet. Cut into small round cakes. Set these cakes in rows on a floured baking tin. Bake in quick oven (425 degrees). These biscuits are best when eaten hot.

Stonewall Jackson (1824-1863)

HERITAGE: Parents died in poverty when he was a child. Grew up as an orphan in Clarksburg, Virginia. Raised by an uncle.

RANK: General.

FOUGHT FOR: Confederacy.

RELIGION: Christian. On his deathbed, he spoke to his wife: *"Please remember me in your prayers, but never forget to use the old petition, 'thy will be done'."*

EDUCATION: West Point graduate – class of 1846. Graduated 17th in their class of 59. Class included such future leaders as Confederate General A.P. Hill and Union General George McClellan.

MARRIAGE: First wife, Eleanor Junkin, died in 1854. Wed Mary Anna Morrison three years later.

CAREER HIGHLIGHTS & TIDBITS: Colonel Sam Fulkerson of the 37th Virginia Infantry had this to say regarding Jackson: *"Our men curse for the hard marching he makes them do, but still...have the most unbounded confidence in him. They say he can take them into harder places and get them out better than any other living man."*
> Commanded a cadet detachment that was present at the execution by hanging of John Brown, the radical abolitionist and insurrectionist.
> Was General Daniel Harvey Hill's brother-in-law.

QUOTABLE QUOTE: In September of 1862, Harper's Ferry surrendered to General Jackson. He stopped his horse in front of the 9th Vermont, removed his hat, and quietly said: *"Boys, don't feel bad. You couldn't help it. It was just as God willed it!"*

SAW ACTION AT: First Battle of Bull Run, Manassas, Shenandoah Valley Campaign, Front Royal, Kernstown, Winchester, Antietam, etc.

LITTLE KNOWN FACT: His final words before dying were: *"Let us cross over the river and rest in the shade of the trees."*

Homemade Biscuits—
Mrs. Hampton's Specialty

2 cups flour	1/3 cup butter
1/2 tsp salt	3/4 cup sour milk
1/2 tsp baking soda	

Sift the flour with the salt in a wooden mixing bowl. Cut in the butter with a fork until the mixture is as fine as corn meal. In a separate bowl combine the sour milk and the baking soda until the baking soda is completely dissolved. Stir this into the flour mixture and continue to stir until a soft dough is formed. Take out of the mixing bowl and knead lightly on a floured surface for 1 minute. Roll out to a 1/4 inch thick sheet and cut with a floured biscuit cutter. Place each biscuit on a greased baking sheet. Bake in a very quick oven (450 degrees) for 12 minutes. This old recipe makes 1-1/2 dozen marvelous Dixie soda biscuits. It originated with the family of Wade Hampton in South Carolina.

Wade Hampton (1818-1902)

HERITAGE: Born in South Carolina.

RANK: General.

FOUGHT FOR: Confederacy.

RELIGION: Christian – He was known to always have his *Bible* at his side when riding into battle.

EDUCATION: Graduated from South Carolina College in 1836.   Followed this by studying law.

MARRIAGE: Unknown.

CHILDREN: Unknown.

CAREER HIGHLIGHTS & TIDBITS: Wounded during the First Battle of Bull Run.
>Wounded again at Seven Pines in May of 1862. Wounded a third time at Gettysburg.
>A fearless warrior and respected by all who knew him.
>Became second-in-command with JEB Stuart's cavalry corps.
>Returned to his South Carolina estate when the war ended.
>Made an effort to rebuild his now-shrunken future.
>Became involved in politics.
>Tried his best to thwart the horrendous, radical Republican reconstruction policies.
>Fought the hate-filled northern politicians who were determined to punish the South and its leaders.

SAW ACTION AT: First Bull Run, Peninsular Campaign, Seven Pines, Antietam, Chambersburg, Gettysburg, etc.

LITTLE KNOWN FACTS: Elected Governor of South Carolina in 1876 by defeating a carpetbagger incumbent. Reelected in 1878. Later became a U.S. Senator.

Whole Wheat Biscuits—
Mrs. Kilpatrick's Best

2 cups whole wheat flour	4 tbls sugar
1 tsp salt	4 tbls shortening, melted
4 tbls baking powder	3/4 cup milk

Sift together the flour, salt, baking powder, and sugar in a wooden mixing bowl. In a separate bowl add the melted shortening to the milk. Blend well. Stir this into the dry ingredients to moisten, making the dough so soft as to be almost sticky. Turn out onto a lightly floured board. Roll or pat out to 1/2 inch thick. Cut into biscuits with biscuit cutter or upside down water glass. Place on well-greased baking sheet. Brush over with a little melted butter. Bake in a moderately quick oven (375 degrees) for 15 to 18 minutes. Serve while hot.

Hugh Judson Kilpatrick (1836-1881)

HERITAGE: Born and raised in New Jersey. Only son of a farmer.

RANK: General.

FOUGHT FOR: Union.

RELIGION: Christian, but many of his horrid deeds—burning, raping, and looting— would suggest otherwise.

EDUCATION: West Point graduate – class of 1861.

MARRIAGE: Unknown.

CHILDREN: Unknown.

CAREER HIGHLIGHTS & TIDBITS: Severely wounded during the Battle of Big Bethel in 1861.
Spent $5,000 in Savannah, Georgia to purchase matches for his men. He told them; *"If after ten years, travelers passing through the Carolinas shall see chimney stacks without houses and the country desolate, and they shall ask, 'Who did this terrible thing?' Some Yankees will answer: 'Kilpatrick's Cavalry!'"*
> His name became widely known as "Kill Cavalry" after the murderous Kilpatrick-Dahlgren raid on Richmond in 1864.
> After looting and burning Little Barnwell, South Carolina, he sent Sherman a caustic note referring to the town as "Burnsville."

QUOTABLE QUOTE: Sherman once declared: *"I know Kilpatrick is a hell of a damned fool, but I want just that sort of man to command my cavalry!"*

SAW ACTION AT: Big Bethel, Richmond, Atlanta Campaign, Sherman's March to the Sea, Carolina's Campaign, etc.

LITTLE KNOWN FACTS: A notorious womanizer.
> An obnoxious leader. Quickly bored those around him with his constant boasting about his innumerable female conquests.

All Night Riser Biscuits—
Mrs. Varina Davis Made These

4 cups milk	3/4 cup yeast
3/4 cup butter	2 tbls sugar
or	1 tsp salt
3/4 cup shortening	flour to suit

Start at night for some of the best old-fashioned breakfast biscuits you have ever tasted. Warm the milk slightly. Melt the butter in it—1/2 butter and 1/2 shortening is good as a rule. Pour into a large wooden mixing bowl. Then add the yeast, sugar, salt, and sufficient flour to make a soft dough. Cover with a thick towel and set aside to rise overnight. In the morning, roll the dough out into a sheet 3/4 of an inch thick. Cut into small round cakes. Set these closely together on a floured baking pan. Let them rise for another 20 minutes. Then place in quick to very quick oven (425 to 450 degrees) and bake for 20 minutes. Split, butter, and eat while hot.

Jefferson Davis (1808-1889)

HERITAGE: Born in Kentucky. 10th child of a settler who had fought in the Revolutionary War.

POSITION: President of the Confederacy.

RELIGION: Christian – Studied at a Roman Catholic seminary in Kentucky. Came close to renouncing his family's Baptist faith.

EDUCATION: West Point graduate – class of 1828. Graduated one year ahead of Robert E. Lee. Also attended Transylvania University.

MARRIAGE: Married the daughter, against his wishes, of future President Zachary Taylor. She died three months later. Remarried in 1848 to Varina Howell, the daughter of a wealthy and prominent Mississippi planter.

CAREER HIGHLIGHTS & TIDBITS: A hero throughout the South during and after the Civil War.

> He was captured by a detachment of Union cavalry.
> The editors of *Harper's Weekly* demanded that he be tried for treason and hanged.
> Never brought to trial after his capture.
> Held in prison for 2 years at Fortress Monroe.
> Mistreated with regularity and treated harshly.
> Allowed to read only his *Bible* and his *Episcopal Prayer Book* the entire time he was in prison.
> Finally released in May of 1867.

QUOTABLE QUOTE: *"... in my opinion, both Mr. Davis and General Lee,"* declared General Jubal Early, *"...did all for the success of our cause which it was humanly possible for mortal men to do."*

SAW ACTION AT: Hero in the Mexican War. Served in Black Hawk War of 1812.

LITTLE KNOWN FACT: His father had fought during the Revolutionary War as the leader of an irregular cavalry troop.

Biscuit Shortcake—
A Meade Family Favorite

2 1/2 cups flour	2 tbls sugar
4 tsp baking powder	5 tbls shortening
1/2 tsp salt	3/4 cup milk

Sift together the flour, baking powder, salt, and sugar in a wooden mixing bowl. Then cut in the shortening with a fork. Add milk and blend everything until smooth dough is obtained. Divide dough into two even portions and place on lightly floured board. Roll each portion out to 1/3 inch thick. Brush over both with melted butter or other shortening. Place one rolled piece on slightly greased baking sheet. Place other on top of the first. Bake in quick oven (425 degrees) for about 20 minutes. Take from oven when done and separate layers. Spread first layer thickly with crushed, sweetened fruit. Replace top layer. Put more fruit over it. Serve with cream or thin custard. This can also be made as individual shortcakes, if preferred, by cutting dough with biscuit cutter or over turned drinking glass before baking.

George Gordon Meade (1815-1872)

HERITAGE: Born in Cadiz, Spain. Father was a U.S. naval agent.

RANK: General.

FOUGHT FOR: Union.

RELIGION: Christian (see quote below).

EDUCATION: West Point graduate – class of 1835.
Was 19th in his class at the academy.

MARRIAGE: Margaretta (Margaret) Sergeant.

CHILDREN: Three sons and four daughters.

CAREER HIGHLIGHTS & TIDBITS: Meade once declared: *"My God, what misery this dreadful war has produced, and how it comes to the doors of almost everyone."*
Grant at one time considered replacing him
Had constant arguments with his subordinates.
Highly praised by President Lincoln for the manner in which he directed Union troops at Gettysburg.
Unruly temper. Flew off the handle at the least provocation.

QUOTABLE QUOTE: Said by his son:*"General Meade's religious principles were exhibited in his daily life, in his intercourse with his fellow men, and the Christian example he set. As far as his outward profession of belief was concerned, he was an active and attentive communicant in our church from an early day, and died in the triumphs of faith in the great Captain of his salvation."*

SAW ACTION AT: Seven Days' Battle, Antietam, Fredericksburg, Chancellorsville, Gettysburg, etc.

LITTLE KNOWN FACT: Wounded during the Battle of Seven Pines in July of 1862. Died a decade later in Philadelphia as a result of old warwounds complicated by pneumonia..

Rich Biscuits—
A Favorite of Robert E. Lee

2/3 cup yeast   flour to suit
1 cup cream   1/2 cup raisins, cut fine
                1/2 cup figs, cut fine

Blend the yeast and cream in a large wooden mixing bowl. Add 2 cups warm flour and beat thoroughly together. Cover the bowl and put it in a warm place to rise. When *light* (well risen), add sufficient flour to make a very soft and pliable dough. Divide the dough into halves. Roll each portion of the dough out into a 1/4-inch thick sheet. Sprinkle the raisins on one of the sheets. Lay the other sheet of dough on top of this. Then sprinkle the figs on top of the second sheet and lightly press them in. Cut into biscuits of various fancy shapes. Lay them on a buttered baking pan and allow to rise until extremely light and fluffy. When ready, place in quick to very quick oven (425 to 450 degrees) and quickly bake until light brown.

Robert E. Lee (1807-1870)
In His Own Words

ON BLACKS: *"There was no doubt that the blacks were immeasurably better off here than they were in Africa – morally, physically, and socially."*

HANDLING AUTHORITY: To General Ambrose Hill when he became enraged with a subordinate: *"Those men are not an army--they are citizens defending their country....When a man makes a mistake, I call him into my tent and use the authority of my position to make him do the right thing the next time."*

ON INTEGRITY: *"There is true glory and a true honor – the glory of duty done, the honor of the integrity of principle."*

ON DUTY: *"Do your duty in all things. You cannot do more; you should never wish to do less."*

ON PROMOTING OFFICERS WHO DRANK: *"I cannot consent to place in the control of others who cannot control himself."*

ADVICE ON GOD: *"Above all things, learn at once to worship your Creator and to do His will as revealed in His Holy Book."*

TO STONEWALL JACKSON'S PASTOR: *"I dread the thought of any student going away from the college without becoming a sincere Christian."*

TO HIS WIFE: *"I tremble for my country when I hear of confidence expressed in me. I know too well my weakness... that our only hope is in God."*

A PERSONAL MAXIM: *"Those who oppose our purposes are not always to be regarded as our enemy."*

TO HIS SON: *"I am unwilling to do what is wrong."*

Beaten Biscuits— As Enjoyed by
General John Bankhead Magruder

4 cups flour	1 tsp salt
1 tsp baking powder	1 tbls shortening
7/8 cup ice water	

Sift together the flour, baking powder, and salt in a wooden mixing bowl. Cut in the shortening with a fork. Add ice water. Knead with hands until a smooth dough is obtained. Turn the dough out onto a board and pat with a rolling pin until it blisters. Keep folding dough together and patting with rolling pin as it spreads on board. This procedure usually takes about 20 minutes. When full of blisters, roll dough out to about 1/4 inch thick. Cut into biscuits with biscuit cutters or an upside down water glass. Prick each biscuit with a fork. Place biscuits on baking sheet. Bake in moderately quick oven (375 degrees) for 15 minutes. Serve while hot with plenty of butter on the side or with gravy over them.

John Bankhead Magruder (1810-1871)

HERITAGE: Born in Port Royal, Virginia.

RANK: General.

FOUGHT FOR: Confederacy.

RELIGION: Christian.

EDUCATION: West Point graduate – class of 1830. Graduated 15th in his class.

MARRIAGE: Wed Esther Henrietta von Kapff.

CAREER HIGHLIGHTS & TIDBITS: Fought heroically in the Seminole War.

Fought in the Mexican War with Winfield Scott's army.

One of the Confederacy's most acclaimed military leaders. Became a celebrity throughout the South because of his significant victory at Big Bethel on June 10, 1861.

Called "Prince John" by those who knew him best while stationed in Newport, Rhode Island.

Loved lavish living, the picture of a Virginia gentleman.

Went into exile in Mexico after the Civil War ended.

Became a m
Major General under Emperor Maxmilian.

Severely wounded

A great favorite of General Winfield Scott.

According to a friend of John H. Edwards: *"Magruder was a born soldier would fight all day and dance all night. He wrote love songs and then sang them."*

SAW ACTION AT: Big Bethel, Seven Days' Battles around Richmond, Chickamauga, Peninsular Campaign, Malvern Hill, etc.

LITTLE KNOWN FACTS: Defiantly refused to ask for a parole when the Civil War ended.

Banned liquor for his troops, but was known to take a sip.

Spoke with a lisp.

7

Homemade Crackers
from the Civil War Era

Plain Crackers—
as Made by Mrs. Anderson

2 cups flour
1/2 tsp salt
1 heaping tsp baking
    powder

4 tbls butter
    (melted)
1 egg white, beaten
1 cup milk

Sift the flour, salt, and baking powder together into a large wooden mixing bowl. Then stir in the melted butter, beaten egg white, and milk. Thoroughly blend everything. Add additional flour as necessary to make a very stiff dough—as stiff as can be rolled out. Pound and knead this dough for a long time. Roll out to the thinness of piecrust. Cut into either round or square pieces to suit. Bake on a floured pan in moderate to moderately quick oven (350 to 375 degrees) or until crackers turn light brown.

NOTE: When these crackers get stale it can be easily remedied. Simply place them back in the oven for a few moments just before they are needed for the table. The crispness will quickly return.

Robert Anderson (1805-1871)

HERITAGE: Born in Kentucky.

RANK: General.

FOUGHT FOR: Union.

RELIGION: Christian.

EDUCATION: West Point graduate – class of 1825.

CAREER HIGHLIGHTS & TIDBITS: A distinguished, white-haired man.
Taught artillery tactics at West Point Military Academy.
Fought heroically in the Mexican War.
Saw combat during the Seminole War.
Became famous throughout the U.S. as *"the hero of Fort Sumter."*
Promoted to Brigadier General in May 1861.
Commander of the garrison at Fort Sumter during the secession crisis.
In command of Union soldiers in Kentucky while the state was supposedly neutral.
A distinguished, soft-spoken man.
Highly respected by all those under his command.
Never known to curse or take an alcoholic drink.
Retired from the military on a disability in October of 1863.

QUOTABLE QUOTE: *"Our Southern brethren have done grievously wrong, they have rebelled...they must be punished and brought back, but this necessity breaks my heart."*

SAW ACTION AT: Fort Sumter in Charleston Harbor.

LITTLE KNOWN FACT: Returned to Fort Sumter on April 14, 1865: *"I restore to its proper place this flag which floated here during peace, before the first act of this cruel rebellion. I thank God I have lived to see this day, and to be here to perform this, perhaps the last act of my life, duty to my country."*

French Crackers—
General J.E. Johnston's Favorite

6 eggs   3/4 cup butter
3/4 cup milk   1/2 tsp baking soda

Blend the eggs and milk in a large wooden mixing bowl. Melt the butter and add it along with the baking soda. Then blend in sufficient flour to mold into a stiff dough. Pound and knead this dough for at least 30 minutes. Roll it out on a floured board. Continue rolling the dough as thin as it can possibly be handled. Cut into any desired shapes and sizes. Bake on a floured pan in a rather quick-to-quick oven (400 to 425 degrees).

Joseph Eagleston Johnston (1807-1891)

HERITAGE: Son of a Revolutionary War veteran. Born in Price Edward County, Virginia. Grew up in Abingdon, Virginia.

RANK: General.

FOUGHT FOR: Confederacy.

RELIGION: Christian – Mother had devotions after the family finished their evening meal. Always prayed with her son nightly before he went to bed.

EDUCATION: West Point graduate – class of 1829. Was 13th in his class of 46 students.
   Early education in an excellent private school founded by father.

CAREER HIGHLIGHTS & TIDBITS: Was but one of 306 West Point graduates who resigned their commissions and fought for the Confederacy.
   Entered the Confederate Army as a second lieutenant of artillery.
   Severely wounded twice in the later part of August of 1862.
   Had an enviable reputation as a Civil War commander.
   One of the elite few who never is known to have lost a battle.

QUOTABLE QUOTE: Said this just prior to Lee's surrender: *"Our people are tired of war, feel themselves whipped, and will not fight. Our country is overrun, its military reserves greatly diminished, while the enemy's military power and resources were never greater, and may be increased to any extent desired."*

SAW ACTION AT: Harper's Ferry, Bull Run, Richmond, Battle of Seven Pines, Vicksburg, The Carolina's Campaign, etc.

LITTLE KNOWN FACTS: Quarreled bitterly with President of the Confederacy, Jefferson Davis.
   Replaced by Davis with General Robert E. Lee, a man who had never even directed a major battle in the Civil War.

Oat Crackers—
a Favorite of Bushrood Johnson

2 cups rolled oats
1 cup graham flour
pinch of salt

pinch of sugar
pinch of baking powder
1 cup cream

Blend all of the above ingredients in a large wooden mixing bowl. The dough should be extremely stiff and hard to work. Lay it on a floured board and roll it out as this as possible. Then cut into round or square shapes of any desired size. Lift each oat cracker carefully and lay in rows on a buttered baking pan. Place in a quick oven (425 degrees) and bake. **NOTE:** These crackers are very nourishing as well as tasty. They were popular during the slavery period in America.

Bushrood Rust Johnson (1817-1880)

HERITAGE: Born and raised in Belmont County, Ohio.

RANK: General.

FOUGHT FOR: Confederacy.

RELIGION: Christian.

EDUCATION: West Point graduate – class of 1840.
    Resigned his U.S. Army commission to fight with the Confederacy.

MARRIAGE: Unknown.

CHILDREN: Unknown.

CAREER HIGHLIGHTS & TIDBITS: Served in the U.S. Army on the frontier.
    Fought in the Seminole War.
    Took part in the Mexican War.
    Resigned from Army in 1847 to teach in the Western Military College in Kentucky from 1848 to 1851.
    Severely wounded at Shiloh on April 6, 1862.
    Captured 130 Union soldiers during the Petersburg Crater Mine explosion in July of 1864.
    His division was shattered at Sailor's Creek on April 6, 1865.
    Punished by being paroled at Appomattox without a command.
    Returned to teaching and became chancellor of the University of Nashville when the Civil War ended.
    Retired to Illinois farm where he eventually died.

SAW ACTION AT: Shiloh, Fort Donelson, Perryville, Stones River, Chickamauga, Knoxville, Drewry's Bluff, The Wilderness, etc.

LITTLE KNOWN FACT: Served in 1868 as professor of engineering mechanics and natural philosophy in the Western Military Institute in Georgetown, Kentucky until 1880

Rye Wafers—
Mrs. Early's Best

 Take a quantity of rye or wheat flour and wet it with water. Salt freely to taste. Knead into a very tight dough. Roll the dough out extremely thin on a well-floured board. Cut into any size or shape desired. Place these wafers on a buttered baking pan. Bake slowly in slow oven (300 degrees) until the crackers become brittle.

Jubal Anderson Early (1816-1894)

HERITAGE: Born in Franklin County, Virginia.

RANK: General.

FOUGHT FOR: Confederacy.

RELIGION: Christian.
   Always read passages from the *Bible* first before going into battle.

EDUCATION: West Point graduate – class of 1837

CAREER HIGHLIGHTS & TIDBITS: Nasty and bitter middle-age bachelor.
   Nicknamed by his troops *"Old Jubilee."*
   A sarcastic way of calling him a disliked, nasty, grouchy old man.
   One of the finest military minds in the Confederate Army.
   Intensely disliked other people and found it difficult to get along.
   Wounded during the fighting at Williamsburg.
   Initially saw action in the Seminole War.
   Led a cavalry force in an attempt to capture Washington for the Confederacy on July 9, 1864.
   Routed by Custer at Waynesboro in March of 1865.
   Union forces under General Wallace blocked his heroic efforts.
   Returned to his Lynchburg law practice in 1867.
   Wrote his autobiography in 1912.

QUOTABLE QUOTE: In reference to the Union Army, on December 15, 1862 He declared: *"I not only wish them all dead, but I wish them all in Hell."*

SAW ACTION AT: First Bull Run, Peninsular Campaign, Second Bull Run, Williamsburg, Antietam, Fredericksburg, Cold Harbor, Chancellorsville, etc.

LITTLE KNOWN FACT: His West Point classmates included General Joseph Hooker (Union), General John Sedgwick (Union), and General Braxton Bragg (confederacy).

Graham Cracker Receipt—
Mrs. Meagher's Best

4 cups milk
 or
4 cups water

2 cups graham flour
1 tsp salt

Bring the milk or water to a boil. Blend the flour and salt together in a large wooden mixing bowl. Scald this by pouring the boiling milk or water over it. Stir hard until well blended and smooth. Then allow to cool a little and knead into as soft a dough as can be handled. Add extra flour if necessary. Then roll the dough out in a sheet nearly 3/4 inch thick (the thinner the better). Cut into round- or square- shaped cakes. Lay these on a hot buttered baking tin and put in very hot oven (450 to 500 degrees is ideal). **NOTE:** Everything depends on the heat in the baking of these wafer crackers. Properly scalded and baked, they will turn out light and delicious. Otherwise, they will turn out tough and rather flat-tasting.

Thomas Francis Meagher (1823-1867)

HERITAGE: Born in Waterford, Ireland.
Expelled from Ireland in 1849 for founding the Irish Confederation in 1840.

RANK: General.

FOUGHT FOR: Union.

RELIGION: Christian – Catholic.

EDUCATION: Studied under Jesuits.
Completed his education in 1843.
Attended Stonyhurst College in Lancashire, England.

MARRIAGE: Wed to beautiful and vivacious red-headed Irish girl named Marjory O'Leary.

CHILDREN: Three - Patrick, Riley, and Kathleen.

CAREER HIGHLIGHTS & TIDBITS: Known to stir up anti-government feelings as a fervent revolutionary nationalist in Ireland.
Successful New York attorney in 1852.
Leader in New York City's Irish community.
Become the editor of a newspaper.
Not well liked by contemporaries due to his abrasive nature.
Held a number of territorial commands after the Civil War.
Temporary Governor of Montana.
Had red hair, and crystal blue, penetrating eyes.
Met his fate in a watery grave due to a boating accident.

SAW ACTION AT: First and Second Bull Run, Fredericksburg, Chancellorsville, The Peninsular Campaign, Antietam, etc.

.LITTLE KNOWN FACT: Leader of the Union Zouaves. These were special troops known for their distinctive colorful uniforms they wore into battle

Graham Crackers—
Mrs. Andrew Johnson's Favorite

1/4 cup butter
4 cups graham flour
1/4 cup sugar

2 cups milk
pinch of salt
pinch of ammonia

Rub the butter and flour together until completely blended. Then add all the other ingredients and stir briskly. Roll the dough out on a well-floured board until it is about 1/8 inch thick. Cut into small envelope-shaped crackers. Lift each cracker carefully and lay on a floured baking pan. Put in a very slow to slow oven (275 to 300 degrees) and bake until they are hard and dry.

NOTE: Ammonia was used in the old days to make the crackers extremely crisp. All ammonia is a water-formed from nitrogen and hydrogen, and quite harmless in its pure form when used in cookies or crackers.

Andrew Johnson (1828-1875)

HERITAGE: Born in Raleigh, North Carolina.
Grew up in abject poverty.
Apprenticed to a tailor as a boy.

POSITION: President Lincoln's Vice-President.
Became the 17th President of the United States.

RELIGION: Christian.
Proclaimed that he believed *"in Almighty God."*
Believed in the infallibility of the *Bible.*

EDUCATION: Very little, if any formal education.
Illiterate. Wife taught him to read and write..

CAREER HIGHLIGHTS & TIDBITS: Offered large reward for the capture of Jefferson Davis after the Civil War ended.
Did not wish to severely punish the southern states as did the radical Republican extremists.
Basically a kind man with no animosity felt toward his defeated Southern brothers.
Started in politics as an illiterate and elected as Mayor of Greenville, Tennessee.
Served in the House of Representatives (1843-1853)
Elected Governor of Tennessee and served from 1853 to 1857.
Appointed Military Governor of Tennessee by President Lincoln.

QUOTABLE QUOTE: His views on the nature of reconstruction are reflected in his 1867 address to Congress. He declared that Blacks posses less *"capacity for government that any other race of people. No independent government of any form has ever been successful in their hands. On the contrary, wherever they have been left to their own devices, they have shown a constant tendency to relapse into barbarism."*

LITTLE KNOWN FACT: Asked that when he died he be buried while *"wrapped in an American flag, with a copy of the Constitution under my head."*

Cracker Thins— as Made by Mrs. Ferrero

8 cups flour   3 cups milk
1/2 cup butter   salt to suit

Blend the flour and butter in a large wooden mixing bowl. Gradually stir in the milk. Salt to taste. The dough should be extremely stiff. Add a little more milk if necessary. Then beat the dough with a rolling pin for at least 30 minutes. After finished beating, let it stand for 2 full hours. Roll out as thin as possible. Cut into small round or square shapes. Place each cracker in rows on a floured baking pan. Bake in quick to very quick oven (425 to 450 degrees). Be careful the crackers do not burn.

Edward Ferrero (1831-1899)

HERITAGE: Born in Spain. Immigrated to the United States.

RANK: General.

FOUGHT FOR: Union.

RELIGION: Christian. Devout Catholic.

EDUCATION: Unknown.

CAREER HIGHLIGHTS & TIDBITS: Was a well known dance instructor in New York City.
> Became militia member in New York City.
> Politically appointed General.
> Served under General Ambrose Burnside in North Carolina.
> Led the Potomac Army troops in Second Bull Run through the fighting in Fredericksburg.
> Joined General Grant's forces in Vicksburg and Knoxville.
> Grant had no confidence in this man.
> Relegated him to a tent and let him only do administrative work.
> Not known for his bravery in the battlefield.
> Usually stayed away from the front where any fighting might be taking place.
> Widely known to be a coward under fire.
> Looked upon with disdain by other military leaders.
> Often found hiding in a dugout area behind the lines.
> Had no military experience.
> His appointment as a General was a terrible political decision.

SAW ACTION AT: Second Bull Run, Fredericksburg, Knoxville, Vicksburg, Petersburg Crater, etc.

LITTLE KNOWN FACT: Has a claim to fame (or notoriety) that most men wouldn't care to have.
> While at Petersburg Crater, he ordered black soldiers under his command to charge the enemy.
> He then promptly abandoned them.

8

Homemade Rolls
During the Civil War

Potato Rolls—
General Grant's Favorite

2 cups potatoes, mashed	pinch of salt
1/2 cup cream	flour to suit

Put mashed potatoes in large wooden mixing bowl. Blend in cream and salt. Slowly add enough flour to make rather stiff dough. Tear off small chunks of dough. Shape into round rolls. Place on buttered baking pan. Bake in quick oven (425 degrees) for about 15 minutes or until lightly browned.

Ulysses Simpson Grant (1882-1885)

HERITAGE: Born in Mt. Pleasant, Ohio. His father, a tanner, was a man of modest means.

RANK: General.

FOUGHT FOR: Union.

RELIGION: Christian (see quote below).

EDUCATION: West Point graduate – class of 1843. Didn't especially stand out as a cadet.

MARRIAGE: Wed Julia Dent in 1848.

CAREER HIGHLIGHTS & TIDBITS: Had several regiments of black troops when he captured Fort Harrison. The *Medal of Honor* was awarded to 14 of them.

>*"This war was a fearful lesson,"* noted Grant, *"and should teach us the necessity of avoiding wars in the future."*

Grant was among many Union men who at one time owned slaves. Others included General Winfield Scott, General George H. Thomas and Commodore Farragut etc.

QUOTABLE QUOTES: *"I believe in the Holy Scriptures and who lives by them will be benefited thereby. Men may differ as to the interpretation, which is human, but the Scriptures are man's best guide."*

"If I thought this war was to abolish slavery I would resign my campaign and offer my sword to the other side."

SAW ACTION AT: Five Forks, Missionary Ridge, Cold Harbor, Shiloh, Fort Donelson, Fort Henry, Petersburg, Richmond, etc.

LITTLE KNOWN FACT: When Confederate President Jefferson Davis sent General Lee under the white flag of truce, he urged Grant to agree to exchange prisoners. Grant ignored the request.

Dinner Graham Rolls—
The Butler Family's Christmas Treat

3 cups graham flour   2 tbls sugar
2 cups flour   1 tsp salt
1 1/2 cups milk

Take large wooden mixing bowl and blend all of above ingredients. Work with the hands until smooth dough is achieved. Grease a square, shallow cake pan. Now form dough into a number of elongated rolls. Lay them, just touching, in pan. Brush over with coating of milk. Bake in moderate oven (350 degrees) for 20 to 25 minutes. When removing from oven, rub each roll with a little butter. Serve while hot.

Benjamin Franklin Butler (1818-1893)

HERITAGE: Born and raised in Deerfield, New Hampshire.

RANK: General.

FOUGHT FOR: Union.

EDUCATION: Unknown, but became a nationally known and influential criminal lawyer in Massachusetts.

CAREER HIGHLIGHTS & TIDBITS: A typical politically-appointed General.

> Dramatic and most effective speaker. Could readily sway others to his way of thinking..
> Always known as a controversial political figure.
> Initially supported Jefferson Davis and the Confederacy.
> Had no known military experience.
> Made absolutely no contribution to the success of the Union during the Civil War.
> His first major military disaster occurred at Fredericksburg.
> Finally discovered to be completely incompetent at Fort Fisher and Petersburg.
> This inability to command finally cost him his command position.
> Became military governor of New Orleans in May of 1862.
> Was dictatorial and corrupt.
> Power-mad individual.
> Issued his notorious "Woman Order."
> According to this order, any woman caught insulting a Union military man would be punished as a prostitute.

QUOTABLE QUOTE: *"I hold the rebellion is treason, and that treason, if persisted in, is death."* (December 24, 1862).

SAW ACTION AT: Big Bethel, Petersburg, Fort Fisher, Fort Hatterag, Fort Clark, New Orleans, Fredericksburg, etc.

LITTLE KNOWN FACT: Hanged a man for merely taking down a Union flag in New Orleans.

Yeast Dinner Rolls—
Favorite of Alexander Stephens

3 cups milk
3 tbls sugar
1 tsp salt

1/2 cup butter
2 egg whites, beaten
2/3 cup yeast

8 cups flour

Bring milk to boil. Put in sugar and salt and let dissolve. Then add butter and stir until completely melted. Allow to cool to lukewarm. Blend in beaten egg whites and yeast. Now pour mixture into a large wooden mixing bowl. Slowly stir in flour. Work into good dough. Put dough on floured board. Knead hard for 20 to 30 minutes. When finished, put dough back in bowl. Cover. Set aside in warm place to rise overnight.

If rolls are wanted for breakfast, break off pieces of the risen dough and mold to any desired shape. Place on buttered tin and allow to double their size. Bake for about 30 minutes. If wanted for lunch, cut up raised dough upon arising in morning. Set in cool place until an hour and one half before you need them. Then mold to shape and place each roll on buttered baking pan. Let them raise double and then bake in moderately quick oven (375 degrees). Serve while hot.

Alexander Hamilton Stephens (1812-1883)

HERITAGE: Born and raised near Crawfordville in Taliafero County, Georgia.

POSITION: Vice-President of the Confederate States of America.

RELIGION: Christian.

EDUCATION: Educated in his town's public schools.
Also attended a number of private schools.
Graduated in 1832 from the University of Georgia in Athens.   Studied law on his own.

CAREER HIGHLIGHTS & TIDBITS: Grandson of a soldier who fought under George Washington in the Revolutionary War.
An astute thinker, he observed that "Liberty once lost will never be recovered without blood."
Prominent lawyer.
Congressman from 1843 to 1859 and 1873 to 1882.
Helped push through the passage of the Kansas-Nebraska Act.
A voice of moderation while serving under Jefferson Davis.
Assisted in drafting a moderate *Confederate Constitution.*
Strongly opposed President Jefferson Davis's attempts at centralization of power.
Also firmly opposed the the suspension of civil rights as Vice-President under Jefferson Davis.
Worked hard to develop a program of prisoner exchange during the Civil War years.
One of the Confederacy's greatest political leaders.
Georgia Governor in 1882.

QUOTABLE QUOTE: He declared early in 1861: *"War I look for as almost certain...Revolutions are much easier started than controlled, and the men who begin them [often] ...themselves become the victims."*

LITTLE KNOWN FACT: Wrote a much-heralded constitutional study of the Civil War.

Cornmeal Rolls—
Mrs. G.E. Pickett's Best

2 1/2 cups cornmeal mush   pinch of salt
1/2 cup cream   3 cups flour

Put well-cooked cornmeal mush into large wooden mixing bowl. Blend in cream and salt. Slowly work in flour until all lumps are gone. Knead into rather stiff dough. Beat and knead very hard for at least 15 minutes. Break off chunks of the dough. Shape in the form of rolls. Place each roll on well-buttered baking tin. Bake in rather quick oven (400 to 425 degrees) until done.

George Edward Pickett (1825-1875)

HERITAGE: Born in Richmond, Virginia.

RANK: General.

FOUGHT FOR: Confederacy.

RELIGION: Christian (see quote below).

EDUCATION: West Point graduate – class of 1846.
Was 59th in his class of 59.
Very little formal education in his youth.
Taught law by an uncle in Illinois.
Obtained appointment to West Point in 1842.

CAREER HIGHLIGHTS & TIDBITS: Served from 1849 to 1856 in a Texas garrison.
Undertook a poorly judged frontal attack as ordered by Robert E. Lee on July 3, 1863.
Could never forgive General Lee for ordering this eventful charge.
Became famous for what is today commonly and inaccurately called *"Pickett's Charge."*
His *"Gamecock Brigade"* won an almost legendary reputation for excellent fighting.
Highly egotistical, he had an underlying hunger for battlefield excitement and glory.

QUOTABLE QUOTE: *"It is finished! Oh, my beloved division! Thousands of them have gone to their eternal home, having given up their lives for the cause they knew to be just. The others , alas, heartbroken, crushed in spirit, are left to mourn its loss."*

SAW ACTION AT: Cold Harbor, Five Forks, Fredericksburg, Gettysburg, Peninsular Campaign, Petersburg, Richmond, Seven Pines and Williamsburg, etc.

LITTLE KNOWN FACT: Wore his hair in perfumed ringlets.

Gluten Roll—
Favorite of Mary Edwards Walker

1 yeast cake, crumbled
2 tbls honey
1 cup water, lukewarm
3 cups gluten flour

1 cup cream, scalded and
      cooled
1 tbls butter, melted
1 tsp salt

Put crumbled yeast cake, honey, and lukewarm water in wooden mixing bowl and stir until completely dissolved. Then stir in cream and melted butter. Gradually add gluten flour and blend thoroughly. Lastly add salt. Knead until dough is smooth and elastic. Place in well-greased bowl and cover. Set aside in warm place, free from drafts, to rise until light – about 2 hours. Then turn out of bowl onto lightly floured board. Break into rolls. Mold nicely. Place on well-greased baking tins. Cover and let rise again until double in bulk – about 1 hour. Bake in moderate oven (350 degrees) for about 20 to 25 minutes.

Mary Edwards Walker (1832-1919)

HERITAGE: Born in Oswego, New York. Father a brilliant, self-taught and exceptionally talented physician.

POSITION: Union doctor, nurse, surgeon.

RELIGION: Devout Christian.

EDUCATION: Graduated from the Syracuse Medical College– the nations first medical school.

MARRIAGE: Wed another physician, Dr. Albert Miller, who had been her classmate in medical school.
> Divorced 13-years later.

CAREER HIGHLIGHTS & TIDBITS: Opened a medical practice with her husband prior to her militate service.
> Only woman and only civilian to be awarded the *Medal of Honor* during the Civil War.
> Her *Medal of Honor* cites her work at First Manassas.
> Began her medical work during the Battle of Chickamauga on September 19, 1863.
> Served in the Union Army Hospital in Chattanooga, Tennessee.
> Tirelessly worked as a volunteer surgeon.
> Often crossed enemy lines to assist soldiers in need of help. Helped as a surgeon during the Battle of Atlanta
> .General W.T. Shermanrecommended her for a *Medal of Honor*. *Medal of Honor* was awarded to her in 1866.
> She proudly wore her medal every day until she died.

SAW ACTION AT: Chickamauga, Battle of Atlanta, First Manassas, Chattanooga, etc.

LITTLE KNOWN FACTS: Captured by Confederate troops on April 10, 1864. Sent to prison as a "spy".
> Exchanged after four months, along with two dozen other Union doctors for 17 Confederate surgeons.

Butter Rolls—
General John D. Imboden's Favorite

1/2 cake yeast	2 tbls sugar
1/4 cup water, lukewarm	1 tsp salt
2 cups milk, scalded	flour to suit
1/2 cup butter	

Crumble and dissolve yeast in lukewarm water. Put the scalding milk into large wooden mixing bowl. Blend in butter, sugar, and salt. Set aside to cool. When milk mixture is lukewarm, stir in the dissolved yeast. Then stir in 3 1/2 cups flour. When mixed thoroughly cover bowl with a thick towel. Set in a warm place to rise. When the mixture is light (has risen) work in enough flour to make soft, pliable dough. Knead well to assure all ingredients are thoroughly blended. Cover again with towel and set aside to rise. It should rise to about double in size. Then turn the dough out on floured board. Roll it out into a 3/4-inch-thick sheet. Take sharp knife and cut dough into pieces 2 1/2 inches long by 1 inch wide. Place strips close together in shallow buttered baking pan. Cover again with towel and let them rise until light. Then take towel off and place pan in rather quick oven (400 to 425 degrees). Bake for 15 minutes.

John Daniel Imboden (1823-1895)

HERITAGE: Born and raised in Virginia.

RANK: General.

FOUGHT FOR: Confederacy.

RELIGION: Christian.

EDUCATION: Unknown for the most part, but was home schooled as a child and young adult.

Self-taught in law.

CAREER HIGHLIGHTS & TIDBITS: Lawyer and legislator.

Took part in the arrest of John Brown at Harper's Ferry.

Struck down with typhoid in the autumn of 1864.

Recovered from typhoid and returned to his military command.

Placed in charge of a Confederate prison in Aiken, South Carolina.

Fair-minded officer who wouldn't allow any mistreatment of Union prisoners.

Helped cover Lee's retreat from Pennsylvania after his unexpected disaster at Gettysburg.

Fought fiercely to protect his native Shenandoah Valley.

A man of great character, intelligence, and a natural leader.

Helped to run a Confederate prison in Aiken, South Carolina. Singled out by Stonewall Jackson as a man who never offered less than his best even after the war.

Became a writer, land developer and practiced law after the war.

The important role he played in the Confederate Army has long been neglected by historians.

SAW ACTION AT: First Bull Run, Gettysburg, Piedmont, New Market, etc.

LITTLE KNOWN FACTS: He and General William E. Jones made a daring raid into West Virginia in April of 1863.

They became heroic notables as a result of what was called *"The Jones and Imboden West Virginia Raid."*

Homemade Rolls—
Rose O'Neil Greenbow's Best

1 1/2 cups flour	1 1/2 cups potatoes, mashed
1/2 tsp salt	2 tbls butter, melted
3 tsp baking powder	2 eggs, well beaten

Sift together the flour, salt, and baking powder in wooden mixing bowl. Stir in mashed potatoes. Moisten with melted butter and well-beaten eggs. Work lightly with hands to form smooth dough. Turn onto slightly floured board. Roll out 1/2 inch thick. Cut into rounds with upside down drinking glass. Brush each roll with melted shortening. Fold over. Place on greased baking sheet. Brush over with egg wash. Bake in moderately quick oven (375 degrees) for 15 to 18 minutes.

Egg Wash for Glazing Rolls

1 egg yolk	1/2 cup cream

Beat egg yolk in small bowl. Add cream and blend thoroughly. Coat surface of each roll with this mixture using soft pastry brush.

Rose O'Neil Greenbow (1815-1864)

HERITAGE: Born and raised in Port Tobacco, Maryland.

POSITION: Confederate spy. Most popular Washington hostess.

RELIGION: Christian.

MARRIAGE: Wed in 1835 at the age of 20 to prominent doctor and historian, Robert Greenbow (1800-1854).

CHILDREN: A daughter, Rose.

CAREER HIGHLIGHTS & TIDBITS: A highly connected hostess on the Washington political scene.

Pro-slavery activist.

Undercover Confederate spy as well.

Close friend of James Calhoun and James Buchanan.

Relayed the First Bull Run battle plans of General Irwin McDowell to Confederate General P.T.G. Beauregard.

One of the most effective Confederate female spies.

Arrested for her activities as a spy by detective Allen Pinkerton in August of 1861.

Subsequently, put under house arrest.

Her home continued to be a bee hive on Confederate intelligence. Finally placed in capitol prison in January of 1862.

Daughter, Rose, was put in prison with her mother.

Continued with her spying activities even while behind bars.

Still found ways to smuggle important intelligence data to her Confederate friends.

Sailed to the South where Jefferson Davis warmly welcomed her.

Accidentally drowned while on a trip from England and France.

LITTLE KNOWN FACTS: Buried with full military honors. Confederate flag was draped over her coffin.

Her coffin was carried by Confederate soldiers.

The marker on her grave, a marble cross, has this epitaph: *"Mrs. Rose O'Neil Greenbow, a bearer of dispatches to the Confederate government."*

Early Morning Yeast Rolls—
A Jefferson Davis Favorite

4 cups flour, sifted   1 tbls shortening
2 tbls sugar   pinch of salt
2 tbls butter   2 cups milk
              1/2 cup yeast

Start making these rolls early in the morning. Begin by blending flour, sugar, butter, shortening, and salt in large wooden mixing bowl. Bring milk to a boil. Stir it in. Allow the mixture to cool to lukewarm. Then blend in yeast. Cover bowl and set aside in warm place to rise. At noon, add sufficient flour to make fine dough. Knead hard and long until the dough is elastic. Let rise again. When light (risen), place dough on a lightly floured board. Roll out into a thing sheet. Cut into small round cakes. Roll each cake until it becomes oblong in shape. Place a little butter on one end and fold over. Put in a buttered baking pan. Again, let the dough rise until double in size. Bake for 10 or 15 minutes in moderately quick oven (375 degrees). When done, brush over the top of each roll with melted butter.

Jefferson Davis (1808-1889)

HERITAGE: Born in Kentucky. 10th child of a settler who had fought in the Revolutionary War.

POSITION: President of the Confederacy (CSA).

RELIGION: Christian – Studied at a Roman Catholic seminary in Kentucky. Came close to renouncing family's Baptist faith.

EDUCATION: West Point graduate – class of 1828. Graduated one year ahead of Robert E. Lee. Also attended Transylvania University.

MARRIAGE: Married the daughter, against his wishes, of future President Zachary Taylor. She died three months later.
  Married Varina Howell, daughter of a wealthy Mississippi planter.

CAREER HIGHLIGHTS & TIDBITS: Married the daughter of his garrison commander in 1835, against her father's wishes.
  Her father was future President Zachary Taylor.
  Because of Taylor's disapproval, the couple moved to Brierfield, a small plantation in Mississippi.
  His wife died three months later of fever.
  Remarried a decade later to Varina Howell, daughter of a prominent Mississippi planter.
  Varina eventually came to be the First Lady of the Confederacy.
  President Andrew Johnson charged that Davis had committed crimes *"worse than murder."*

QUOTABLE QUOTE(S): *"The time for compromise has now passed. The South is determined to maintain her position, and make all who oppose her smell southern powder and feel southern steel."* (February 16, 1861)

SAW ACTION AT: A hero in the Mexican War.
  Made a name for himself while in command of a Mississippi regiment of volunteers during the 1847 Battle of Buena Vista.

LITTLE KNOWN FACT: Spent two years in prison at Fortress Monroe without even being tried for anything.

German Yeast Rolls—
As Made by Mrs. Hooker

3 cups milk
1 cup yeast
8 cups flour
3 eggs

1/2 cup butter
chopped almonds to suit
cinnamon to suit
sugar to suit

Set sponge as follows: pour 2 cups warm milk into large wooden mixing bowl. Add yeast and enough flour to make a rather stiff batter. Cover with towel. Set aside in a warm place to rise. When it has sufficiently risen, add eggs and blend. Work the butter into remaining flour. Slowly stir it in. Lastly, pour in remaining milk and stir well. Sweeten to taste by adding a little sugar (use very little: the greater part of the sweetness of these rolls should be on the top). *Knead dough hard.* When ready, use fingers. Press dough out very thin. Cut into round cakes or shape with hands into balls. Place in rows on buttered baking pan. Brush over the top of each roll with melted butter. Then sprinkle on almonds, cinnamon, and sugar. Bake in moderate oven (350 degrees).

Joseph Hooker (1814-1879)

HERITAGE: Born in Hadley, Massachusetts.

RANK: General.

FOUGHT FOR: Union.

RELIGION: Christian – Never without his *Bible* at his side. Never would go into battle before reading his *Bible* while alone in his tent.

EDUCATION: West Point graduate – class of 1837. Ranked in the middle of his class.
>Classmates included future Generals as John Sedgwick (Union), Jubal Early (Confederacy), and Braxton Bragg (Confederacy).

CAREER HIGHLIGHTS & TIDBITS: George Armstrong Custer said this: *"Hooker's career is exemplified by that of a rocket, he went up like one and came down like a stick."*
>Rumored to have been drunk during the Battle of Chancellorsville when defeated by General Lee.
>Denied the accusation, blaming the loss on himself. He said: *"For once, I lost confidence in Joe Hooker."*
>As commander of the army of the Potomac, he had 133,000men under his leadership fighting at Chancellorsville, VA.
>Hoped to defeat General Lee's force of 60,000 men, but was unsuccessful.
>Defeated by Lee in May of 1863.
>A cocky, self-confident individual.

QUOTABLE QUOTE: In April of 1862, he said this: *"My plans are perfect. May god have mercy on General Lee for I will have none!"*

SAW ACTION AT: Resaca, Cassville, Pine Mountain, Second Bull Run, South Mountain, Antietam, Chancellorsville, Gettysburg, Atlanta Campaign, etc.

LITTLE KNOWN FACT: A tall, handsome officer who often stepped on the toes of his senior officers with his biting criticism.

9

Muffins Made During
the War Between the States

Rolled Oats Muffins—
Mrs. Patrick R. Cleburne

1 cup milk, scalded
2/3 cup rolled oats
3 tbls maple syrup
1/2 teaspoon salt

2 tbls butter, melted
1 1/2 cups flour
4 tsp baking powder
1 egg, well beaten

Put the scalded milk and rolled oats into large wooden mixing bowl. Let stand for 10 minutes. Stir in maple syrup, salt, and melted butter. Beat thoroughly. Sift flour and baking powder together. Stir into mixture in bowl. Beat in frothy egg. Pour batter into a well-buttered muffin tin. Fill each cup about 2/3 full. Bake in rather quick oven (400 to 425 degrees) for 20 to 30 minutes.

NOTE: Never cut open a muffin of any type—especially those made with meals. Pass knife lightly around it to pierce the crust. Then break open with the fingers.

Patrick R. Cleburne (1828-1864)

HERITAGE: Immigrated to America from Ireland in 1849 when just 21 years of age.

RANK: General.

FOUGHT FOR: Confederacy.

RELIGION: Christian.

EDUCATION: West Point graduate.

MARRIAGE: Married twice – first wife died during childbirth.

CAREER HIGHLIGHTS & TIDBITS: Served in the British Royal Army prior to coming to the United States.
> Became a successful druggist in the United States.
> Studied law and became an attorney in Little Rock, Arkansas.
> Organized a group of volunteers prior to outbreak of the Civil War Called themselves *"The Tall Rifles of the Confederacy"*.
> Seized the Little Rock Arsenal at that time.
> Impressively battled at Shiloh and was rewarded with a promotion to Brigadier General.
> Known as the *"Stonewall Jackson of the West."*

QUOTABLE QUOTE: *"Boys, don't be discouraged. That is not the first charge that was ever repulsed. Fix bayonets and give them steel!"*

SAW ACTION AT: Shiloh, Richmond, Kentucky (wounded), Perryville, Stones River, Chickamauga, Missionary Ridge, The Atlanta Campaign, Franklin, Tennessee (killed in action).

LITTLE KNOWN FACT: Just six weeks before he was killed in the Battle of Franklin, Tennessee on October 4, 1864 he said: *"If this cause that's so near to my heart is doomed to failure, I pray that heaven may let me fall with it, with my face toward the foe, and my arm battling for that which I know to be right."*

Muffins—
As Made for John S. Mosby

1/3 cup sugar
1/4 cup shortening
2 eggs
2 1/2 cups flour

4 tsp baking powder
1/2 tsp salt
1/2 cup walnuts, chopped
3/4 cup milk

Cream the sugar and shortening in wooden mixing bowl. Add eggs, one at a time. Beat thoroughly, while adding. In separate mixing bowl, sift together flour, baking powder, and salt. Add this and chopped walnuts, alternately, with milk, to mixture in first bowl. Beat everything together until smooth. Put into well-greased muffin tins. Bake in moderately quick oven (375 degrees) for about 25 minutes. Serve while hot with butter. **NOTE:** Never cut open a muffin of any type—especially those made with meals. Pass knife lightly around it to pierce the crust. Then break open with the fingers.

John Singleton Mosby (1833-1916)

HERITAGE: Born and raised in Virginia.

RANK: Captain.

FOUGHT FOR: Confederacy.

RELIGION: Christian.

EDUCATION: Attended University of Virginia.
Arrested and jailed for shooting another student.
`Released when it was found that the other student had "provoked" him.
Studied law while in jail with the help of his attorney.

CAREER HIGHLIGHTS & TIDBITS: On March 9,1863 Mosby's Rangers pulled off a daring exploit.
Raided a Union camp at the Fairfax County Courthouse.
Captured Brigadier General Edwin Stoughton while he was sleeping.
Mosby awoke Stoughton with a slap and shouted, *"Get up General and come with me!"*
Stoughton jumped from bed and bellowed: *"What is this? Don't you know who I am, sir?"*
"I reckon I do, General. You ever heard of Mosby?"
"Yes, have you caught him?"
"No, but he's caught you!"

QUOTABLE QUOTE: *"My men had no camps...They would scatter for safety and gather at my call like Children of the Mist."*

SAW ACTION AT: First Bull Run, and many other places. Primarily undertook raids all over Virginia with "irregulars."

LITTLE KNOWN FACT: Also captured in his famous raid at the Fairfax County Courthouse were two captains, 38 privates, and 58 horses. Not one of his cavalrymen was either killed or wounded in this famous and heroic escapade!

Whole Wheat Muffins—
As Beecher Liked Them for Breakfast

2 cups whole-wheat flour	1/2 tsp salt
1 tsp baking powder	2 tbls butter, melted
1 tsp baking soda	1 egg
2 tbls sugar	1 1/2 cups sour milk

Mix but do not sift in wooden bowl the whole-wheat flour, baking powder, baking soda, sugar, and salt. Stir in melted butter, unbeaten egg, and sour milk. Beat only enough to make smooth, lump-free batter. Lightly grease muffin tin. Fill each cup about 2/3 full. Bake in quick oven (425 degrees) for about 25 minutes. Makes 12 nice muffins.

NOTE: Never cut open a muffin of any type—especially those made with meals. Pass knife lightly around it to pierce the crust. Then break open with the fingers.

Henry Ward Beecher (1813-1887)

POSITION: Clergyman, reformer.

RELIGION: Christian – Protestant minister. Attended Lane Theological Seminary.

CAREER HIGHLIGHTS & TIDBITS: Brother of Harriet Beecher Stowe, author of *Uncle Tom's Cabin*.

> Outspoken opponent of slavery.
> Advocated letting slavery "wither away" in the slave states.
> Fiery and famed pastor of the Plymouth Congregational Church in Brooklyn, New York.
> Probably best known Protestant minister of his day.
> The most hated and reviled minister in America because of his public stand on the slavery issue.
> Became well-known editor of the *Independent* in 1861.
> Toured and lectured widely in England throughout 1863.
> His lectures are credited with obtaining the sympathy of Great Britain for the Union cause.
> Highest paid preacher in America in his time.
> Was the man behind the shipping of rifles to anti-slavery proponents in Kansas during 1854-59.
> Carbines were secretly shipped in boxes labeled *"Bibles."*
> Such weapons became widely known as *"Beecher's Bibles!"*
> A disreputable scoundrel when it came to other men's wives.
> Developed a national reputation for his astounding speaking and preaching skills.
> Regularly drew astounding crowds of 2500 people to his church services every Sunday.

QUOTABLE QUOTE: Referring to the rifles being shipped South, he declared there was *"more moral power in one of these instruments so far as the slaveholders were concerned than in 100 Bibles."*

LITTLE KNOWN FACTS: Sued for $100,000 by newspaper editor Theodore Tilton over an affair Beecher was having with his wife.

> The *Louisville Courier* called him nothing more than *"A dunghill covered with flowers."*

171

Berry Muffins—
A Velazquez Christmas Favorite

1/2 cup sugar	3 tsp baking powder
4 tbls shortening	1/2 tsp salt
3 egg yolks	2/3 cup milk
2 1/2 cups flour	1 cup blackberries

3 eggs, stiffly beaten

Put sugar, shortening, and egg yolks in wooden mixing bowl. Cream together until light. Sift together in separate bowl the flour, baking powder, and salt. Add these dry ingredients, alternately, with milk, to the mixture in first bowl. Beat until smooth. Stir in blackberries. Lastly, fold in stiffly beaten egg whites. Put in mixture in well-greased muffin tins. Fill each cup about 2/3 full. Bake in quick oven (425 degrees) for about 25 minutes. Serve while hot.

NOTE: Never cut open a muffin of any type—especially those made with meals. Pass knife lightly around it to pierce the crust. Then break open with the fingers.

Loreta Janra Valezquez (1847-1897)

HERITAGE: Born in Cuba to a wealthy aristocratic family. Father said to own a plantation in both Cuba and Mexico.

RANK: Lieutenant and spy.

FOUGHT FOR: Confederacy.

RELIGION: Christian – Catholic faith.

EDUCATION: Home-schooled in New Orleans.

MARRIAGE: Wed against her parents wishes at 14 years of age. Married a young, Confederate officer 1856.

CHILDREN: None.

CAREER HIGHLIGHTS & TIDBITS: A fiercely, independent young woman.
> Not overly good looking.
> Proceeded to join the army, along with her husband.
> She was cleverly disguised as a man.
> Went under the fictitious name of Harry Buford.
> Husband killed early in the war.
> Velazquez stayed on as a Confederate army officer.
> Raised and led her own special volunteer battalion.
> Served under the name of Lieutenant Harry Buford.
> Eventually exposed as a women in 1863.
> Continued to do in valuable work for the Confederacy as a spy behind the Union lines.

SAW ACTION AT: First Bull Run, Fort Donelson, Manassas, Shiloh, Balls Bluff, etc.

LITTLE KNOWN FACT: Years after the Civil War ended, in 1876, she wrote and published a book called *Women in Battle*. Disappeared shortly thereafter.

Mrs. Hampton's Peanut Muffins— As Eaten by Her Family

2 cups flour, sifted
3 tbls sugar
2 1/2 tsp baking powder
1/2 tsp salt

1/2 cup peanuts, chopped
1 egg, beaten
1 cup milk
3 tbls peanut oil

Sift together in wooden mixing bowl sifted flour, sugar, baking powder, and salt. Stir in the chopped peanuts. In separate bowl, combine well-beaten egg, milk, and peanut oil. Make well in the middle of dry ingredients. Pour liquid mixture into well. Stir just enough to lightly blend everything. The mixture should have a rather rough appearance. Fill greased muffin pans 2/3 full. Bake in rather quick oven (400 to 425 degrees) for about 20 to 30 minutes or until golden brown. Makes approximately 12 muffins.

NOTE: Never cut open a muffin of any type—especially those made with meals. Pass knife lightly around it to pierce the crust. Then break open with the fingers.

Wade Hampton (1818-1902)

HERITAGE: Born in Millwood, the distinguished family estate near Columbia, South Carolina.

Son and grandson of extremely wealthy planters.

Descended from family of Revolutionary War patriots

RANK: General.

FOUGHT FOR: Confederacy.

RELIGION: Christian – Constantly seen reading his Bible while riding into battle.

EDUCATION: Graduated from South Carolina's College in 1836.

MARRIAGE: Unknown.

CHILDREN: Unknown.

CAREER HIGHLIGHTS & TIDBITS: Wounded during the First Battle of Bull Run.

Wounded a second time at Seven Pines in May of 1862.

Wounded a third time at Gettysburg.

A fearless warrior, admired and respected by all who know him.

Fought with JEB Stuart cavalry corps.

Rose quickly to be Stuart's second-in-command.

Returned to South Carolina when the Civil War ended.

Tried to rebuild his estate and shrunken future.

Became involved in politics.

Made an effort to thwart the horrendous Radical Republican Reconstruction policies.

SAW ACTION AT: First Bull Run, Seven Pines, The Peninsular Campaign, Antietam, Chambersburg, Gettysburg, etc.

LITTLE KNOWN FACT: Elected Governor of South Carolina in 1876 by defeating the carpetbagger incumbent. Reelected in 1878.

Buttermilk Muffins—
General Ewell's Favorite

4 cups buttermilk   1 tsp salt

2 eggs   flour to suit

          1 tsp baking powder

Pour the buttermilk into large wooden mixing bowl. Beat eggs well. When light, harshly whip into the milk. Add salt and enough flour to make thick batter. Lastly, dissolve baking powder in little hot water. Stir lightly into batter. Pour batter into buttered muffin rings about 2/3 full. Bake at one in rather quick oven (400 to 425 degrees).

NOTE: Never cut open a muffin of any type—especially those made with meals. Pass knife lightly around it to pierce the crust. Then break open with the fingers.

Richard Stoddard Ewell (1817-1872)

HERITAGE: Born in Georgetown, Washington D.C.

RANK: General.

FOUGHT FOR: Confederacy.

RELIGION: Christian.

EDUCATION: West Point graduate. Was 13th in his class of 1840.

CAREER HIGHLIGHTS & TIDBITS: Started military career as a Lieutenant Colonel in the Virginia forces.
> Became a Colonel in the Confederate Army.
> Initially gained valuable military experience by fighting during the Mexican War.
> Led the Second Brigade at First Bull Run.
> Won important engagements at Cross Keys and Winchester.
> Severely wounded and lost a leg in the Battle of Groveton in August of 1862.
> Captured by General Sheridan in April 6, 1865 at Sayler's Creek.
> Imprisoned at Fort Warren until his release on August 19, 1865.

QUOTABLE QUOTE: Grumpy and on edge all of the time, General Lee relieved him of command after the bloody Wilderness Battle. Lee said: *"I think his health and nervous system have been shaken by his great injury and, though active and attentive, that he cannot without breaking himself down and undergo the arduous duties of corps command."*

SAW ACTION AT: First Bull Run, Winchester, Cross Keys, The Peninsular Campaign, Cedar Mountain, Second Bull Run, Gettysburg, Spotsylvania, Sayler's Creek, The Wilderness, etc.

LITTLE KNOWN FACTS: Once declared that *"it don't hurt a bit to be shot in a wooden leg."* Had lost a leg earlier in the war.
> A nervous man who jumped around on his wooden leg and cursed mightily when a shell exploded close to him.

Popover Muffins—
Mrs. McClernand's Best

2 cups flour   2 eggs, well beaten
1 tsp butter   1 tsp salt
                2 cups milk

Put flour into large wooden mixing bowl. Rub in butter. Then add milk, frothy beaten eggs, and salt. Stir well until everything is thoroughly blended. When ready, put mixture into individual buttered cups or a muffin tin. Fill each cup about 2/3 full. Bake in rather quick oven (400 to 425 degrees) for 15 minutes. Serve while hot in sweet sauce or fruit jam.

NOTE: Never cut open a muffin of any type—especially those made with meals. Pass knife lightly around it to pierce the crust. Then break open with the fingers.

John Alexander McClernand (1802-1900)

HERITAGE: Born and raised in Breckinridge County, Kentucky. Son of a farmer.

RANK: General.

FOUGHT FOR: Union.

RELIGION: Christian.

EDUCATION: In and out of a variety of local schools due to his responsibilities on the farm.
Studied law for a period of time.

CAREER HIGHLIGHTS & TIDBITS: Lawyer, Democratic politician and newspaper editor.
Led 30,000 troops in January of 1803 on an unauthorized and controversial *"Arkansas Post Expedition."*
For this insubordination, his command was disbanded by General Grant early in 1863.
U.S. House of Representatives (1843 to 1851) (1859 to 1864).
Left his seat in Congress to become a General in the Union Army.
Fought early in the Mexican War.
Often seen as an ineffective leader.
Known to be overbearing and egotistical.
Politically ambitious as an army officer.
Close friend of President Lincoln.
Despised by Generals Grant, Halleck, Sherman, Admiral David Dixon Porter and a multitude of other military leaders.
Intensely disliked by all of these men because he was no more than *"a politically appointed General"* of little worth.
Relieved of his command by General Grant on June 19, 1863.

SAW ACTION AT: Fort Henry, Fort Donelson, Shiloh, Vicksburg, Red River Campaign, Siege of Jackson, Arkansas Post, Battle of Port Gibson, Sabine Cross Roads, Big Black River Bridge, etc.

LITTLE KNOWN FACT: As a Democratic politician, he proposed war appropriations after the Battle of First Bull Run.

Hominy Muffins—
As Made by Mrs. Pemberton

2 cups hominy (boiled and cold)	2 tsp salt
	2 tbls honey
3 cups sour milk	3 eggs
1/2 cup butter	1 tsp baking powder

1 3/4 cups flour

Put hominy in large wooden mixing bowl. Beat until a smooth paste. Stir in milk. Then melt butter and add it along with salt and honey. Beat eggs thoroughly. When light, add to batter. Dissolve baking powder in little hot water. Stir it in. Lastly, blend in flour. Stir well. Pour battered into well-buttered muffin rings. Fill each about 2/3 full. Bake at once in rather quick oven (400 to 425 degrees). They should not take more than 20 minutes.

NOTE: Never cut open a muffin of any type—especially those made with meals. Pass knife lightly around it to pierce the crust. Then break open with the fingers.

John Clifford Pemberton (1814-1881)

HERITAGE: Born in Philadelphia, Pennsylvania, to a prominent, influential Quaker family.

RANK: General.

FOUGHT FOR: Confederacy.

RELIGION: Christian – Quaker.

EDUCATION: West Point graduate – class of 1837

MARRIAGE: Wed a lovely Southern girl named Martha Thompson of Norfolk, Virginia, in 1848.

CAREER HIGHLIGHTS & TIDBITS: Cited for bravery many times during the Mexican War.
> Refused U.S. Army commission upon graduation from West Point.
> Instead went down to Virginia to fight for his wife's native State.
> Joined the Confederate Army in April of 1861.
> Commanding General at Vicksburg in 1863.
> Heroically defended Vicksburg, Mississippi, from General Grant's siege that began on May 18, 1863.
> Ultimately forced to accept Grant's *"Unconditional Surrender"* terms of July 4.
> Because of this humiliating defeat, many southerners, because of his northern ties, suspected him of some sort of treachery.

QUOTABLE QUOTE: On July 3, 1863, while fighting in Vicksburg he said: *"I know my people [Northerners]. I know their peculiar weaknesses and their national vanity; I know we can get better terms from them on the Fourth of July than on any other day of the year."*

LITTLE KNOWN FACTS: One of 306 U.S. Military Academy (West Point) graduates who resigned their U.S. Army commission and fought instead for the Confederacy.
> Fort Pemberton, in Greenwood, Mississippi, was constructed in his honor.

Creole Style Corn Muffins—
As Eaten by the Henry Wise Family

1 1/2 cups flour   1 egg, well beaten
3 tsp baking powder   1/4 cup butter, melted
1 tsp salt   1 cup milk
3 tbls sugar   1 tbls green pepper, chopped fine
3/4 cup corn meal   1 tsp onion, chopped fine
1-cup cheese, grated

Take a large wooden mixing bowl and sift together flour, baking powder, salt, and sugar. Stir in corn meal and blend well. Combine beaten egg, melted butter, and milk in another bowl. Pour into dry ingredients. Stir vigorously until all flour is dampened. Blend in green pepper, onion, and cheese. Pour batter into well-greased muffin tins. Fill each cup about 2/3 full. Bake in rather quick oven (400-425 degrees) for 25 to 30 minutes. Recipe makes 12 lovely muffins. This same batter can be used to make crispy Creole puffs. Simply drop batter from wooden spoon into kettle of hot deep grease. Fry until golden brown. **NOTE:** Never cut open a muffin of any type—especially those made with meals. Pass knife lightly around it to pierce the crust. Then break open with the fingers.

Henry Alexander Wise (1807-1876)

RANK: General.

FOUGHT FOR: Confederacy.

RELIGION: Christian.

EDUCATION: Unknown, except for the fact that he studied law.

MARRIAGE: Unknown.

CHILDREN: Unknown.

CAREER HIGHLIGHTS & TIDBITS: Lawyer and politician before war broke out.
>Minister to Brazil from 1844 to 1847.
>Served in Congress.
>Governor of Virginia from 1850 to 1860.
>Ordered the execution of John Brown for his part in the raid on Harper's Ferry.
>Initially opposed secession.
>Nevertheless he offered his services of Jefferson Davis who was the President of the Confederate States of America.
>Distinguished himself during the Battle of Petersburg against Grant's first assault.

QUOTABLE QUOTE: *"Country be damned. There is no country. There has been no country. General, for a year or more, you are the country to these men. They have fought for you...there are still thousands left who will die for you."*

SAW ACTION AT: Western Virginia, Virginia, Roanoke Island in North Carolina, Petersburg, Richmond, etc.

LITTLE KNOWN FACTS: One son mortally wounded while fighting at Roanoke Island, North Carolina.
>Surrendered with Robert E. Lee at Appomattox.

Cornmeal Muffins—
General Robert E. Lees Favorite

2 cups corn meal	1 tsp salt
1 cup flour	3 eggs
3 tsps baking powder	1 tbls shortening
2 tbls sugar	2 1/2 cups milk

Put the corn meal and flour in large wooden mixing bowl. Blend together. Stir in baking powder, sugar, and salt. Separate whites and yolks of eggs. Beat both by themselves. Add to bowl of ingredients. Melt shortening and stir it in. Pour in milk. Beat entire mixture with large wooden spoon. Pour into buttered muffin tins. Fill each cup about 2/3 full. Bake in rather quick oven (400 to 425 degrees). Less than 30 minutes should suffice. These muffins are always best when eaten hot.

NOTE: Never cut open a muffin of any type—especially those made with meals. Pass knife lightly around it to pierce the crust. Then break open with the fingers.

Robert Edward Lee (1807-1870)
From the Man Himself

On one occasion, shortly before the battle Fredericksburg, General Lee stood on a hill quietly observing the beautiful land. He told his staff: *"It's something those Yankees do not understand, will never understand. Rivers, hill, valleys, fields, even towns: To those people they're just markings on a map from the war office in Washington. To us, they're where our ancestors fought. They are birth places and burial places. They're the places where we learned to walk, to talk, to pray. They're places where we made friendships and fell in love. They're the incarnation of all our memories and all that we love."*

When General Lee once joined a group of soldiers who were holding a prayer meeting, he said: *"Don't jump to attention. I am only a poor sinner saved by the grace of God through faith in the Lord Jesus Christ."*

Lee had this to say regarding the *Bible*: *"There are things in the Old Book which I may not be able to explain, but I fully accept it as the infallible Word of God, and receive its teachings as inspired by the Holy Spirit."*

"Madam, do not train up your children in hostility to the government of the United States. Remember, we are one country now. Dismiss from your mind all sectional feeling, and bring them up to be Americans." – **While he was the President of Washington College, Lexington, Virginia, 1867.**

To his daughter, Mildred on, Christmas Day in 1862: *"Gain knowledge and virtue and learn your duty to God and your neighbor. That is the great object of life."*

Said to Reverend J. William Jones: *"With calm satisfaction, trust in God and leave the results to Him."*

To his son, Robert Jr.: *"Above all things, learn to worship your Creator and to do His will as revealed in His Holy Book."*
"I am unwilling to do what is wrong."
"My whole trust is in God... "

Muffins—
Mrs. Zollicoffer's Best

2 tbls cream of tarter	1 tsp baking soda
6 cups flour	1 tsp salt
2 eggs, beaten	4 cups milk

Sift cream of tarter with flour into large wooden mixing bowl. Beat eggs very light and add to flour in bowl. Dissolve baking soda in little warm water and put it in. Add salt and, lastly, milk. Stir briskly until smooth batter is evident. Pour into buttered muffin rings. Fill each cup about 2/3 full. Bake in rather quick oven (400 to 425 degrees) for about 20 minutes.

NOTE: Never cut open a muffin of any type—especially those made with meals. Pass knife lightly around it to pierce the crust. Then break open with the fingers.

Felix Kirk Zollicoffer (1812-1862)

HERITAGE: Born and raised in Tennessee.

RANK: General.

FOUGHT FOR: Confederacy.

RELIGION: Christian.

EDUCATION: Graduated from high school, but never attended college.

MARRIAGE: Unknown.

CHILDREN: Unknown.

CAREER HIGHLIGHTS & TIDBITS: Former newspaper editor.
Fought in the Seminole War.
Commanded an East Tennessee brigade.
Former newspaper editor.
Severely near-sighted.
Almost blind.
Got confused and rode his horse into the Union lines.
Killed in his first major battle at Logan's Crossroads.
Shot point-blank in the chest by Union General Speed Fry.
Very shy, unassuming individual.
Whig politician.
Served in the House of Representatives (1853 to 1859).
Strong advocate of states' right.
Tried to avoid a North-South confrontation.
Took part in important peace-conference held in Washington D.C.

SAW ACTION AT: Logan's Crossroads, Kentucky, etc.

LITTLE KNOWN FACT: Always wore a white coat into battle on dark, rainy nights.

Graham Muffins—
General O. Howard's Favorite

3 cups graham flour
1 cup wheat flour
2 tbls sugar

1 tsp salt
1 tbls shortening
3/4 cup yeast

4 cups milk

 Put both types flour in large wooden mixing bowl. Blend well. Stir in sugar and salt. Melt shortening and add it also. Then briskly stir in yeast and milk. Harshly beat mixture with large wooden spoon. Cover and set in warm place to rise overnight. In the morning, pour into muffin rings. Fill each about 2/3 full. Bake for 20 minutes in rather quick oven (400 to 425 degrees). Break, butter, and eat while still hot.

NOTE: Never cut open a muffin of any type—especially those made with meals. Pass knife lightly around it to pierce the crust. Then break open with the fingers.

Otis Howard (1830-1908)

HERITAGE: Born and raised in Maine.

RANK: General.

FOUGHT FOR: Union.

RELIGION: Christian.

EDUCATION: Bowdion College and a West Point graduate.

CAREER HIGHLIGHTS & TIDBITS: Taught mathematics at West Point from 1859 to 1861.
> Had his arm shot off during the Battle of Fair Oaks.
> Superintendent of West Point from 1880-1882.
> Howard University, which he founded, was named after him.
> President of Howard University from 1869 to 1874.
> Earned the *"Thanks of Congress"* for his fighting and heroism at Gettysburg.
> Devoted to the cause of Negro betterment.
> Routed by Stonewall Jackson's flank attack in the Battle of Chancellorsville.
> Driven back with heavy losses during the Battle of Cemetery Hill.
> An honest man but a terrible administrator.

QUOTABLE QUOTE: *"Defeat was the best thing that could have happened to us; for it humbled us and made us make better preparations which led in time to a final victory."*

SAW ACTION AT: First Bull Run, Peninsular Campaign, Antietam, Fredericksburg, Chancellorsville, Gettysburg, Missionary Ridge on Lookout Mountain, The Atlanta Campaign, etc.

LITTLE KNOWN FACTS: Lost an arm while leading his men during the Battle of Fair Oaks in the Peninsular Campaign.
> Won the Congressional Medal of Honor for his heroic deeds while under enemy fire.

Bacon Muffins—
As Made by Mrs. Ashby

2 cups flour	1egg, well beaten
4 tsp baking powder	1 cup milk
2/3 tsp salt	2 tbls butter, melted

1 cup bacon, crisp and broken

Sift together in wooden mixing bowl the flour, baking powder, and salt. Blend in beaten egg, milk, and melted butter. Mix well until nice smooth batter is made. Set aside and prepare well-greased muffin tins. Put in generous tablespoon of batter for each muffin. Then add a portion of bacon. Cover with more batter. Fill each cup about 2/3 full. Bake in moderately quick oven (375 degrees) for about 20 minutes. Serve hot.

NOTE: Never cut open a muffin of any type—especially those made with meals. Pass knife lightly around it to pierce the crust. Then break open with the fingers.

Turner Ashby (1828-1862)

HERITAGE: Born in Fauquier County, Virginia.
Father was officer during the Revolutionary War.

RANK: General.

FOUGHT FOR: Confederacy.

RELIGION: Christian.

EDUCATION: Unknown.

MARRIAGE: Unknown.

CHILDREN: Unknown.

CAREER HIGHLIGHTS & TIDBITS: Stonewall Jackson's most trusted cavalry commander.
Best known for his courage and resourcefulness.
Raised a volunteer cavalry unit in 1859 and went to Harper's Ferry in an effort to stop John Brown.
One of the Shenandoah Valley's wealthy planters and grain dealers.
An extremely influential, local, political leader.
Favored slavery, but opposed secession.
Disguised himself and went to Chambersburg, Pennsylvania as a spy to gather intelligence information.
Displayed exceptional leadership qualities throughout the War.
Member of the 7th Virginia cavalry after June of 1861.
He and his men had the responsibility of defending the Upper Potomac border.

SAW ACTION AT: First Bull Run, Stonewall Jackson's Shenandoah Valley Campaign, Winchester, Front Royal, etc.

LITTLE KNOWN FACT: Killed while trying to protect Stonewall Jackson as he retreated from the Shenandoah Valley on June 6, 1862.

Corn Meal Muffins—
As Made For Gail Borden's Family

4 tbls shortening	4 tsp baking powder
4 tbls sugar	1/2 tsp salt
1 egg, well beaten	1 cup corn meal
1 cup flour	1-1/4 cups milk

Put shortening and sugar in wooden mixing bowl. Using fork, cream these together until light. Stir in beaten egg. Sift together flour, baking powder, and salt in a separate bowl. Then blend corn meal. Slowly add dry mixture, alternately with the milk, to the first mixture in wooden bowl. Beat together thoroughly. Pour batter into well-greased muffin tins. Fill each about 2/3 full. Bake in moderately quick oven (375 degrees) for about 25 minutes. Serve while hot.

Gail Borden (1801-1875)

HERITAGE: Born in Norwick, New York while Thomas Jefferson was President of the United States. Lived in Mississippi and Texas.

POSITION: Businessman. Inventor of Borden's Condensed Milk, still to be found on today's supermarket shelves.

RELIGION: Christian (see quote below).

EDUCATION: Unknown.

CAREER HIGHLIGHTS & TIDBITS: Helped to secure Texas independence.

> Part-time surveyor in 1814 at the age of 14 years.
> Worked twenty long years (1831 to 1851) perfecting a method of condensing milk.
> Finally was able to obtain a patent for condensed milk in 1856.
> Built America's first condensed milk plant in New Jersey.
> Became wealthy by supplying his canned condensed milk to the Union Army of the Potomac.
> First sale to Army of the Potomac was for 500 pounds of condensed milk. This was at that time the largest order his company had ever received.
> Union army desperately needed his milk for field rations due to its long shelf life.
> One son, Lee, joined the Confederate Army and rode with the Texas cavalry.
> John Gail, his other son, fought for the Union.

QUOTABLE QUOTE: *"My success in life can only be attributed to my sincere belief in God and to the fine Christian upbringing my mother provided me as a child."*

LITTLE KNOWN FACT: Wrote this inscription found on the marker over his grave in New York City:

> *"I tried and failed,*
> *I tried again and again,*
> *and succeeded."*

10

Yesteryear's Favorite Layer Cakes

Three-Layer Cake
Mrs. Hooker's Best

1 1/2 cups sugar	1 tsp baking powder
1 cup butter, soft	1/2 tsp salt
3 eggs	1/2 tsp cloves
1 1/4 cups raspberry jam	1 tsp cinnamon
3 cups flour, sifted	1/2 tsp nutmeg
1/2 tsp baking soda	1 cup buttermilk

Put sugar and butter in a large wooden mixing bowl and beat to light creamy mixture. Add eggs, one at a time. Beat thoroughly. Lastly, beat in the raspberry jam. Now sift together the flour, baking soda, baking powder, salt, and spices. Add these dry ingredients in 3 parts, alternately with buttermilk. Beat thoroughly after each part is put in.

Butter 3 round 9-inch cake pans. Line them with buttered, lightly floured paper. Pour equal amounts of batter into each of 3 pans. Bake in moderate oven (350 degrees) for 30 to 40 minutes, or until a toothpick inserted in center comes out clean. Then take out of the oven. Set the pans on wire racks to cool for 10 minutes. Turn cakes out of the pans and set aside until cold. When completely cold spread each layer with old fashioned frosting. Set 1 layer on the other and cover the entire cake with the same. It is made as follows:

1 cup sugar	pinch cream of tarter
1 egg white, beaten	lemon juice or vanilla to suit

Mix sugar with 1/4 cup hot water in saucepan and bring to boil. Boil until it strings. Do not stir. Slow pour this into the stiffly beaten egg white and blend. Now stir in cream of tartar. Beat thoroughly. Lastly, flavor with your choice of lemon juice or vanilla. When thick and smooth, spread over the cake.

NOTE: This frosting hardens quickly. Spread immediately after making it.

Joseph Hooker (1814-1879)

HERITAGE: Born in Hadley, Massachusetts.

RANK: General.

FOUGHT FOR: Union.

RELIGION: Christian – Never without his *Bible* at his side. Never would go into battle before first reading his *Bible* while alone in his tent.

EDUCATION: West Point graduate – class of 1837. He was ranked in the middle of his class.

CAREER HIGHLIGHTS & TIDBITS: Most officers would never ride a white horse into battle because of the tempting target it presented to the enemy, but not fearless Joe Hooker.
> Rode a massive white horse into battle at Antietam.
> Said that such a horse *"made it easy for my men to recognize me."*
> Aptly named *"Fighting Joe"* as a result of his many daring exploits on the battlefield.
> Defeated General Braxton Bragg at the Battle of Lookout Mountain in Chattanooga, Tennessee, on November 4, 1863.
> Had 133,000 men under his command during the fighting at Chancellorsville, Virginia.
> Hoped to defeat Robert E. Lee's force of 60,000 men, but was unsuccessful.

QUOTABLE QUOTE: Once said: *"May God have mercy on General Lee, for I will have none."* Subsequently defeated by Lee at Chancellorsville in May of 1863.

SAW ACTION AT: Seven Days' Battles, Second Bull Run, South Mountain, Antietam, Chancellorsville, Gettysburg, Lookout Mountain (Chattanooga), Atlanta Campaign, Mill Creek Gap, Resaca, etc.

LITTLE KNOWN FACT: Classmates at West Point included future Generals John Sedgwick (Union), Jubal Early (confederacy), and Braxton Bragg (confederacy)

Layer Cake—
Mrs. Pickett's Best

10 egg whites, beaten   2 cups flour
10 egg yolks, beaten   2 lemon rinds (grated)
2 cups sugar   juice of 1 lemon

Put separately beaten egg whites and yolks in large wooden mixing bowl. Sir in sugar and flour. Lastly, blend in grated rinds and lemon juice. When mixed well together, pour batter in large shallow buttered and floured pans. Bake in moderate to moderately quick oven (350 to 375 degrees) in thin layers. When cold, fill and frost with:

3 egg whites   large orange
3 cups powdered sugar   a little lemon juice

Put egg whites in broad, cool dish. Throw small handful of powdered sugar on them. Begin whipping. When stiff, take out enough to cover top of the cake and set aside. Add to rest the juice of the orange and half the grated ring. Beat until stiff. When the cake is nearly cold, spread this between layers.

Now take icing, set aside. Beat in a little lemon juice and, if needed, more sugar. This meringue should be much stiffer than that spread between the cakes as a filling.

George Edward Pickett (1825-1875)

HERITAGE: Born in Richmond, Virginia.

RANK: General.

FOUGHT FOR: Confederacy.

RELIGION: Christian (see quote below).

EDUCATION: West Point graduate – class of 1846.
Was 59th in his class of 59.
Very little formal education in his youth.
Taught law by an uncle in Illinois.
Obtained appointment to West Point in 1842.

CAREER HIGHLIGHTS & TIDBITS: Served from 1849 to 1856 in a Texas garrison.
Undertook a poorly judged frontal attack as ordered by Robert E. Lee on July 3, 1863.
Could never forgive General Lee for ordering this eventful charge.
Became famous for what is today commonly and inaccurately called *"Pickett's Charge."*
His *"Gamecock Brigade"* won an almost legendary reputation for excellent fighting.
Highly egotistical, he had an underlying hunger for battlefield excitement and glory.

QUOTABLE QUOTE: *"It is finished! Oh, my beloved division! Thousands of them have gone to their eternal home, having given up their lives for the cause they knew to be just. The others , alas, heartbroken, crushed in spirit, are left to mourn its loss."*

SAW ACTION AT: Cold Harbor, Five Forks, Fredericksburg, Gettysburg, Peninsular Campaign, Petersburg, Richmond, Seven Pines and Williamsburg, etc.

LITTLE KNOWN FACT: Wore his hair in perfumed ringlets.

Sponge Cake—
As Made by Mrs. Wallace

3 egg yolks   1 1/2 cups flour
1 cup sugar   2 tsp baking powder
1/2 cup milk   1/2 tsp salt
1 tsp vanilla extract   4 tbls butter, melted
            3 egg whites, beaten until stiff

Put egg yolks in wooden mixing bowl with sugar. Beat until thick and yellow. Stir in milk and vanilla extract. Sift together the flour, baking powder, and salt. Gradually stir this into mixture in wooden bowl. Add melted butter. Lastly fold in stiffly beaten egg whites. Grease and flour 2 large cake pans. Turn batter mixture into pans. Bake in moderate oven (350 degrees) for 15 to 20 minutes. Set aside to cool. Then put chocolate pudding between the layers. Cover top layer with Chantilly Cream (see below)

Mrs. Wallace's Chantilly Cream

1 egg, white only   2 tbls currant or quince jelly

Place egg white and jelly together in large wooden mixing bowl. Beat until stiff, like whipped cream. Pile on top of cake and sprinkle thickly with coconut.

Lew Wallace (1827-1905)

HERITAGE: Born and raised in Brookville, Indiana.

RANK: General.

FOUGHT FOR: Union.

RELIGION: Christian.

EDUCATION: Unknown – primarily self-educated. as he was both a newspaper reporter and a lawyer.

MARRIAGE: Unknown.

CHILDREN: Unknown.

CAREER HIGHLIGHTS & TIDBITS: Was both a newspaper reporter and a lawyer.
> Served with distinction in the Mexican War.
> Commended by General Grant for saving Washington when it was about to be captured.
> Served on the court-martial board that tried and convicted the assassins of President Lincoln.
> Headed the court-martial of Captain Henry Wirz, commandant of Andersonville, the infamous prison-of-war camp in Georgia.
> Wirz was unfairly tried, convicted, and hanged.
> Governor of New Mexico from 1778 to 1881.
> Published his *Autobiography* one year after his death.

SAW ACTION AT: Romney, Harper's Ferry, Fort Donelson, Shiloh, Monocasy, etc.

LITTLE KNOWN FACTS: Published quite a number of books. Included are such titles as *The Boyhood of Christ* (1888) and *The Fair God* (1873).
> Became famous as the author of *Ben Hur* (1880)

Honey Molasses Stack Cake—
Mrs. Winfield Scott's Favorite

2/3 cup molasses   3 tsp baking powder
1/2 cup honey   2 tsp baking soda
2/3 cup butter   1 tsp cinnamon
3 eggs   1 tsp nutmeg
6 cups flour   1/4 tsp salt
2/3 cup buttermilk

Put molasses, honey, and butter in wooden mixing bowl. Using fork, cream them together. Beat in one egg, then the other. In separate bowl, sift together flour, baking powder, baking soda, cinnamon, nutmeg, and salt. Add these dry ingredients, alternately, with buttermilk to the mixture in first bowl. Grease and flour 6 round 9-inch baking pans. Put an equal amount of batter in each pan. Pat neatly into place. Bake in rather quick oven (400 degrees) until lightly browned. Set aside to cool. When cooled, take from pans. Thickly spread chunky applesauce or apple butter on each layer and stack layers, one on top of the other. Serve when ready.

Note: During the Civil War Period each invited wedding guest was expected to bring one layer for such a cake. The height of the finished cake determined the amount of esteem the community held for the new bride.

Winfield Scott (1786-1866)

HERITAGE: Born near Petersburg, Virginia.

On family estate the year after James Madison and a number of other Founding Fathers drew up the *Constitution.*

RANK: General.

FOUGHT FOR: Union.

RELIGION: Christian.

EDUCATION: Tutored at home as a child and young adult. Attended William and Mary College.

Studied law under a prominent attorney in Petersburg, Virginia.

MARRIAGE: Unknown.

CHILDREN: Unknown.

CAREER HIGHLIGHTS & TIDBITS: Appointed to be General-in-Chief of the United States Army in 1841.

Grant was one of his junior officers during the Mexican War.

Developed a close friendship with Grant while serving with him.

Campaigned for temperance while in the Peace Time Army.

Was old, fat, and in poor health during the Civil War.

Couldn't even get on a horse because his obesity.

Held no field command as a result of all this.

Presented Grant with a gift in 1865. Inscribed on the card accompanying the gift: *"From the oldest to the greatest General."*

Had the utmost respect and admiration for General Philip Kearney.

Called General Kearney (1814-1862) *"The bravest and most perfect soldier I have ever known."*

Wrote two volumes of his memories.

Retired in 1861 after almost 50 years in the military.

LITTLE KNOWN FACT: Became, in 1852, the first officer since George Washington to hold the rank of Lieutenant General.

Applesauce Cake—
The Forrest Family Christmas Favorite

1 cup shortening	2 tsp nutmeg
2 cups brown sugar	3 tsp cinnamon
2 1/3 cups applesauce	1 tsp mace
2/3 cup molasses	1 tsp allspice
4 eggs, well beaten	1 tsp cloves
6 tbls lemon juice	2 pounds raisins
4 cups flour	1 cup whole wheat flour
4 tsp baking soda	1 pound apples, sliced thin
1 3/4 tsp salt	1 cup walnuts, chopped

Put shortening and brown sugar in large wooden mixing bowl. Beat together until they are nicely creamed. Stir in applesauce, molasses, beaten eggs, and lemon juice. Blend well. In a separate bowl, sift some flour and take out 4 cups. Sift these 4 cups again with baking soda, salt, nutmeg, cinnamon, mace, allspice, and cloves. Add this gradually to batter in first bowl and beat thoroughly. Dredge raisins in whole-wheat flour. Now add raisins to mixture. Put thin layer of batter in paper-lined baking pan. Cover with layer of sliced apples and chopped walnuts. Cover with another layer of batter. Repeat with sliced apples and chopped nuts. The last layer should be of batter. Bake in slow to moderately slow oven (300 to 325 degrees) for about 2 hours.

Nathan Bedford Forrest (1821-1877)

HERITAGE: Born in Tennessee.
     Father was a blacksmith.
     Settled on the Tennessee frontier in 1806.

RANK: General.

FOUGHT FOR: Confederacy.

RELIGION: Christian – Brought up in a fundamental, Christian home.

EDUCATION: Very little, if any, formal education.

CAREER HIGHLIGHTS & TIDBITS: Brigadier General James R. Chamberlain reported that he faced enemy fire more than 100 times.
     One source claims that 27 horses were shot out from under him during various battles.
     Another source says 39 horses were shot out from under this dauntless warrior.
     General Lee was asked who he believed was the greatest General on either side of the Civil War. Without hesitation he responded, *"A man I have never met. General Nathan Bedford Forrest."*
     A man with few real friends. Would allow only a select few to really get to know him.
     Had the most penetrating eyes.
     Could savage another man with merely a look.
     If looks could ill as the saying goes then Forrest could do it.

QUOTABLE QUOTES: *"Whenever you see something blue, shoot at it, and do all you can to keep up the scare."*
     "War means fighting, and fighting means killing."

SAW ACTION AT: Fort Donelson, Murfreesboro, and Parker's Crossroad, Chickamauga, Brice's Crossroads, Tupelo, Selma, etc.

LITTLE KNOWN FACT: When the war ended, General Forrest remarked: *"I did all in my power to break up the government, but I have found it a useless undertaking, and am now resolved to stand by the government as earnestly and honestly as I fought it.*

Coconut Cake—
As Made by Mrs. Stevens

1 cup butter   1 cup milk
2 cups powdered sugar   1 1/2 tsp baking powder
4 egg whites, beaten   3 cups flour
            1/2 coconut, finely grated

Cream butter and sugar in large wooden mixing bowl. Lightly fold in stiffly beaten egg whites. Blend in milk. Sift baking powder into flour and add this. Lastly, stir in grated coconut. When well blended, pour batter in large, shallow buttered and floured pans. Bake in moderate oven (350 degrees) in thin layers. When cold fill and frost with following:

3 egg whites   1 cup powdered sugar
            1 coconut, grated

Put egg whites in a broad, cool dish. Throw small handful powdered sugar on them. Begin whipping. When stiff, blend in half the grated coconut. Lay this between the layers of the cake. Mix other half of the grated coconut with 4 tablespoons of powdered sugar. Strew this thickly on top of cake.

Thaddeus Stevens (1792-1868)

HERITAGE: Born in Danville, Vermont.
Father was abusive and an alcoholic.
Brought up in abject poverty.
Settled in Pennsylvania in 1816.

POSITION: Radical Republican Politician.

EDUCATION: Graduated from Dartmouth in 1814.
Later studied law and taught school in York, Pennsylvania.

CAREER HIGHLIGHTS & TIDBITS: Not very well liked by any of his colleagues.
Avoided and despised by everyone who knew him.
Said to be a *"stern disciplinarian"* and a man who beat his children and his wife.
A radical and controversial lawyer in his day.
Anyone who disagreed with him and see everything his way was considered to be an enemy.
Founder and leader of the Radical Republicans.
Hell-bent to destroy every vestige of the Southern way of life.
Great debater, slick-tongued, and vindictive.
Gained fame in the North due to his ferocious anti-South oratory.
Had an undying hatred for the South.
Instrumental in getting a bill passed providing free public schools all over America.
Instrumental in getting passage of the infamous and hateful *Radical Reconstruction Act.*
Opposed the Compromise of 1860.
Opposed the Fugitive Slave Law.
A leader in the movement to impeach President Andrew Jackson.
Chairman of the House Ways and Means Committee.
Controlled all military appropriations during the Civil War.

LITTLE KNOWN FACTS: Born with a clubfoot. His brother had two clubfeet.
Was ridiculed and shunned as his clubfoot was seen as *"a sign of the devil.*

Cornstarch Cake—
A Favorite of David Hunter

2 cups butter	1 tsp baking soda
2 cups sugar	(dissolved in hot water)
3 egg whites, beaten	2 tsp cream of tartar
3 egg yolks, beaten	1/2 cup cornstarch
1 cup milk	2 cups flour

Cream butter and sugar in large wooden mixing bowl. Stir in separately beaten egg whites and yolks. Then stir in milk and baking soda. Now sift cream of tartar and cornstarch with flour. Gradually stir into mixture. Blend all ingredients well. Pour batter into small buttered and floured tins. Bake in moderate to moderately quick oven (350 to 375 degrees).

NOTE: This kind of cake tends to dry and sour in 2 or 3 days. It is excellent to eat for 24 hours after baking. When cold, spread favorite jam or jelly between layers and over the top.

David Hunter (1802-1806)

HERITAGE: Born in Washington, D.C.

RANK: General.

FOUGHT FOR: Union.

RELIGION: Christian.

EDUCATION: West Point graduate.

MARRIAGE: Unknown.

CHILDREN: Unknown.

CAREER HIGHLIGHTS & TIDBITS: Served with distinction in the Mexican War.
>Served as Major Paymaster.
>Held a number of territorial commands.
>Seriously wounded in the Battle of First Bull Run.
>Lincoln overrode his May 1862 order to free the slaves he had authorized to form the 1st South Carolina regiment.
>Lincoln said this action was "unauthorized."
>Invited by Lincoln to accompany him on his inaugural trip to Washington.
>President over many court-martial boards.
>Presided over the trial of President Lincoln's assassins.
>Later accompanied Lincoln's body to Springfield.
>Commander of the Department of the South.
>Freed all slaves in Union hands in his department.
>Retired in 1866 and lived in Washington, D.C.

SAW ACTION AT: First Bull Run where he was badly wounded.

LITTLE KNOWN FACT: Authorized the 1st South Carolina – the first all-negro regiment in the Civil War

Jelly Layer Cake—
Philip Kearney's Favorite

1 cup butter   6 egg yolks, beaten
2 cups sugar   1 cup milk
6 egg whites, beaten   1 1/2 tsp baking powder
4 cups flour

Cream butter and sugar in a large wooden mixing bowl. Stir in separately beaten egg whites and yolks. Blend in milk. Sift baking powder into the flour and add last. When well blended, pour batter in large, shallow buttered and floured pans. Bake in moderate oven (350 degrees) in thin layers. Spread when cold, between the layers, and over the top with fruit, jelly, or jam.

Philip Kearney (1814-1862)

HERITAGE: Born and raised in New York State.
Grew up in socially prominent New York family.

RANK: General.

FOUGHT FOR: Union.

RELIGION: Christian – a devout Methodist lay preacher.

EDUCATION: Graduate of Columbia College

CAREER HIGHLIGHTS & TIDBITS: Inherited a lot of property and a rather large fortune in 1836.
  Always had a rather romantic dream of becoming a cavalry officer.
  Studied cavalry tactics in France and fought in Algiers.
  Went against his family's wishes and volunteered for the Union army.
  He had an outstanding military record.
  Wounded and lost an arm in the Mexican War.
  Aide-de-camp to Commander-in-Chief Winfield Scott.
  Always rode into battle on a distinctive dapple-gray horse.
  Dashing cavalry officer whose men wore a unique diamond-shaped scarlet *"Kearney Patch."*
  When once asked by Confederate troops to surrender, he refused and was shot in the back as he rode away.
  Died while in combat just as he had hoped and prayed to do.

QUOTABLE QUOTE: Kearney's motto was: *"Dulce et decorum est propatria mori (It is sweet to die for one's country)".*

SAW ACTION AT: Williamsburg, Seven Pines, Second Bull Run, Chantilly, etc.
  Killed during the battle of Chantilly while reconnoitering in September of 1862.).

LITTLE KNOWN FACT: Union General Winfield Scott called Kearney, *"The bravest and most perfect soldier I have ever known.*

11

Other Cakes Enjoyed
by the Blue and the Gray

Lady Cakes—
The Davis Family Recipe

1 cup butter	1 tsp vanilla
2 1/2 cups sugar	1 tsp almond flavoring
6 eggs	3 cups flour

 Cream butter and sugar. Add eggs, one at a time, beating well. Add flavoring. Mix flour into the batter, 1 cup at a time. Grease and flour an 11x17 inch sheet pan. Pour in the batter and bake in moderate oven (350 degrees) for 20 to 25 minutes. Cool and trim to uniform thickness. Ice with warm divinity icing as found below. Cool until icing is set but not completely hard. Carefully cut into squares or diamonds.

Divinity Icing—
As Made by Mrs. Davis

2 cups sugar	1/4 tsp corn syrup
1/2 cup water	2 egg whites
1/4 tsp cream of tartar	6 marshmallows

Boil sugar, water, cream of tartar, and corn syrup to 240 degrees. Beat whites until very stiff. Add chopped marshmallows. Pour hot syrup over whites. Beat until marshmallows dissolve. Pour over cake while still warm enough to pour smoothly.

Jefferson Davis (1808-1889)

HERITAGE: Born in Kentucky. Tenth child of a settler who had fought during the Revolutionary War.

POSITION: President of the Confederate States of America (CSA).

RELIGION: Christian – Studied at a Roman Catholic seminary in Kentucky. Came close to renouncing his family's Baptist faith.

EDUCATION: West Point graduate – class of 1828. Graduated one year ahead of Robert E. Lee. Also attended Transylvania University.

MARRIAGE: Wed the daughter, against her father's wishes of future President Zachary Taylor. She died three months later. Married again to Varina Howell, daughter of a wealthy, Mississippi planter.

CAREER HIGHLIGHTS & TIDBITS: Hated and feared by President Andrew Johnson.

> Captured by a Union cavalry detachment.
> After his capture, the editors of *Harper's Weekly* were vengeful: *"Mr. Davis must be tried for treason. If convicted, he must be sentenced. If sentenced, he must be hanged."*
> Wrongly imprisoned for two years at Fortress Monroe. Harshly treated and often mistreated.
> Only allowed to read his *Bible* and his *Episcopal Prayer Book* while in prison.
> Controversy over his unjust imprisonment grew to international proportions.

QUOTABLE QUOTE: On April 29, 1861 he said: *"We feel that our cause is just and holy...in independence we seek no conquest...all we ask is to be let alone."*

SAW ACTION AT: Hero in the Mexican War. Served in the Black Hawk War in the 1830s.

LITTLE KNOWN FACT: Had a dog named after him. The 6th Iowa Regiment named their mongrel mascot, *"Jeff Davis.*

Coconut Almond Fruit Cake—
As it was Made for James Longstreet

1/2 cup butter	1/4 tsp vanilla
1 cup sugar	1 1/2 cups flour
2/3 cup coconut, grated	1/4 tsp salt
2/3 cup almonds, chopped	2 tsp baking powder
1/4 cup lemon peel, candied	1 cup cream
1/4 cup orange peel candied	3 egg whites, beaten

Using a fork, cream butter and sugar in wooden mixing bowl. Then add coconut, chopped, almonds, candied lemon and orange peels, and vanilla. Stir everything together well. Sift together in a separate bowl flour, salt, and baking powder. Add this alternately with cream to the ingredients in first bowl. Blend thoroughly. Lastly, fold in stiffly beaten egg whites. Put batter into well-greased loaf pan. Bake in moderate oven (350 degrees) for about 30 minutes.

James Longstreet (1821-1904)

HERITAGE: Born in South Carolina. Raised in Georgia and Alabama. Son of a farmer.

RANK: General.

FOUGHT FOR: Confederacy.

RELIGION: Christian – once said this*: "I am pleased to say: I believe in God, the Father, and his only Son, Jesus Christ, our Lord. It is my custom to read one or more chapters of my Bible daily for comfort, guidance, and instruction."*

EDUCATION: West Point graduate – class of 1842.
Graduated near the bottom of his class.

CAREER HIGHLIGHTS & TIDBITS: He and General Grant served together at Jefferson Barracks in the 1840's.
The men their wives developed a close and lasting friendship while on duty there.
General Lee considered him to be one of his most reliable commanders.
Lee affectionately dubbed him his *"Old War Horse."*
Fought in Mexican War under the command of Zachary Taylor.
Routed General Pope's troops at Bull Run on June 30, 1862.
Commanded more than half of Lee's troops in summer of 1862.

QUOTABLE QUOTE: Comment to Lee regarding surrender to Grant: *"General, unless he offers us honorable terms, come back and let us fight it out!"*

SAW ACTION AT: Petersburg, Richmond, Chickamauga, Williamsburg, Seven Pines, Fredericksburg, Antietam, First and Second Bull Run, Knoxville, etc.

LITTLE KNOWN FACT: Accompanied General Winfield Scott on his March to Mexico City during the Mexican War. Served in Scott's Paymaster Corps.

Coffee Butterscotch Cake—
As Made by Mrs. Forrest

1/2 cup butter
1 1/3 cups brown sugar
2 eggs
1 tsp vanilla extract

1 3/4 cups flour
2 1/2 tsp baking powder
1/4 tsp baking soda
1/2 cup cold strong coffee

Using a fork, cream butter in wooden mixing bowl. Slowly stir in brown sugar. Add unbeaten eggs, one at a time, beating mixture well after each addition. Lastly, stir in vanilla. Sift together in a separate bowl flour, baking powder, and baking soda. Add these dry ingredients, alternately, with coffee, to first bowl. Blend everything thoroughly. Put batter into well-greased 8-inch square baking pan. Bake in moderate oven (350 degrees) for about 50 minutes. When done, set aside to cool. When cold, cover top with favorite frosting.

Nathan Bedford Forrest (1821-1877)

HERITAGE: Born in Tennessee. Father a blacksmith – died when Forrest was 16 years old. Family had settled on the Tennessee frontier in 1806.

RANK: General.

FOUGHT FOR: Confederacy.

RELIGION: Christian – Brought up in a fundamental Christian home where there was a nightly Bible reading.

EDUCATION: Very little, if any, formal education.

CAREER HIGHLIGHTS & TIDBITS: The name Nathan Bedford Forrest became so famous during the Civil War that it symbolized the entire Confederate cause.

> General Sherman angrily declared: *"Follow Forrest to the death even if it costs 10,000 lives and breaks the Federal Treasury."*
> Most aggressive, and best known cavalry rider during the War.
> One example of General Forrest's daring deeds took place on May 2, 1863. A teenage girl, Emma Sansom, heroically guided his troops, while under fire, across Black Creek near Gadsen.
> The very next day they captured Union Colonel Straight and 1,466 men near Cedar Bluff.

QUOTABLE QUOTE: On November 30, 1864 he was insulted by a fellow General who had lost a leg during the Battle of Chickamauga, and the use of an arm at Gettysburg. Forrest told him in no uncertain terms: *"General Hood, if you were a whole man, I'd whip you to within an inch of your life."* He then turned and walked away.

SAW ACTION AT: Fort Donelson, Murfreesboro, Parker's Crossroad, Chickamauga, Bryce's Crossroad, Tupelo, Selma, etc.

LITTLE KNOWN FACT: Forrest offers this: *"I went into the army worth a million and a half dollars and came out a beggar."*

Coffee Loaf Cake—
Mrs. Hooker's Special Christmas Treat

3/4 cup butter	1/2 tsp mace
2 1/4 cups brown sugar	1/2 tsp cinnamon
3 ounces chocolate, melted	1/2 tsp salt
3 cups flour	1 c. strong coffee, black and cold
4 tsp baking powder	4 eggs

Put the butter and brown sugar in large wooden mixing bowl. Beat together until nicely creamed. Stir in melted chocolate. Sift together in separate mixing bowl the flour, baking powder, mace, cinnamon, and salt. Stir this in with ingredients in first bowl, alternately, with cold coffee. Drop in eggs, one at a time, beating each in thoroughly. Set aside momentarily. Grease and lightly flour large loaf pan. Put mixture in pan. Bake in moderate oven (350 degrees) for about 50 minutes. When done, let cake cool in pan. Then turn out on plate. Cover entire cake with special coffee frosting as made below.

Mrs. Hooker's Coffee Frosting Recipe

1 cup black coffee, very strong	powdered sugar as required
1 tbls vanilla	2 cups walnuts, chopped

Put the cold black coffee and vanilla in wooden mixing bowl. Beat in enough powdered sugar until mixture becomes stiff enough to spread. Spread liberally on top and sides of cake. Sprinkle top of cake thickly with chopped walnuts.

Joseph Hooker (1814-1879)

HERITAGE: Born in Hadley, Massachusetts.

RANK: General.

FOUGHT FOR: Union.

RELIGION: Christian – Never without his *Bible* at his side. Would never go into battle without first reading passages from his Bible while alone in his tent.

EDUCATION: West Point graduate – class of 1837.

MARRIAGE: Unknown.

CHILDREN: Unknown.

CAREER HIGHLIGHTS & TIDBITS: *"Hooker's career is exemplified by that of a rocket,"* declared Captain George Armstrong Custer. *"He went up like one and came down like a stick."*

Declared in April of 1862: *"My plans are perfect. May God have mercy on General Lee for I will have none!"*.

In April of 1862, President Lincoln told Hooker: *"General: I have placed you at the head of the Army of the Potomac...I have heard, in such a way as to believe it, of your recently saying that both the army and the government needed a dictator. Of course it was not for this, but in spite of it, that I have given you the command. Only those Generals who gain successes can set up dictatorships. What I now ask of you is military successes, and I will risk the dictatorship."*

SAW ACTION AT: Second Bull Run, Chancellorsville, Gettysburg, Lookout Mountain, Antietam, Resaca, Pine Mountain, Mill Creek Gap, Seven Days' Battles, South Mountain, etc.

LITTLE KNOWN FACT:. Said to have been heavily drinking during the battle of Chancellorsville when he was unexpectedly and soundly defeated by General Lee.

Soft Fruit Cake—
A Favorite of the Johnston Family

2/3 cup dried apricots, chopped
1 cup dried apples, chopped
1 cup prunes, chopped
1 cup dried figs, chopped
1 cup raisins
2 1/4 cups sugar
3/4 cup water
3/4 cup butter
1/2 cup peanuts, crushed
2 tsp vanilla

3 eggs, well beaten
3/4 cup milk
2 1/4 cups flour
1/2 tsp baking soda
1 tsp nutmeg
1/2 tsp cloves
1/2 tsp cinnamon
3 tsp baking powder
1 tsp salt
2 tbls orange peel, shredded

Put into a kettle the chopped apricots, apple slices, prunes, figs, and raisins. Add 1/2 cup sugar water. Stir together and bring to boil. Cover and let simmer 10 minutes. Take kettle from stove. Drain off liquid and discard. Set fruit mixture aside to cool. Put remaining 1 3/4 cups sugar and butter in wooden mixing bowl and beat until creamy. Add peanuts and mix well. Blend in beaten eggs and milk. Sift some flour in a separate bowl. Measure out 2 1/4 cups. Sift this again (into the first bowl) with baking soda, nutmeg, cloves, cinnamon, baking powder, and salt. Add fruits from kettle. Blend everything thoroughly. Lastly, stir in shredded orange peel and vanilla. Line a large tube pan with oiled paper. Pour mixture into pan. Bake in moderately slow oven (325 degrees) for 1 hour. Reduce temperature to very slow (250 degrees) and continue baking 30 minutes more.

Albert Sidney Johnston (1803-1862)

HERITAGE: Born in Washington, Kentucky.

RANK: General.

FOUGHT FOR: Confederacy.

RELIGION: Christian. Attended Sunday School and church regularly as a child.

EDUCATION: West Point graduate – class of 1826.

MARRIAGE: Unknown.

CAREER HIGHLIGHTS & TIDBITS: Secretary of War for the Republic of Texas from 1838 to 1840.
> Wounded in his leg at Shiloh on April 6, 1862, on the first day of the fighting.
> Subsequently died from this injury.
> His loss was called *"irreparable"* by Jefferson Davis.
> Davis once called him *"the greatest soldier...then living."*
> Turned down an offer by Lincoln to be General Winfield Scott's second-in-command.
> Instead chose to become a full General in the Confederate cause.
> Oversaw the retreat of Confederate forces from Nashville.

QUOTABLE QUOTE: *"I hoped and expected that I had others who would prove Generals, but I knew I had one, and that was Sidney Johnston,"* said *Jefferson Davis in September of 1861.*

SAW ACTION AT: Shiloh.

LITTLE KNOWN FACT: Appointed to be the commander of the Texas Army. This resulted in a duel with another officer who believed that he should have been given the promotion instead of Johnston.

Mrs. Stuart's Fruit Loaf—
A Favorite of Her Son Jeb

1/2 cup butter	2 cups flour
1 cup sugar	3 tsp baking powder
2 egg yolks	1/2 tsp salt
1 cup raisins	1/2 cup milk
1/4 cup citron, chopped	2 egg whites, beaten stiff

Cream the butter in a wooden mixing bowl. Gradually add sugar, alternately, with the egg yolks while constantly stirring. Blend in the raising and chopped citron. In a separate bowl, sift together the flour, baking powder, and salt. Add these dry ingredients, alternately, with the milk and blend everything thoroughly. Lastly fold in the stiffly beaten egg whites. Put batter into a buttered loaf pan. Bake in moderate oven (350 degrees) for 45 minutes.

Note: Other fruits such as apples, blueberries or cherries, or a combination of these, were sometimes added to this recipe for a change when Mrs. Stuart desired to do so for her family.

James Ewell Brown (JEB) Stuart (1833-1864)

HERITAGE: Born on Laurel Hill Plantation, Patrick County, Virginia. 7th of 10 children. Family was wealthy.

RANK: General.

FOUGHT FOR: Confederacy.

RELIGION: Christian – quiet and not vocal about his religious beliefs (see quote below).

EDUCATION: West Point graduate – class of 1854. Was 13th in his class of 46. Initially home-schooled as a youngster and attended Emory and Henry College prior to entering West Point in 1850.

CAREER HIGHLIGHTS & TIDBITS: One of General Lee's favorite cadets when Lee was the superintendent of West Point.

Had a crush on Lee's daughter. Never did anything about this because a cadet simply should not ask the man in charge of the school if he could *"court"* his daughter.

After being mortally wounded at Yellow Tavern on May 11, 1864, he shouted to his troops: *"Go back! Go back! Do your duty as I have done mine, and our country will be safer. Go back! Go back! I had rather die than be whipped."*

Never doubted that he was fighting for *"the will of the Almighty."*

QUOTABLE QUOTE: Said as he lay dying: *"If it were God's will, I should like to live longer and serve my country. If I must die, I should like to see my wife first, but if it His will that I die now, I am ready and willing to go if God and my country think that I have fulfilled my destiny and done my duty."*

SAW ACTION AT: Gettysburg, First and Second Bull Run, First and Second Manassas, Fairfax, Westminster, Yellow Tavern, Carlisle, Harper's Ferry, etc.

LITTLE KNOWN FACT: His father-in-law was Union General Philip St. George Cooke, also a cavalry leader.

Rich Steamed Fruit Cake—
Mrs. Sherman's Christmas Best

4 cups raisins
1 cup dried apples, marmalade
1 cup dried cherries, diced
1 cup dried apricots, diced
1 cup figs, chopped
1 cup brandy
1 cup butter
1/2 cup molasses
1 cup brown sugar
3 cups peanuts, chopped

6 eggs
1/2 cup grape jelly
1 square unsweetened
chocolate, melted
1 1/2 tsp baking powder
1/4 tsp salt
1/2 tsp allspice
1/2 tsp nutmeg
1 tsp cinnamon
2 cups walnuts, chopped

Put raisings, apples, cherries, apricots, and figs into a large bowl. Pour in brandy (or grape juice) and let soak overnight. Start the next morning by putting butter and brown sugar in a large wooden mixing bowl. Beat until they are nicely creamed. Then add eggs, one at a time, beating mixture thoroughly. Stir in the orange marmalade, grape jelly, and melted chocolate. In a separate mixing bowl, sift together half the flour with the baking powder, salt, allspice, nutmeg, and cinnamon. Stir this into the mixture in the first bowl. Sift the rest of the flour over the soaked fruit. Stir well to blend nicely. Now add this to the batter in the first bowl. Lastly stir in the chopped almonds and halved pecans. Place in loaf pans lined with well-greased brown paper. Cover tightly. Set in larger pan of water in oven and let steam slowly for 6 hours. Then uncover and bake in very slow oven (250 degrees) for about 1 hour. Makes 3 nice fruitcakes.

William Tecumseh Sherman (1820-1891)

HERITAGE: Born in Lancaster, Ohio. Son of an Ohio Supreme Court Justice.

RANK: General.

FOUGHT FOR: Union.

RELIGION: Christian – He and his wife were Roman Catholics.

EDUCATION: West Point graduate – class of 1840. Sixth in his class. Attended private academy as a boy.

MARRIAGE: Unknown.

CHILDREN: Unknown.

CAREER HIGHLIGHTS & TIDBITS: When undamaged Savannah, Georgia, peacefully surrendered in 1864, he sent a telegram to President Lincoln in December. It read, *"I beg to present you as a Christmas gift the city of Savannah."*

Columbia, South Carolina, didn't enjoy such a fate. Sherman's troops ruthlessly sacked and burned the lovely city.

He declared: *"They [Southerners] cannot be made to love us, but they can be made to fear us!"*

On September 17, 1863 he emphatically stated: *"I would make this war as severe as possible, and show no symptoms of tiring until the South begs for mercy."*

QUOTABLE QUOTE(S): *"To secure the safety of navigation of the Mississippi, I would slay millions—on that point I am not only insane, but mad!"* *"Follow [Nathan Bedford] Forrest to the death if it costs 10,000 lives and breaks the [federal] Treasury."* He didn't succeed.

LITTLE KNOWN FACT: Had three horses shot out from under him during the fighting at Shiloh.

Date-Nut Loaf—
The Vallingham Family Recipe

1 1/2 cups flour
5 tsp baking powder
1 1/2 tsp salt
1/4 tsp baking soda
1/2 cup brown sugar

1 1/2 cups milk
1/4 cup molasses
1 1/2 cups graham flour
1 cup dates, chopped, dredged in
graham flour

1 cup walnuts, chopped

Sift together in a wooden mixing bowl the flour, baking powder, salt, and baking soda. Stir in brown sugar, milk, and molasses. Add graham flour, dredged dates, and chopped walnuts. Beat all ingredients thoroughly until nicely blended. Grease a loaf pan. Pour batter into loaf pan. Bake in moderately quick oven (375 degrees) for 1 hour.

Clement Laird Vallandigham (1820-1870)

HERITAGE: Born and raised in Lisbon, Ohio.

POSITION: Democratic politician, Ohio attorney, journalist.

RELIGION: Christian.

EDUCATION: Studied in his youth at the New Lisbon Academy. Attended Jefferson's College in Pennsylvania. Privately pursued legal studies in Ohio.

MARRIAGE: Unknown.

CHILDREN: Unknown.

CAREER HIGHLIGHTS & TIDBITS: Strongly opposed the Civil War from the very beginning.
>   Congressman from 1858 to 1863.
>   Fearless and outspoken individual.
>   Convicted of treason in 1863 by a vehement Lincoln Administration cabal.
>   This came about because of his making derogatory comments about President Lincoln and the war effort.
>   Unjustly and illegally sentenced to two years in prison.
>   Lincoln commuted the sentence and banished him to the Confederacy.
>   Strenuously opposed any and all of the horrendous Radical Republican Reconstruction policies.

QUOTABLE QUOTE: *"You have not conquered the South. You never will. War for the Union was abandoned; war for the Negro openly begun and with stronger battalions than before. With what success: Let the dead at Fredericksburg ... answer."*

LITTLE KNOWN FACT: Hurt Democratic chance to defeat Lincoln by forcing the insertion of an anti-war amendment in their campaign platform.

Ginger Bread—
As Mrs. Lyons Made It

1 cup molasses	3 cups flour
1/2 cup butter	2 tsps baking powder
1/2 cup sugar	1/4 tsp salt
1 cup water, boiling	2 tsp cinnamon
1 cup walnuts, chopped	1 tsp ginger
1 cup raisins, chopped	2 eggs, well beaten

Put the molasses into a wooden mixing bowl with the butter and sugar. Pour in the boiling water and stir well. Let this cool thoroughly, then add the walnuts and raisins. Sift together the flour, baking powder, salt, cinnamon, and ginger. Add this to the mixture and stir until blended. Lastly, stir in the beaten eggs. Grease and flour a shallow baking pan. Put the gingerbread mixture in the baking pan and bake in moderate oven (350 degrees) for 40 minutes. Let cool and cut in squares. Gingerbread is probably one of the oldest forms of cake known. It was formerly made of rye flour kneaded with ginger and other spices, and sweetened with honey.

Nathaniel Lyon (1818-1861)

HERITAGE: Born in Ashford, Connecticut. Spent childhood working on the family farm.

RANK: General.

FOUGHT FOR: Union.

RELIGION: Christian. Once said: *"The Bible in which I believe is no doubt the most wonderful thing God has given me."*

EDUCATION: West Point graduate – class of 1841.

MARRIAGE: Unknown.

CAREER HIGHLIGHTS & TIDBITS: Fought in Mexican War.
Fought in the Seminole War.
A fiery, irascible man, best suited to be a soldier.
Strongly supported Lincoln and the Republican Party.
Career soldier who firmly believed in the necessity of preserving the Union.
Commandant of the U.S. Arsenal in St. Louis, Missouri.
Saved Missouri for the Union by capturing the pro-secessionist mob at Camp Jackson in May of 1886.
Known as the *"Savior of Missouri."*
Willed all of his property and belongings to the government in an effort to assist in the war effort.
Flags were flown at half-mast when his funeral train stopped in Cincinnati, Philadelphia, New York, and Hartford.
Assigned to holster the weak defenses of the St. Louis Arsenal. Here was stored 90,000 pounds of gun powder, 60,000 muskets, and was close to the Federal sub-treasury that housed more than a million dollars in gold and silver.

LITTLE KNOWN FACTS: Killed during the Battle of Wilson's Creek in 1861.
First Union General to die in battle during the Civil War.
Once, disguised as a farm woman, he spied on a military camp.

Fruit Cake—
Lincoln's Favorite

1 cups butter	1 tsp cinnamon
2 cups sugar	4 cups flour
6 egg yolks, beaten	1 tbls rose water
1 tsp baking soda	Double handful citron, chopped
2 cups sour cream	and floured
1 nutmeg, grated	6 egg whites, beaten

Cream butter and sugar in large wooden mixing bowl. Mix in beaten egg yolks. Dissolve baking soda in little hot water and stir it into sour cream. Then add sour cream and spices. Next, blend in flour and then rose water. Now stir in citron. Finally, add fluffy beaten egg whites and stir well. Pour batter into deep loaf tins or large shallow pans lined with well-buttered paper. Bake in very slow to slow oven (275 to300 degrees) for at least 2 hours.

Abraham Lincoln(1809-1865)
His Views on Religion

ACCORDING TO WILLIAM H. HERADON: *"Lincoln was a deep-grounded infidel. He disliked and despised churches. He never entered a church except to scoff and ridicule."*

THE BIBLE: *"In regard to this great Book, I have but one thing to say. I believe the Bible is the best gift God has given to man. All the good religion gave to the world was communicated through this book."*

In his second inaugural address on March 4, 1865: *"Both sides read the same Bible, and pray to the same God; and each invokes his aid against the other. It may seem strange that any men should dare to ask a just God's assistance in wringing their bread from the sweat of other men's faces; but let us judge not that we be not judged."*

PRAYER: When General Lee marched into Pennsylvania, everyone in Washington was panic-stricken—everyone that is except the President. Lincoln remained perfectly calm. He later explained to a General who had been wounded at Gettysburg: *"I went to my room...and got down on my knees before Almighty God and prayed...Soon a sweet comfort crept into my soul that God Almighty had taken the whole business into His own hands."*

GOD: On December of 1862, he declared: *"We are now on the brink of destruction. It appears to me that the Almighty is against us."*

On June 18, 1864 he said this: *"We accepted this war for the worthy object...of restoring the national authority over the whole national domain...and the war will end when that object is attained. Under God, I hope it never will until that time."*

JUDGEMENT: *"Fondly do we hope—fervently do we pray—that this mighty scourge of war may speedily pass away. Yet if God wills that it continue...so it must be said 'the judgments of the Lord are true and righteous altogether.'*

Silver Tube Cake—
Mrs. William Jones' Best

2 cups sugar
1 cup butter
3 cups flour

1 cup milk
1 tsp almond extract
8 egg whites, stiffly beaten

3 tsp baking powder

Put sugar and butter into large wooden mixing bowl and beat to light creamy mixture. Then sift together flour and baking powder 3 times. Alternately beat this and milk into the bowl. Blend in almond extract. Lastly, fold in fluffy beaten egg whites. Pour batter into well-buttered tube pan. Bake in moderate oven (350 degrees) for about 50 minutes. When the cake is done, prepare the icing.

2 cups powdered sugar
4 tbls cream

1/2 tsp vanilla
1 cup coconut, grated

Put the sugar into wooden mixing bowl. Gradually add cream and beat steadily. Add vanilla. When beaten to a good spreading consistency, spread all over cake. Sprinkle heavily with grated coconut.

William Edmonson "Grumble" Jones
(1824-1864)

HERITAGE: Born in the Middle Fork of the Holsten River in Washington County, Virginia.

RANK: General.

FOUGHT FOR: Confederacy.

RELIGION: Christian.

EDUCATION: West Point graduate – class of 1848. 12th in a class of 48. Graduated from Emory and Henry College in Virginia in 1844.

MARRIAGE: His young wife was washed from his arms in a shipwreck shortly after their marriage.

CAREER HIGHLIGHTS & TIDBITS: Earned name *"Grumble Jones"* because he was irascible and constantly complained.
> Disliked by General J.E.B. Stuart although Stuart respected him.
> Stuart called him *"The best outpost officer in the army."*
> He referred to Stuart as *"that young whipper-snapper."*
> Became "embittered, whining, complaining, and suspicious" as a result of his wife's untimely death.
> A plain-dresser, not at all flamboyant.
> Had a legendary talent for using profanity.
> An extremely strict disciplinarian whose men respected him, but detested him.

QUOTABLE QUOTE: General John D. Imboden wrote that Jones *"was an old army officer brave as a lion...and was known as a hard fighter. He was a man, however, of high temper, morose, and fretful...never would admit the possibility of defeat..."*

SAW ACTION AT: Cedar Mountain, Groveton, Second Bull Run, Gettysburg, etc.

LITTLE KNOWN FACT: Never washed his beard and mustache.

Simple Pound Cake—
As Made by Mrs. Gatling

1 1/2 cups butter
2 cups sugar
9 egg whites, beaten

9 egg yolks, beaten
2 tsps baking powder
4 cups flour

Cream butter and sugar in large wooden mixing bowl. Carefully stir in separately beaten egg whites and yolks. Sift baking powder through flour. Gradually blend flour until batter is smooth. Pour batter in well buttered and floured loaf pan. Put in the oven and bake in slow oven (300 degrees)

Richard Jordan Gatling (1828-1903)

HERITAGE: Born and raised at Money's Neck, his father's North Carolina plantation.
  Father a wealthy planter and slave owner.

POSITION: Physician, inventor, school teacher, merchant.

RELIGION: Christian. Regular church attendee.

EDUCATION: Home schooled as a child. A brilliant student.
  Attended Ohio Medical College. –
  Studied both medicine and dentistry.
  Graduated in 1850 with medical degree.

MARRIAGE: Unknown.

CHILDREN: Unknown.

CAREER HIGHLIGHTS & TIDBITS: Patented the revolving 6-barrel hand-cranked Gatling machine gun on November 4, 1862.
  The weapon's military potential was initially ignored by President Abraham Lincoln.
  His new weapon could fire an astounding 250 rounds a minute.
  A few of these guns were first tried aboard Union ships during the siege of Petersburg.
  Gatling sincerely believed that wars would cease to exist in the future because of the devastating weapon he had created.
  Suspected of having Confederate sympathies.
  As a teenager, he helped his father invent a machine for sowing cotton, another for thinning young cotton plants.
  Invented a steamboat screw propeller in 1839 at the age of 21. Invented a steam-driven plow in 1857.

LITTLE KNOWN FACTS: Called a hypocrite by those who thought him to be pacifist.
  Opened a factory in Hartford, Connecticut in 1870 to produce his machine gun.

Angel Cake—
As Made by General Ellsworth's Mother

7 egg whites   3/4 cup pastry flour
3/4 tsp cream of tartar   1 1/2 tsp baking powder
1 cup sugar   Few grains salt
            1 tsp vanilla extract

Put egg whites in wooden mixing bowl. Beat harshly with wire beater until whites foam. Add cream of tartar. Continue beating until whites stiffen. Gradually add sugar by folding into stiff egg whites with a spatula. Then proceed to sift together four times the pastry flour, baking powder, and salt in a separate bowl. Fold these dry ingredients into stiff egg whites. Lastly stiff in vanilla. Bake in well-greased tube pan in moderate oven (350 degrees) for 45 to 60 minutes.

Elmer Ephraim Ellsworth (1837-1861)

HERITAGE: Born in Saratoga County, New York.
Direct descendant of Reverend Richard Denton (1603-1662), founder of the first Presbyterian Church in the New World.

RANK: General.

FOUGHT FOR: Union.

RELIGION: Christian.

CAREER HIGHLIGHTS & TIDBITS: Started working as a clerk in a Chicago store.
Was a glib, fast-talking salesman type of individual.
Highly egotistical with a flair for grandiose showmanship.
Worked as an election aide during Lincoln's campaign for the Presidency.
Helped Lincoln win the election.
As a result, they became close friends.
Organized a most unusual and colorful Union military unit in New York City called the Zouaves.
His men wore odd exotic Algerian uniforms patterned after French units.
His regiment was best known for its flamboyant military drills.
Looked and acted rather prissy while undertaking military training exercises and when marching at public events.
His Zouave regiment once did a special performance for President Lincoln at the White House in 1860.
His unit helped occupy Alexandria, Virginia.
Shot after tearing down a Confederate flag atop the Marshall house.

LITTLE KNOWN FACT: Was first publicized Union casualty during the Civil War.

Nut Loaf—
General Edward Aylesworth Perry's Favorite

1 cup butter	3 tsp baking powder
2 cups sugar	3 cups flour
4 egg whites, beaten	2 cups chopped hickory nuts
4 egg yolks, beaten	

or

1 cup ice water	2 cups chopped white walnuts

Cream butter and sugar in large wooden mixing bowl. Add separately beaten egg whites and yolks. Beat together hard for at least 5 minutes. Now blend in ice water. Sift baking powder in flour and blend with bowl ingredients. Lastly, add nuts. Stir well. Pour the batter in well-buttered and floured loaf pan. Bake in very slow oven (275 to 300 degrees).

Edward Aylesworth Perry (1831-1889)

HERITAGE: Born and raised in Richmond, Berkshire County, Massachusetts.

RANK: General.

FOUGHT FOR: Confederacy.

RELIGION: Christian (see quote below).

EDUCATION: Initially entered Yale Class of 1854. Dropped out within a year. Studied law in Alabama and admitted to bar in 1857.

CAREER HIGHLIGHTS & TIDBITS: Led his own brigade at Fredericksburg and Chancellorsville.
Once taught school in Alabama.
Spent most of his time alone as a child.
Had few friends even as an adult.
Extremely shy and quite introverted.
Become Governor of Florida after the Civil War.
Served as Governor for four years beginning in 1885.
Practiced law in Florida after the Civil War ended.
Stricken with typhoid fever at the time of the Gettysburg Campaign.
Rather handsome, heavily bearded individual.
Lost more men at Gettysburg than any other Confederate brigade.

QUOTABLE QUOTE: *"God gives a man all the strength he needs to face all of the things in this life. A man is free to believe or not to believe in the Bible. I personally choose to believe in the Good Book and make an effort to always go along with the Lord's will in everything!"*

SAW ACTION AT: Frayser's Farm, Fredericksburg, The Wilderness, Chancellorsville, the Seven Pines, etc.

LITTLE KNOWN FACT: Wounded twice – once at Frayser's Farm in 1862 and again during fighting at the Wilderness in 1864

Applesauce Fruit Nut Loaf Cakes—
A Favorite of the Morgan Family

1 1/2 cups rolled oats
1 cup applesauce
1/4 cup molasses
     or
1/4 cup honey
1 cup brown sugar
1 cup raisins
1 cup candied fruit

1 cup candied cherries
1 cup walnuts, chopped
2 1/2 cups flour, sifted
1 tsp baking soda
1 tsp salt
1 tsp cinnamon
3/4 tsp cloves
1/2 tsp nutmeg

Put rolled oats into a large wooden mixing bowl. Stir in applesauce, molasses or honey, and brown sugar. In another bowl blend fruits, nuts, and 1/2 cup flour. Sift remaining 2 cups flour with baking soda, salt, and spices. Then combine ingredients in the mixing bowl and stir until thoroughly blended. Pour batter into 2 well-buttered loaf pans, which have been lined with buttered paper. Bake in a slow to moderate oven (300 - 325 degrees) for 1 hour. Take out of the oven and set on wire racks to cool for 10 minutes. Then remove cakes from pans. Set aside for 2 or 3 days before serving. This type of old-fashioned cake will stay moist and fresh tasting for a long time.

John Hunt Morgan (1825-1864)

HERITAGE: Born in Alabama. Raised on farm in Kentucky.

RANK: General.

FOUGHT FOR: Confederacy.

RELIGION: Christian. Brought up in strict, Christian home.   Always read *Bible* and prayed before retiring for the night.

EDUCATION: All of his formal education was undertaken in what was called "common schools." Today we know them as public schools.

CAREER HIGHLIGHTS & TIDBITS: Enlisted in the Army of the Confederacy when the Civil War broke out.

Gained a measure of fame as a scout.

Commanded the Kentucky Cavalry as a colonel at Shiloh in 1862. Became quite famous as a raider.

Took more than 400 prisoners in Mississippi and Tennessee. Rewarded by being given command of a brigade.

Started out on July 4th on bold 800-man raid into Union territory. Covered 1,000 miles in 24 days of riding.

Captured 1,200 Union prisoners

Lost less than 100 of his raiders.

Captured 1,800 prisoners during the Stones River Campaign in December of 1862.

Destroyed more than two million dollars worth of Union military supplies – only 2 of his men were killed and 24 wounded.

Heroic exploits earned hi a promotion to Brigadier General and the command of his own cavalry division.

Captured by federal troops in Lisbon, Ohio on July 26

Escaped from Ohio penitentiary in November.

SAW ACTION AT: Shiloh, Stones River Campaign, commanded a cavalry detachment and led many raids into Tennessee and Kentucky.

LITTLE KNOWN FACT: His luck finally ran out – Killed in Greeneville, Tennessee on September 4, 1884.

Boston Cream Cake— Favorite of William Evarts

1 tbls butter	1/4 tsp salt
1/2 cup milk	2 eggs
1 cup flour	1 cup sugar
1 tsp baking powder	1 tsp vanilla

Add butter to milk in a saucepan and heat in a larger pot of hot water. Take a large wooden mixing bowl and sift together the flour, baking powder, and salt. In another bowl, beat eggs until thick. Then gradually beat in sugar. Add vanilla. Gradually beat in hot milk-butter mixture. Fold in flour and blend thoroughly. Pour batter into an 8-inch square-baking pan greased with butter. Bake in moderate oven (350 degrees) for 40 to 50 minutes. While this is baking, proceed to make filling as follows:

2/3 cup sugar	2 cups milk, scalded
1/3 cup flour	1 egg, slightly beaten
1/8 tsp salt	1 tsp vanilla

Mix sugar, flour, and salt in saucepan. Gradually pour on scalded milk and set in larger pan of hot water. Allow to cook until mixture is smooth and thick (about 15 minutes). Stir constantly while cooking. Pour over beaten egg in a mixing bowl. Stir well. Return to saucepan. Cook for 2 more minutes. Stir in the vanilla. Split warm cake and spread cream filling between layers. Sift 1/4 cup powdered sugar over top. This cake is enough for 8-10 people.

William Maxwell Evarts (1818-1901)

HERITAGE: Born in Boston, Massachusetts.

POSITION: Union public official.

RELIGION: Christian. Attended church regularly.

EDUCATION: Law degree – college or university unknown.

MARRIAGE: Unknown.

CHILDREN: Unknown.

CAREER HIGHLIGHTS & TIDBITS: Widely-known New York City attorney.

Became a member of the new Republican party.

Secretary of the Union Defense Committee in 1860.

This was a moderate group of citizens fighting against a total split between the North and the South.

Possessed a great legal mind. An unsurpassed orator.

One of the important government prosecutors against Jefferson Davis at the end of the Civil War.

Part of the powered legal team that President Andrew Johnson used to defend him during his impeachment trial.

Became one of the most prominent attorneys in America.

Because of his phenomenal legal skills, he is given the credit for keeping Johnson from being impeached and thrown out of office. Rewarded with an appointment to be the Attorney General of the United States from 1867 and 1868.

Served as Secretary of State under President Rutherford Hayes from 1877 to 1881.

LITTLE KNOWN FACTS: Sent to England in 1863 and again 1864 by Union government.

Instructed to use his influence to forcibly persuade the British to stop building and equipping ships for the Confederate navy.

Old Fashioned Pound Cake—
A Beauregard Favorite

2/3 cup butter   1 cup eggs
2 cups flour   1 1/2 cups sugar
1 tsp baking powder   1/2 tsp nutmeg
1/8 tsp salt   2 tbls orange juice
                1 tsp brandy

Cream butter with flour in large wooden mixing bowl. In separate bowl, add baking powder and salt to eggs. Beat until light and fluffy. Add sugar and nutmeg gradually. Beat well. Put into bowl with creamed flour. Using wooden spoon, stir until everything is blended thoroughly. Add orange juice and brandy, stirring with long, light strokes. Turn into buttered and floured shallow cake tin. Bake in moderate oven (350 degrees) for 1 hour.

Pierre Gustave Toutant Beauregard
(1818-1893)

HERITAGE: Creole. Born in Louisiana's St. Bernard Parish.
Family extremely wealthy.

RANK: General.

FOUGHT FOR: Confederacy.

RELIGION: Christian. Roman Catholic.

EDUCATION: West Point graduate – class of 1838.
Second in his class.

CAREER HIGHLIGHTS & TIDBITS: Became the Confederacy's first war hero with his successful assault on Fort Sumter.
Bombardment of this fort was ordered by a telegram from Confederate President Jefferson Davis.
Highly thought of as a military tactician.
After a victory at Manassas, Confederate President Jefferson Davis met with Beauregard and other Generals at the Wilcox Tavern in Fairfax, Virginia on October 1, 1861.
This is where Beauregard is said to have redesigned the Confederate flag.

QUOTABLE QUOTES: *"We must do something or die in the attempt. Otherwise, all will be shortly lost."*
While fighting in Corinth, Mississippi, he declared, *"If defeated here we lose...our cause."*

SAW ACTION AT: Fort Sumter, Manassas, Bull Run, Shiloh, Petersburg, Richmond, Charleston, Corinth and at Drewry's Bluff, Virginia, etc.

LITTLE KNOWN FACTS: After the Civil War ended, he rejected numerous offers of senior command positions in the Egyptian Army.
Always a gentleman, he allowed Union Major Robert Anderson to fire a 100-gun salute to the American flag before it was lowered at Fort Sumter.

Coconut Loaf—
As Made by Mrs. Garfield

1 cup butter	6 egg whites, beaten
2 cups sugar	2 cups flour
6 egg yolks, beaten	5 cups coconut, finely grated

Cream butter and sugar in large wooden mixing bowl. Lightly stir in separately beaten egg yolks and whites. Blend in flour. Lastly, stir in grated coconut. When all ingredients are well blended, pour batter into greased and floured loaf pan. Bake in moderate oven (350 degrees). Frost with the following:

1 coconut grated   1 1/2 cups sugar
milk of the coconut

Blend grated coconut with sugar and coconut milk. Set in oven until sugar melts. Then stir well and spread between layers and on top of cake.

James Abram Garfield (1831-1881)

HERITAGE: Born and raised in Ohio in a little log cabin on the frontier.

RANK: General.

FOUGHT FOR: Union.

RELIGION: Christian – was a lay preacher and President of a Christian college.

EDUCATION: Williams College in Massachusetts. A brilliant student, graduated with honors in 1856.

CAREER HIGHLIGHTS & TIDBITS: Pulled himself up by his bootstraps from a poor childhood.
> Became a lay preacher.
> Later, became a Union General.
> Finally, the President of the United States.
> Was General William Rosecran's chief-of-staff during the Chickamauga campaign.
> Had a horse shot out from under him while fighting at Chickamauga.
> Elected lieutenant colonel of a company of Hiram College students attached to the 42nd Ohio Volunteers.
> Elected President of the United States in close election in 1880.
> Assassinated in 1861.

QUOTABLE QUOTE(S): *"Better to lose a million men in battle than to allow the government to be overthrown."*

SAW ACTION AT: Middle Creek, Pound Gap, Shiloh, Chickamauga, etc.

LITTLE KNOWN FACTS: Had to borrow money in order to attend college. Became President of Hiram College, a school founded by the Disciples of Christ, when just 26 years old.

12

Cookie Specialties
from Kitchens of Long Ago

Ginger Snaps—
A Davis Family Favorite

2 1/4 cups shortening	6 cups flour
3 cups sugar	4 1/2 tsp soda
3 eggs	1 1/2 tbls ginger
3/4 cup molasses	

Cream shortening and sugar. Add eggs and molasses. Add flour, which has been sifted with spices. Form into 3/4 inch balls. Roll in sugar and place two inches apart on greased cookie sheets. Bake in moderate oven (350 degrees) for 10 to 20 minutes. Cool and store in airtight containers. Makes 16-dozen ginger snaps.

Jefferson Davis (1808-1889)

HERITAGE: Born in Kentucky.

Tenth child of a settler who had fought in Revolutionary War.

POSITION: President of the Confederate States of America.

RELIGION: Christian. Studied at Roman Catholic seminary in Kentucky. Came close to renouncing his family's Baptist faith.

EDUCATION: West Point graduate – class of 1828. Graduated one year ahead of Robert E. Lee.

Also attended Transylvania University.

MARRIAGE: Married the daughter, against her father's wishes, of future President Zachary Taylor. She soon after died.

Second wife was Varina Howell, daughter of a prominent Mississippi planter.

CAREER HIGHLIGHTS & TIDBITS: Served honorably in the Mexican War and the in the Black Hawk War in the 1830s.

Was kept in prison at Fortress Monroe after his capture when the Civil War was over.

Held in solitary confinement for two years with only his *Bible* and *Episcopal Prayer Book* to read.

An international outcry forced his release.

Multi-millionaire financer Cornelius Vanderbilt and Horace Greeley, *New York Tribune* journalist, helped secure his freedom.

QUOTABLE QUOTE: *"Were the things to be done over again, I would do as I then did. Disappointments have not changed my convictions."*

LITTLE KNOWN FACTS: On May 2, 1865 he held his final meeting with his war cabinet at the Burt Stark Mansion in Abbeville, South Carolina.

Here the Confederacy was officially dissolved.

Abbeville holds the distinction of being known as "the birthplace and the death of the Confederacy."

Peanut Cookies—
As Eaten by Horace Greeley

2 tbls butter

1 cup sugar

2 eggs, well beaten

2 tsp baking powder

2 cups flour

1/4 cup milk

1 cup peanuts, chopped

1/2 tsp salt

1 tsp lemon juice

Using a fork, cream butter in a wooden mixing bowl while gradually adding sugar. Then add beaten eggs and blend thoroughly. In a separate bowl, sift together baking powder, salt, and flour. Stir this in with first mixture. Then add milk, chopped peanuts, and lemon juice. Blend everything well. Drop batter from tip of a spoon onto well-greased cookie sheet. Leave about 1 inch space between each cookie. Place a half peanut on top of each. Bake in slow oven (300 degrees) for 12 to 15 minutes.

Horace Greeley (1811-1872)

HERITAGE: Born and raised in Amherst, New Hampshire.
Son of a New England farmer and laborer.

POSITION: *New York Tribune* journalist and editor.

RELIGION: Christian – Once declared: *"It is impossible to mentally or socially enslave a Bible-reading people. The principles of the Bible are the groundwork of human freedom."*

CAREER HIGHLIGHTS & TIDBITS: Strong supporter of the constitutional right of various states to secede from the Union.
This view did not make him very popular with his northern counterparts.
Founded the *New York Tribune* at age 30.
Had previously started the *New Yorker*, with Jonas Winchester in 1834.
Called by *Harper's Weekly*: *"the most perfect Yankee the country ever produced."*
Opposed slavery as morally deficient and economically regressive.

QUOTABLE QUOTE: *"The right to secede may be a revolting one, but it exists nevertheless...We hope never to live in a Republic where one section is pinned to the other section by bayonets. If the Declaration of Independence justified the secession of 3,000,000 colonists in 1776, I do not see why the Constitution ratified by the same men would not justify the secession of 5,000,000 Southerners from the Federal Union in 1861."*

LITTLE KNOWN FACTS: Greeley and multi-millionaire, Cornelius Vanderbilt, helped financially to get Confederate President Jefferson Davis released from prison.
Opposed the Mexican War.
Advocated the impeachment of Andrew Jackson.

Brown Sugar Honey Molasses Drop Cookies—A McDowell Family Favorite

1 cup brown sugar

3 1/2 cups flour

1 1/2 tsp baking soda

1 cup butter

1 cup molasses

1 tsp ginger

1/2 cup honey

2 eggs

1 tsp cinnamon

1/2 cup water, boiling

Using a fork, cream brown sugar and butter together in a wooden mixing bowl. Stir in molasses. Then stir in eggs, one at a time. In a separate bowl, sift together flour, baking soda, ginger, and cinnamon. Add these dry ingredients, alternately, with boiling water, to those in first bowl. Blend everything thoroughly. Drop by spoonfuls on greased cookie sheets. Bake in moderate oven (350 degrees) for 12 to 15 minutes. Makes 4-dozen cookies.

Irvin McDowell (1818-1885)

HERITAGE: Born in Ohio. Raised in France.

RANK: General.

FOUGHT FOR: Union.

RELIGION: Christian. Raised in firmly-based Christian family.

EDUCATION: West Point graduate – class of 1838.
Initially educated in France.

CAREER HIGHLIGHTS & TIDBITS: Favorite of the Lincoln Administration.
Especially liked by Secretary of the Treasury, Salmon P. Chase.
Union forces under his command were routed in the Battle of First Bull Run near the Manassas railway junction.
Soundly defeated by Confederate troops led by General Joe Eagleston Johnson and General Beauregard.
Came under heavy criticism for his disastrous performance at Second Bull Run.
Relieved of his command as a result of those defeats.
Exonerated after an investigation.
Never again given a field command.

QUOTABLE QUOTE: Elihu B. Washburne, Illinois Congressman, offers this: *"I went to the tent of General McDowell and had quite a conversation with him. I never had much of an opinion of him as a General, and I left his tent with a feeling of great sadness and sort of prescience of coming disaster."*

SAW ACTION AT: Manassas Junction, Bull Run, Peninsular Campaign, etc.

LITTLE KNOWN FACT: Actions at Bull Run twice almost brought his career to an inglorious end.

Sugar Cookies—
James Andrews Favorites at Christmas

1 cup butter	4 cups flour
2 cups sugar	4 tsp baking powder
1 tsp vanilla	1/4 tsp salt

1 cup milk

Cream butter and sugar in wooden mixing bowl. Blend in vanilla. In a separate mixing bowl, sift together flour, baking powder and salt. Add this, alternately, with milk, to the butter mixture in first bowl. Blend everything well and set aside to chill for 15 minutes. Then roll out on lightly floured board to a 1/8 inch thick sheet. Cut into cookies with floured cookie cutter or an upside down drinking glass. Lay cookies on greased baking sheets. Bake in rather quick oven (400 degrees) for 10 to 12 minutes. Makes 12 to 13 dozen 2-inch cookies.

James Andrews

HERITAGE: Born and raised in Cedar Mills, Ohio.
Father was farmer-preacher.

RANK: Captain.

FOUGHT FOR: Union.

RELIGION: Christian. Raised by Christian parents. Referred to by his men as *"A Bible-totin man of God."*

EDUCATION: Attended public school in or near his community.

CAREER HIGHLIGHTS & TIDBITS: Led his men on daring raid against Confederates on April 1, 1862.
Stole *The General*, a Confederate locomotive.
Confederates took another locomotive, *The Texas* and chased Andrews and his men riding *The General*.
Andrews and his men were eventually captured after a long pursuit on the rails.
Eight of these heroic raiders were eventually set free in an exchange of prisoners.
Eight of the raiders, including Andrews, were executed.
They were hanged near the Oakland Community Cemetery in Atlanta, Georgia.
The state of Ohio later erected a monument to honor the raiders.
This can be seen today in Chattanooga, Tennessee.
Inscribed on it are the names of the men.

QUOTABLE QUOTE: Train conductor, Fuller, made this observation about Andrews: *"He died bravely and without fear or remorse."*

LITTLE KNOWN FACT: Andrews and his men were the first to ever be awarded the *Medal of Honor*.

Drop Sponge Cookies—
As Made by Mrs. George Henry Thomas

1 3/4 cups powdered sugar
4 egg yolks, beaten
1 cup flour

1 lemon, all the juice,
   and 1/2 the rind
4 egg whites, beaten

Blend sugar into custard-like beaten egg yolks. Beat together for 10 minutes. Then stir in lemon juice and rind. Now alternately stir in flour and fluffy egg whites. Beat hard for a full 30 minutes. Have a broad and shallow baking pan lined with buttered paper. Drop spoonfuls of batter on the paper. Try one first. If it runs, add a little more flour and beat the mixture hard for a few more minutes. Bake in a moderately quick oven (375 degrees) for about 12 minutes until the cookies are a delicate yellowish-brown color.

Lady Fingers—
As Prepared by Mrs. Thomas

Prepare exact same batter as shown above under *Drop Sponge Cookies*. Instead of dropping batter on the buttered paper, form each cookie in long narrow strip. Then bake in moderately quick oven (375 degrees). Ladyfingers are especially good when dipped in caramel or chocolate frosting.

George Henry Thomas (1816-1870)

HERITAGE: Born and raised in Southampton, Virginia.

RANK: General.

FOUGHT FOR: Union.

RELIGION: Christian.

EDUCATION: West Point graduate – class of 1840.
Briefly studied law prior to his appointment to West Point. Graduated from West Point with later-to-be Generals N.E. Ewell and W.T. Sherman.

CAREER HIGHLIGHTS & TIDBITS: Fought in the Seminole War in Florida.
Extensive action in the Mexican War.
Promoted twice for his gallantry during the fighting at Buena Vista and Monterey.
Served in Texas in the 2nd Cavalry.
A few of his later-to-gain-fame fellow officers were Generals Robert E. Lee, Fitzhugh Lee, and Albert Sidney Johnston.
Called *"The Rock of Chickamauga"* because of the way he held off a ferocious Confederate attack.
A large, powerfully-built man.
Soundly criticized for being overly-deliberate in making decisions regarding war maneuvers.
Nicknamed "Slow Trot" because of this.
Troops serving under this man truly loved him. Affectionately called him "Paps" or "Pa-Pa."

SAW ACTION AT: Shenandoah Valley Campaign, Logan's Crossroad, Shiloh, Corinth, Perryville, Stones River Campaign, Chickamauga, Missionary Ridge, etc.

LITTLE KNOWN FACT: Once wounded while fighting Indians. On leave to convalesce when the Civil War started.

Honey Cookies—
Abraham Lincoln Ate These in 1831

2/3 cup shortening
1/2 cup sugar
1 cup honey, strained
1 egg beaten
1/2 cup sour milk

5 cups flour
1 tsp baking soda
1/2 tsp salt
1/2 tsp nutmeg
1/2 tsp cinnamon

1/2 tsp cloves

Cream shortening and sugar in wooden mixing bowl. Add honey and blend thoroughly. Stir in beaten egg and sour milk. Now sift together in separate bowl flour, baking soda, salt, nutmeg, cinnamon, and cloves. Combine these dry ingredients with liquids in wooden mixing bowl. Blend well. Set aside and let chill. When chilled, put dough on floured board. Roll out to 1/4 inch thick. Cut out cookies with cookie cutter or upside down drinking glass. Put cookies on greased baking tins and bake in moderate oven (350 degrees) for about 10 minutes. Makes about 4-dozen 2 ½-inch cookies.

Abraham Lincoln(1809-1865)
The Man

LINCOLN'S UNCANNY FORESIGHT: *"...shall we...expect some transatlantic giant, to step the ocean, and crush us a blow? Never! All the armies of Europe, Asia, and Africa combined...could not by force take a drink from the Ohio, or make a track on the Blue Ridge...At which point then is the approach of danger to be expected? I answer; if it ever reaches us, it must spring up amongst us."*

HIS PROPHETIC DREAM: President Lincoln and his wife were spending part of a quiet afternoon visiting with friends at the White House. It was Good Friday, April 14, 1865. He described a haunting dream he had recently experienced: *"About ten days ago I retired very late...I soon began to dream. There seemed to be a deathlike stillness about me. Then I heard subdued sobs as if a number of people were weeping. I thought I had left my bed and wandered downstairs. There the silence was broken by the same pitiful sobbing, but the mourners were invisible. I went from room to room. No living person was in sight, but the same mournful sounds of distress met me as I passed along. Every object was familiar to me, but nowhere could I see the people who were grieving as though their hearts would break. I was puzzled and alarmed. Determined to find the cause of a sate of things so mysterious and so shocking, I kept on until I arrived at the East Room. There I met with a sickening surprise. Before me was a catafalque, on which rested a corpse wrapped in funeral vestments. Around it were stationed soldiers who were acting as guards; and there was a throng of people, some gazing mournfully at the corpse, whose face was covered, others weeping pitifully. 'Who is dead in the White House?' I demanded of one of the soldiers. 'The President,' was his answer. 'He was killed by an assassin.' Then came a loud burst of grief from the crowd, which awoke me from my dream. It is only a dream but it has strangely annoyed me, however. Let us say no more about it"*

Abraham Lincoln was shot at Ford's Theater April 14, 1865. He died early the next day at the Peterson House across the street

Currant Cookies—
A Favorite of John Hunt Morgan

1 cup butter
1 1/2 cups sugar
4 egg yolks, beaten
1/2 teaspoons baking soda

1 cup currants, floured
1/2 lemon, juice and grated rind
1 teaspoon cinnamon
4 egg whites, beaten

4 cups flour

Cream butter and sugar in large wooden mixing bowl. Stir in custard-like beaten egg yolks. Dissolve baking soda in a little hot water and add it. Gradually stir in flour. Follow by adding currants, lemon juice and rind, and cinnamon. Lastly, blend in fluffy egg whites with quick, light strokes. When ready, drop from spoon onto well-buttered, paper-lined baking pan. Leave enough space between the cookies to prevent them from running together. Bake in moderate oven (350 degrees) until done or for about 10 minutes.

John Hunt Morgan (1825-1864)

HERITAGE: Born in Alabama. Raised on farm in Kentucky.

RANK: General.

FOUGHT FOR: Confederacy.

RELIGION: Christian. Brought up in strict, Christian home.   Always read *Bible* and prayed before retiring for the night.

EDUCATION: All of his formal education was undertaken in what was called "common schools." Today we know them as public schools.

CAREER HIGHLIGHTS & TIDBITS: Enlisted in the Army of the Confederacy when the Civil War broke out.

Gained a measure of fame as a scout.

Commanded the Kentucky Cavalry as a colonel at Shiloh in 1862. Became quite famous as a raider.

Took more than 400 prisoners in Mississippi and Tennessee.   Rewarded by being given command of a brigade.

Started out on July 4th on bold 800-man raid into Union territory.

Covered 1,000 miles in 24 days of riding.

Captured 1,200 Union prisoners

Lost less than 100 of his raiders.

Captured 1,800 prisoners during the Stones River Campaign in December of 1862.

Destroyed more than two million dollars worth of Union military supplies – only 2 of his men were killed and 24 wounded.

Heroic exploits earned hi a promotion to Brigadier General and the command of his own cavalry division.

Captured by federal troops in Lisbon, Ohio on July 26

Escaped from Ohio penitentiary in November.

SAW ACTION AT: Shiloh, Stones River Campaign, commanded a cavalry detachment and led many raids into Tennessee and Kentucky.

LITTLE KNOWN FACT: His luck finally ran out – Killed in Greeneville, Tennessee on September 4, 1884.

Sugar Cookies—
Mrs. Reynolds Made These

1 cup butter	3 eggs, beaten
2 cups sugar	3 tsp baking powder
6 tbls milk	5 1/2 cups flour
2 tsp vanilla extract	1 tsp salt

Cream butter in wooden mixing bowl. Gradually add sugar and work together with a fork until a creamy mixture is obtained. Blend together milk, vanilla extract, and beaten eggs in second bowl. In yet a third bowl, sift together baking powder, flour, and salt. Then add these dry ingredients, alternately, with milk-egg mixture to butter-sugar mixture in first bowl. Blend everything well. Set aside to chill. When thoroughly chilled, put dough on lightly floured board. Roll out to about 1/4 inch thick. Cut into cookies with floured cookie cutter or upside down water glass. Lightly grease baking tin and place cut cookies on them. Sprinkle with sugar. Bake in moderately quick oven (375 degrees) for about 10 to 12 minutes. Makes 4-dozen 2-inch cookies.

Alexander Reynolds (1817-1876)

HERITAGE: Not known.

RANK: General.

FOUGHT FOR: Confederacy.

RELIGION: Christian (see quote below).

EDUCATION: West Point graduate – class of 1838.

MARRIAGE: Unknown.

CHILDREN: Unknown.

CAREER HIGHLIGHTS & TIDBITS: A balding man with heavy gray sideburns running down his entire face.
Stood at around six feet tall and on the slender side.
Saw action during the Seminole War.
Was discharged from the army after being accused of having serious *"account discrepancies"* in 1865.
Later reinstated after an investigation into the charges.
Kicked out of the U.S. Army once again when he went to join the Confederate forces.
Known to have a wonderful sense of humor and took few things seriously.
Joined the Egyptian Army in 1869, after the Civil War ended.   Became Chief of Staff of the Egyptian army in 1875.

QUOTABLE QUOTE: *"I often get on my knees and pray to the Almighty. I talk to God often. I know Jesus is my Savior and this means everything to me."*

SAW ACTION AT: Commanded a brigade at Vicksburg, Chattanooga and during the Atlanta Campaign..

LITTLE KNOWN FACT: Began going bald at an early age.

Ring Jumbles—
A Favorite of General Wilson

2 cups butter
2 cups sugar
4 egg yolks, beaten

1/4 cup lemon juice
5 cups flour
4 egg whites, beaten

Cream the butter and sugar in a large wooden mixing bowl. Add the custard-like beaten egg yolks and then blend in the lemon juice. Stir well. Gradually blend in half the flour (2 1/2 cups). Lastly, very lightly stir in the frothy egg whites alternately with the remaining half of the flour. Have the bottom of a broad shallow pan lined with buttered paper. Use a tablespoon to form regular rings of the batter in the baking pan. Leave a hold in the center of each cookie. Bake in a moderately quick oven (375 degrees). Sift powdered sugar over the jumbles as soon as they are done baking.

NOTE: Rose water or vanilla may be substituted in place of the lemon juice called for above.

James Harrison Wilson (1837-1925)

HERITAGE: Born and raised in Illinois.

RANK: General.

FOUGHT FOR: Union.

RELIGION: Christian.

EDUCATION: West Point graduate – class of 1860.

MARRIAGE: Unknown.

CAREER HIGHLIGHTS & TIDBITS: Led a cavalry corps in 1864 and 1865.

> One of the Union's outstanding commanders.
> Led a cavalry corps in 1864-1865.
> Served under General W.T. Sherman, General David Hunter, and General George McClellan.
> Was the instigator of numerous spectacular raids during the siege of Petersburg.
> Instrumental in destroying many miles of vital railroad track throughout the South.
> Known to be a daring, relentless leader as well as a brilliant strategist and commander.
> Wrote many of the army's training manuals in later life.
> Only Union General to outmarch and outmaneuver Confederate General Nathan Bedford Forrest in a raid on Selma, Alabama.
> Re-enlisted to fight in the Spanish-American War.
> Helped suppress the Boxer Rebellion

SAW ACTION AT: Siege of Atlanta, Selma, Petersburg, Sherman's *"March to the Sea."*

LITTLE KNOWN FACT: Men under his command were instrumental in the capture of Confederate President Jefferson Davis.

Almond Macaroons—
George Armstrong Custer'sFavorite

Prepare almonds the day before you make these cookies. Blanch in boiling water. Strip off skins. Pound when cold – a few at a time – in a mortar. Add a little rose water from time to time. When beaten to smooth paste, stir in 1-tablespoon bitter almond extract for every 3 1/2 cups sweet almonds used. Cover and set away in a cold place until the next day. For every 3 1/2 cups of these nuts allow:

> 2 1/2 cups powdered sugar   1 tsp nutmeg
> 8 egg whites, beaten

The next day, stir sugar, nutmeg, and well-beaten whites together. Then gradually whip in almond paste. Line a broad, shallow baking pan with buttered paper. Drop spoonfuls of this mixture far enough apart to prevent their running together. Sift powdered sugar thickly on each macaroon. Then bake in a slow to moderately slow oven (300 to 325 degrees) for about 10 minutes until delicate brown.

NOTE: Test a little mixture first, to make sure it is the right consistency. Drop 1 spoonful on buttered paper. If the butter runs in irregular shapes, beat in more sugar. This shouldn't happen, however, if the above blend is already properly beaten.

George Armstrong Custer (1839-1876)

HERITAGE: Grandfather was Hessian mercenary named Kuster. Settled in Pennsylvania after Revolutionary War.

Father a farmer, later migrated to Ohio.

RANK: General.

FOUGHT FOR: Union.

RELIGION: Christian.

EDUCATION: West Point graduate – class of 1861.

Ranked 34th in his class of 34.

CAREER HIGHLIGHTS & TIDBITS: Had 11 horses shot out from under him, yet was wounded only once during the Civil War.

A tall, handsome, Bible-believing cavalry man

Had since childhood dreamed only of being a soldier.

Best known for his curly, blond, flowing locks.

Was unbelievably courageous.

Served on the staff of General's Kearney, Smith and McClellan.

Few people realize that he was only 37 when he died.

Gained lasting fame in what history calls *"Custer's Last Stand."* This is where he and his army were meticulously slaughtered by Sitting Bull's warriors at Little Big Horn on July 23, 1876.

QUOTABLE QUOTE: At Cedar Creek, Virginia, on September 19, 1864, he was in charge of the 1st cavalry. He declared: *"This is the bulliest day since Christ was born."*

SAW ACTION AT: Bull Run, Peninsular Campaign, Gettysburg, Winchester, Fisher's Hill, Cedar Creek, Dinwiddle Courthouse, Five Forks, Appomattox, etc.

LITTLE KNOWN FACTS: Few military men saw as much action as did he during the Civil War.

More than 10,000 Confederate prisoners were captured under his command

Caraway Cookies—
As Eaten by General Burnside

1 cup butter
1 cup sugar
2 eggs, well beaten
1 tbls milk
1 cup flour

1/4 tsp baking soda
1/4 tsp salt
1/2 tsp ginger
2 tbls orange rind, grated
1 tbls caraway seeds

Cream the butter and sugar in wooden mixing bowl. Stir in beaten eggs and milk. Sift flour and measure out 1 cup. Then again sift with baking soda, salt, and ginger. Add to first mixture. Stir in grated orange ring and caraway seeds. Add sufficient flour to form soft dough. Blend thoroughly. Set aside to chill overnight. In the morning, turn dough out on lightly floured board. Roll out into sheet 1/2 inch thick. Cut into cookies with cookie cutter or upside down water glass. Lightly grease baking sheets. Place cooking on sheet and bake in rather quick oven (400 degrees) for 10 minutes. Makes about 75 cookies.

Ambrose Everett Burnside (1824-1884)

HERITAGE: Born in Liberty, Indiana. Family of modest means. Father elected to Indiana senate.

RANK: General.

FOUGHT FOR: Union.

RELIGION: Christian. Attended village seminary.

EDUCATION: Father used his political influence to obtain his son an appointment to West Point.
 Graduated with the class of 1847.

CAREER HIGHLIGHTS & TIDBITS: Close friend of President Abraham Lincoln.
 A handsome six-foot fellow with flamboyant whiskers and fluffy sideburns.
 Had genial nature and ability to make friends in high places.
 In November of 1862, Lincoln put him in command of the Army of the Potomac in place of General McClellan.
 Burnside protested that he wasn't able to take on such a huge responsibility.
 Future events proved him all too correct in his self-appraisal.
 A forceful looking six-foot fellow with flamboyant whiskers and fluffy sideburns.
 An incorrigible prankster

QUOTABLE QUOTE: Confederate General George Edwards said this: *"I can't help feeling sorry for old Burnside – proud, plucky, hard-headed old dog, I always liked him."*

SAW ACTION AT: First Bull Run, Antietam, Fredericksburg, The Wilderness, Spotsylvania, Knoxville, Cold Harbor, Petersburg, etc.

LITTLE KNOWN FACT: Jilted by his fiancé who left him standing at the church.

Coriander Cookies—
A Favorite of the Hallecks

7 cups flour
2 tbls coriander seed,
ground or beaten
1 cup butter

3 cups sugar
1 cup cream (or milk)
1 1/2 tbls baking powder
4 eggs, beaten

Put the flour in large wooden mixing bowl. Stir in crushed coriander seeds. Rub butter in flour until thoroughly blended. Dissolve sugar in cream and baking powder in a little hot water. Add both to bowl and stir well. Lastly, blend in beaten eggs. This mixture should be just stiff enough to roll. Put on floured board and roll out into thin sheet. Cut into variously shaped small cookies. Place the cookies on a buttered baking pan. Bake in a moderately quick oven (375 degrees) for about 10 minutes.

NOTE: Caraway seeds may be substituted for coriander seeds if desired.

Henry Wager Halleck (1815-1872)

HERITAGE: Born and raised in Oneida, New York. Son of prosperous farmer.

RANK: General.

FOUGHT FOR: Union.

RELIGION: Christian.

EDUCATION: West Point graduate – class of 1839. He was third in his class. Bachelor degree from Union College in New York.

CAREER HIGHLIGHTS & TIDBITS: Offered rank of Major General in the Union Army in August of 1861.
> This was done at the urging of George Winfield Scott.
> Served in California during the Mexican War.
> Ineffective in Washington's social scene due to his inability to play the political game.
> Advisor to President Lincoln in 1862.
> His title was commander-in-chief.
> Described his roll in Washington as *"political Hell."*
> Retired from military in 1854 and began California law practice. Refused a seat on the California Supreme Court as well as the office of United States Senator.

QUOTABLE QUOTE: On March 20, 1862 he declared: *"The character of the war has very much changed within the last year. There can be no peace but that which is enforced with the sword. We must conquer the rebels, or be conquered by them. This is the phase which the rebellion has now assumed."*

SAW ACTION AT: Shiloh, Corinth. Led his troops so cautiously on Corinth, Mississippi, that General Beauregard's troops, though greatly outnumbered, were able to get away with little harm.

LITTLE KNOWN FACT: A genius with literary talent. Translated Domini's *Vie de Napoleon* while on sea voyage to California.

Crisp Delights—
As Made by Mrs. Robert E. Lee

1 cup butter
3 cups sugar
6 egg whites, beaten

6 egg yolks, beaten
flour to suit
lemon juice to suit

Cream butter and sugar in large wooden mixing bowl. Stir in separately beaten egg whites and yolks. Then gradually blend in sufficient flour to make batter stiff enough to be molded with floured hands. Flavor with enough lemon juice to suit individual taste. Mold into small round cookies. Flatten and then place on shallow buttered pan. Bake in rather quick oven (400 to 425 degrees) for about 6 to 8 minutes.

Robert Edward Lee(1807-1870)
From the Mouths of Others

Confederate General James Longstreet, Appomattox Court House, April 9, 1865: *"The road was packed by standing troops as he approached, the men with hats off, heads and hearts bowed down. As he passed they raised their heads and looked upon him with swimming eyes. Those who could find voice said good-bye, those who could not speak, and were near, passed their hands gently over the sides of Traveller."*

Major Charles Marshall, one of General Lee's Aides: *"In the midst of this awful scene, General Lee...rode to the front of his advancing battalions. His presence was the signal for one of those outbursts of enthusiasm which none can appreciate who have not witnessed them."*

Mary Custis Lee – when Lee resigned his U.S. Army commission on April 21, 1861: *"My husband has wept bitter tears of blood over this terrible war, but as a man of honor and a Virginian, he must follow the destiny of his state."*

General Winfield Scott: *"Lee is the greatest military genius in America."*

Gamaliel Bradford: *"Lee had one intimate friend – God."*

English military critic, Colonel Henderson: *"Lee stands out as one of the greatest soldiers of all times...undoubtedly one of the greatest, if not the greatest who ever spoke the English tongue."*

Stonewall Jackson told Colonel Boteler: *"So great is my confidence in General Lee ... I am willing to follow him blindfolded"*

General Grant: *"All the people except a few political leaders in the South will accept whatever he does as right and will be guided to a great extent by his example."*

Almond Cookies—
Abe Lincoln's Favorite

1/2 cup butter
2 cups sugar
5 egg yolks, beaten
3/4 cup sour milk
1 tsp baking soda

2 cups flour
2 tbls rose water
1 3/4 cups almonds, blanched
    and chopped small
5 egg whites, beaten

Cream the butter and sugar in large wooden mixing bowl. Stir in beaten egg yolks and milk. Dissolve baking soda in a little boiling water and add it along with flour, rose water, and almonds. Lastly, quickly and lightly blend in fluffy beaten egg whites. Have a broad and shallow baking pan ready. It should have buttered paper lining the bottom. Drop tablespoonfuls of mixture in shape of rings or round cookies. Space far enough apart to prevent cookies from running together. Bake immediately in moderately quick oven (375 degrees) for about 10 minutes.

NOTE: Lincoln enjoyed a variety of these cookies. Grated coconut or shopped walnuts were substituted for the almonds. If you decide to try this, add a pinch of salt to recipe.

Abraham Lincoln (1809-1865)
The Man

BLACK AND WHITE MIXING: June 21, 1857: *"Judge Douglas is especially horrified at the thought of the mixing blood by the white and black races: agreed for once—a thousand times agreed. There are white men enough to marry all the white women, and black men enough to marry all the black women; and so let them be married."*

INTERMARRIAGE: On September 18, 1858 during the first Lincoln-Douglas Debates: *"I give him [Douglas] the most solemn pledge that I will to the very last stand by the law of the State [of Illinois] which forbids the marrying of white people with Negroes."*

ON THE CONSTITUTION: *"Our safety, our liberty, depends upon preserving the Constitution...The people...are the rightful masters of both the congress and the courts, not to overthrow the Constitution, but to overthrow the men who pervert the Constitution."*

PROPHETICALLY TOLD FRIENDS IN 1864: *"This war is eating my life out. I have a strong impression that I shall not live to see the end."*

IN THE "WAR OF NORTHERN AGGRESSION IN NORTH CAROLINA" AUTHORS SHIPMAN AND HOWELL SAID THIS: *"Lincoln was responsible for Sherman's orders to wage unconscionable war against women, children, and even beasts of the field. After death, his policies caused much of the financial destruction of the South."*

LINCOLN SPOKE IN PEORIA ILLINOIS: *"Free them and make them socially and politically our equals? My own feelings will not admit this ...We cannot make them our equals."*

LITTLE KNOWN FACTS: The same flag hauled down from Fort Sumter was the flag used to drape the President's booth at Ford's Theater.
Lincoln's wife came from a slaveholding family.

Rice-Flour Cookies—
A Favorite of Fitz-John Porter

4 egg yolks, beaten
2 1/2 cups powdered sugar
1 tbls orange-flower water
1 lemon, juice and 1/2 grated rind

1 cup ground rice
2 cups flour
1 cup butter
4 egg whites, beaten

Put custard-like beaten egg yolks into large, wooden mixing bowl. Blend in sugar and beat together for 10 full minutes. Then stir in orange-flower water, lemon juice and lemon rind. Set bowl aside and proceed as follows: Blend ground rice and flour together in another bowl. Rub in butter until everything is thoroughly blended. Now alternately stir mixture and the fluffy beaten egg whites into the ingredients in the first bowl. When everything is blended, begin to beat hard. Continue for at least 30 minutes. Put in buttered patty-pans and bake in a moderate oven (350 degrees) for about 10 minutes.

Fitz-John Porter (1822-1901)

HERITAGE: Born and raised in Portsmouth, New Hampshire.
Son a navy captain.
Nephew of the famed Admiral David Porter.

RANK: General.

FOUGHT FOR: Union.

RELIGION: Christian.

EDUCATION: West Point graduate – class of 1845.

CAREER HIGHLIGHTS & TIDBITS: Taught artillery and cavalry at West Point from 1849 to 1855.
Wounded in the Mexican War.
Distinguished himself at Malverna Hill during the Peninsular Campaign.
Chief of Staff to General Albert Sidney Johnston in the 1860-1861 Utah Expedition.
Inspected the defenses of Charleston and restored rail lines north of Washington, D.C.
Commanded the siege of Yorktown as a Brigadier General.
Fought against Stonewall Jackson in the Shenandoah Campaign of 1862.
Was not, according to most historians, a competent battlefield commander.
Served as Commissioner of Public Works in New Jersey after the war ended.

SAW ACTION AT: Second Bull Run, Malvern Hill, Antietam, etc.

LITTLE KNOWN FACTS: Blamed for Union defeat at Second Bull Run by General John Pope.
Had failed to attack Jackson's right flank as ordered.
Relieved of his command in November of 1862.
Convicted of disobeying battle orders.
Finally cashiered (dismissed from the military) in 1863.

Sour Cream Cookies—
A Christmas Favorite of Jefferson Davis

2/3 cup brown sugar
1 egg, well beaten
1 cup heavy sour cream
2 1/4 cups flour
1/2 tsp baking soda
1 1/2 tsp baking powder

1/4 tsp salt
1/4 tsp cinnamon
1/4 tsp nutmeg
1/2 cup butter
1/2 cup pecans, chopped
1/2 cup raisins, chopped

Blend in large wooden mixing bowl the brown sugar, beaten egg, and sour cream. In a separate mixing bowl, sift together flour, baking soda, baking powder, salt, cinnamon, and nutmeg. Cut in butter with a fork. Now combine mixtures and thoroughly blend. Add chopped nuts and raisins. Grease some baking sheets. Drop batter from a teaspoon onto baking sheets. Bake in moderate oven (350 degrees) until cookies are delicate brown. Makes about 6 dozen 2 1/2 inch cookies.

Jefferson Davis (1808-1889)

HERITAGE: Born in Kentucky. Tenth child of settler who fought in Revolutionary War.

POSITION: President of the Confederacy (CSA).

RELIGION: Christian. Studied at Roman Catholic seminary in Kentucky. Came close to renouncing family's Baptist faith.

EDUCATION: West Point graduate – class of 1828. Graduated one year ahead of Robert E. Lee. Also attended Transylvania University.

MARRIAGE: First married in 1835 to the daughter of future President Zachary Taylor. She died three months later. Remarried in 1845 to Varina Howell, daughter of a prominent Mississippi planter.

CAREER HIGHLIGHTS & TIDBITS: Made a name for himself by commanding a regiment of Mississippi volunteers in the 1847 Battle of Buena Vista.
> Captured by a Union cavalry detachment when the war ended.
> Never brought to trail after his capture.
> Finally released from prison after many public outcries.
> Many notable individuals helped financially to secure his release.
> These included Cornelius Vanderbilt, a man who made $10 million in the steamboat industry during the Civil War.
> Another was Horace Greeley, famed *New York Times* journalist.

QUOTABLE QUOTE: On July 7th, 1864, he declared: *"We are fighting for independence, and that, or extermination, we will have...We will govern ourselves...if we have to see every Southern plantation sacked, and every Southern city in flames."*

LITTLE KNOWN FACTS: Initially a reluctant secessionist.
> Urged to retaliate against the North for their inhuman treatment of Confederate POWs. Davis responded, *"The inhumanity of the enemy to our prisoners can be no justification for a disregard by us of the rules of civilized war and Christianity."*

13

Pie Crusts and Pastries
in Homes During the Civil War

Pie Crust—
Favorite of John Charles Fremont

4 cups flour	3/4 cup ice water
1 cup shortening	1 cup butter

Sift flour into a deep wooden mixing bowl. With a broad-bladed knife or a small sharp "chopper", cut up shortening in the flour until it is as fine as dust. West flour with the ice water and form into a stiff dough. Work it with a large wooden spoon until no longer possible. Make it into a roll or ball with floured hands. Knead dough into shape with as few strokes as necessary to achieve desired end. Lay lump on floured board and roll out into very thin sheet. Always roll away from yourself with a quick, light action. When thin enough, stick bits of butter in regular close rows all over sheet of dough. Use knife for this purpose rather than hands. Sprinkle flour lightly over the sheet. Tightly roll dough into close folds as you would a sheet of music. Flatten it enough so the rolling pin can take hold, and again roll the dough out as thin as before. Baste again with bits of butter and sprinkle lightly with flour as you did previously. Roll the sheet of dough up again. Then roll it out again. Continue the buttering, flouring, and rolling up and rolling out operation until the butter is all used up. It should be done 4 times for best results.

It is best, when you can spare the time, to lay the roll, when all the butter has finally been used up, in a very cold place for 15 minutes or so before rolling it out into the finished crust. Let it stand on ice for an hour in hot weather. This is said to make the crust flakier as well as much firmer.

The dough is now ready to use in making piecrust. Roll into thin sheet. Butter pie plates or pans. Lay sheet of dough lightly within them. Cut off evenly around the edges of the pan after neatly fitting. Gather up scraps left from trimming and make into another sheet simply by rolling out together.

If the pies are to have a top crust, fill the pan with fruit, pumpkin, or whatever you have ready. Lay sheet of dough on this and cut around edges to fit. Press down edges.

Bake in moderate oven (350 degrees) until crust is light brown. Be particularly careful to have heat even or lower crust will turn clammy and raw.

286

John Charles Fremont (1813-1890)

HERITAGE: Born and raised in South Carolina.

RANK: General.

FOUGHT FOR: Union.

RELIGION: Christian. Raised in strict Christian family.

EDUCATION: Unknown.

CHILDREN: Unknown.

MARRIAGE: Unknown.

CAREER HIGHLIGHTS & TIDBITS: Well-known explorer, political leader, and General in the Union army.

> Used Kit Carson, noted mountain man, as his guide in his historic trek west along the Oregon Trail in 1842.
>
> His more spectacular expedition in 1843-184 through the western territories made him a national hero.
>
> Later led expeditions to determine railroad routes across America.
>
> The *"California Battalion"* was made up of expedition members during the Mexican War.
>
> Became wealthy during the California Gold Rush of 1849.
>
> Given command of the Department of the West in July of 1866.
>
> His administration was found to be corrupt, reckless, and dangerously flamboyant.
>
> A total failure in the 1862 Shenandoah Valley Campaign.
>
> Relieved of command when he refused to serve under General John Pope, an old adversary.
>
> President of the Memphis and El Paso Railroad (1865 to 1873). Went bankrupt during this period of time.
>
> Territorial Governor of Arizona from 1878 to 1883.

LITTLE KNOWN FACTS: He was the favorite candidate of the Radical Republicans to run against President Abraham Lincoln in 1864

> Withdrew from the race in September.

Puff Paste—
As Made by Mrs. Lomax

4 cups flour
1 cup soft butter

1 egg yolk, beaten
1/2 cup ice water

Put flour into a large wooden mixing bowl. Beat in 1 tbls of soft butter, custard-like beaten egg yolk, and ice water. Use large wooden spoon to mix this to a smooth, heavy, paste-dough. Flour pastry board. Mold dough into ball and lay it on board. Roll out as thin as possible. Always roll away from yourself with a quick, light action. Put rest of the soft butter in the center of sheet. Flatten it. Then fold the four corners of the dough well over it. Flour lightly and again roll out, this time more carefully than before, so as not to break the sheet. Should it give way, flour the broken spot and it will not stick to the rolling pin. When very thin, sprinkle lightly with flour, fold up, and again roll out. This should be done 4 times in all. Then tightly roll the dough up and set in a cool place (refrigerate) for 1 full hour.

After the cooling period, roll out dough for the last time. Cut into small tartlet shells. Bake these shells before they are filled. Bake in a very hot oven (450 degrees) for 6 minutes. Bake in slow oven (300 degrees) for 25 to 30 minutes. When lightly tanned, take from the oven. Brush over the still hot crust with a beaten egg. Let cool and fill with tartlet fillings.

NOTE: This delicate crust can be used for the tops of regular pies as well as tartlet shells. The bottom crust of pies is usually made of plainer pastry. But this can be used for both upper and lower piecrusts if desired.

288

Lunsford Lindsey Lomax (1835-1913)

HERITAGE: Born in Newport, Rhode Island.

RANK: General.

FOUGHT FOR: Confederacy.

RELIGION: Christian. Raised in "God-fearing family."

EDUCATION: West Point graduate – class of 1856. Previously attended schools in Richmond and Norfolk, Virginia.

CAREER HIGHLIGHTS & TIDBITS: Handsome young man with crystal, unexpressive eyes.
> Could easily be mistaken for a blind man.
> Often unnerved others with his stare.
> Spent time gaining military experience on the Western frontier as an Indian fighter.
> Father was already an army officer from Virginia when the Civil War started.
> Applied for and was given a commission as a captain in the Confederate Army.
> Highly thought of as a young military leader.
> Appointed Assistant Adjutant General to General Joseph S. Johnston
> He, along with General Johnston, later surrendered after the Carolina's Campaign.
> Became President of a small Virginia college at the end of the War.
> Served as commissioner of Gettysburg National Park.

SAW ACTION AT: The Wilderness, Petersburg, Gettysburg, Woodstock, and the Carolina's Campaign, etc.

LITTLE KNOWN FACTS: Helped compile the *Official Records* of the Gettysburg Campaign.
> Captured by Union Forces at Woodstock.
> Escaped and rejoined the Confederate Army.

Basic Pie Recipe—
Of Mrs. Hood

One-Crust Pie
1 1/2 cups sifted flour
3/4 tsp salt
1/2 cup shortening
3 to 4 tbls cold water

Two-Crust Pie
2 1/4 cups sifted flour
1 tsp salt
3/4 cup shortening
5 to 6 tbls cold water

Sift together flour and salt in wooden mixing bowl. Cut in shortening with two table knives until mixture resembles coarse corn meal. Sprinkle water, 1 tbls at a time, over small portions of the mixture with fork. Press flour particles together as they absorb water. *Do not stir.* Use only enough water to hold pastry together. Press all together lightly with your fingers. Chill at least 30 minutes before rolling.

To make pie shell: Form dough into ball on lightly floured pastry board. Roll lightly. Work always from the center out in all directions, into a circle about 1/8 inch thick and 2 inches larger in diameter than top of pie plate. Then fold in half. Carefully place in ungreased pie plate, having folded edge of pastry at center of plate. Unfold pastry. Fit loosely to plate. Trim pastry with scissors or knife. Leave about 1 inch of pastry over rim of pie plate. Fold edge under. Make a standing rim. If unbaked pie shell is called for in recipe, the shell is ready to be filled. If baked pie shell is called for, prick entire surface with a fork to remove air bubbles. Chill about 30 minutes. Bake in a very quick oven (450 degrees) about 15 minutes. Cool and fill.

To make a two-crust pie: Divide dough into two portions. Put slightly less than half into the ball to use for lower crust. Proceed to make shell as directed above. Trim pastry even with plate rim. Then fill unbaked pie shell. Moisten edge of crust with cold water. Then roll rest of pastry into circle 1/8-inch thick and 2 inches larger in diameter than top of pie plate. Fold circle in half. Make several slits with knife in center of fold to let steam escape from the pie during baking. Lay on filling with folded edge of pastry at center point of pie plate. Unfold and fit evenly over filling. Trim edges. Leave 1/2-inch overhang. Fold edge of upper crust under lower crust. Press edges together. Bake as directed in pie recipe.

To make tart shells: Roll pastry to 1/8-inch thickness. Cut into rounds with floured cutter or upside down drinking glass. Fit pastry circles over backs of 12 ungreased 3-inch muffing pans. Trim to fit. Prick well with fork. Bake, pastry side up at 425 degrees about 15 minutes. Remove from oven and lift shells from pan.

John Bell Hood (1831-1879)

HERITAGE: Born and raised in Owensville, Kentucky.

RANK: General.

FOUGHT FOR: Confederacy.

RELIGION: Christian. Baptized into Episcopal Church by General Leonidas Polk.

EDUCATION: West Point graduate – class of 1853. Near the bottom of his class. 52nd in a class of 54.

CAREER HIGHLIGHTS & TIDBITS: Brigadier General when leading his "Texas Brigade" (March of 1862) at Gaine's Mill.
>Lost the use of an arm while fighting at Gettysburg.
>Leg amputated at the Battle of Chickamauga.
>So badly maimed was Hood that he thereafter rode into battle strapped to his horse with a special leather harness.
>An inspiration to his men throughout the Civil War.
>"Hood's Brigade" became famous and was the unit all others aspired to emulate.
>Died in bed with yellow fever, just after the terrible epidemic of 1878, and not on the battlefield as he would have chosen.

QUOTABLE QUOTE(S): On November 30, 1864 General Nathan Bedford Forrest said this: *"General Hood, if you were a whole man, I'd whip you within an inch of your life."*

SAW ACTION AT: Gaine's Mill, Second Bull Run, Antietam, Chickamauga, Fredericksburg, Gettysburg, Yorktown, Franklin, etc.

LITTLE KNOWN FACT: Confided in General Leonidas Polk that he wished to be baptized just before the Battle of Resaca. Polk, known as *"the Fighting Bishop"* performed the baptismal service. The crippled Hood leaned on his crutch while a horse bucket full of water was used by Polk as *"consecrated water."*

Sesame Pastry—
As Made by Mrs. Sherman

5 tbls olive oil	1 tbls lemon juice
2 tbls sugar	1 cup flour
1/4 tsp salt	1/4 tsp baking powder

Put 1/4 cup cold water into large wooden mixing bowl. Beat in olive oil, sugar, salt, and lemon juice. Sift flour and baking powder together. Now blend these with ingredients in the bowl. Work the mixture well until it forms smooth, pliable dough. Turn the dough out on lightly floured board. Roll out into 1/8-inch thick sheet. Cut neatly into 2-inch squares. Then prepare filling as follows:

1/4 cup almonds, chopped fine	1/4 cup coconut, toasted
1/4 cup sesame seeds	1/4 cup honey
	3 drops almond extract

Blend above ingredients in wooden mixing bowl. Put small ball of mixture in center of each pastry square. Fold squares over filling. Have 4 corners overlap in center to form triangle. Press firmly together to close. Brush each with beaten egg. Sprinkle lightly with sesame seeds. Place in shallow, buttered, baking pan. Bake in very slow oven (275 degrees) for about 20 minutes, or until golden brown. When done remove from the oven. Sprinkle with powdered sugar. Serve hot or cold.

NOTE: This recipe makes about 36 small pastries. It was one of Mrs. Sherman's very best concoctions.

William Tecumseh Sherman (1820-1891)

HERITAGE: Born in Lancaster, Ohio.
　　Son of Ohio Supreme Court Justice.

RANK: General.

FOUGHT FOR: Union.

RELIGION: Christian – brought up in Christian-centered family.　　Taught　to never doubt the infallibility of the *Bible.*

EDUCATION: West Point graduate – class of 1840.　6th in his class.
　　Attended a private academy as a boy.

CAREER HIGHLIGHTS & TIDBITS: His troops maimed, murdered, burned, and totally destroyed everything as they marched through Louisiana.
　　Innumerable atrocities (shooting unarmed civilians, raping women, etc.) were commonly committed by this man's soldiers.
　　In 1864 he declared, *"We cannot change the hearts of those people of the South, but we can make war so terrible, make them so sick of war, that generations would pass away before they would again appeal to it."*
　　"The mass of the people South will never trouble us again.　They have suffered terrifically, and now I feel disposed to befriend them."

QUOTABLE QUOTE: *"When I go through South Carolina it will become one of the most horrible things in the history of the world.　The devil himself couldn't restrain my men in that state."*

SAW ACTION AT: First Battle of Bull Run, Shiloh, Vicksburg, Chattanooga, Atlanta Campaign, The Carolina Campaign, etc.

LITTLE KNOWN FACTS: Despised throughout the South and referred to as *"that bastard!"*
　　Observed the destruction of Atlanta and the corpses of women and children in the streets and declared it to be *"a beautiful sight."*

Pie Shell—
As Made by Mrs. Pope

1 cup plus 2 tbls sifted flour

1/2 tsp salt

6 tbls lard

2 1/2 tbls cold water (about)

Sift flour once. Measure. Add salt. Sift together in bowl. Cut in 4 tbls shortening very thoroughly. Use light strokes of two knives. (Mixture should first become fluffy and fine like meal, and then start to clump together.)

Add remaining tbls of shortening in several pieces. Chop in lightly just until divided into pieces the size of large peas. Sprinkle in water, a small amount at a time. Mix mightily with blender or fork. When all particles are moistened, press pastry into a cake. Cover with damp cloth. Let stand 15 to 30 minutes. Roll out on lightly floured board to 1/8-inch thick. Fit loosely in 9-inch pie pan. Trim pastry 1 inch large than pan. Fold edge to form a standing rim. Flute with fingers. Prick pastry with fork. Prick all over and thoroughly around bottom curve of pan. Bake in hot oven (450 degrees) 10 to 12 minutes, or until slightly browned.

John Pope (1822-1892)

HERITAGE: Born in Louisville, Kentucky.

RANK: General.

FOUGHT FOR: Union.

RELIGION: Christian.

EDUCATION: West Point graduate – class of 1842.

CAREER HIGHLIGHTS & TIDBITS: Only Union commander who operated against the Army of Northern Virginia to gain the personal animosity of General Robert E. Lee.

> Served under Zachary Taylor in the Mexican War.
> Thoroughly outwitted and outfought by General Lee, Stonewall Jackson and James Longstreet in Second Battle of Bull Run.
> Retreated to Washington's defenses after disastrous Battle of Chantilly on September 1, 1862.
> A furious Lincoln cashiered him the very next day.
> Succeeded General McClellan as Senior Commander of the Virginia Theater of War in the summer of 1862.
> Alienated his troops when he questioned their courage under fire: *"I have come to you from the West, where we have always seen the backs of our enemies; from an army whose business it has been to seek the adversary and to beat him when he was found; whose policy has been attack and not defense."*

SAW ACTION AT: New Madrid, Missouri, Corinth, Second Bull Run, Battle of Chantilly, etc.

LITTLE KNOWN FACTS: His defeat at Second Bull Run ruined his military career.

> Blamed all of his misfortunes on subordinates.
> Could never take the responsibility for his failures.
> Believed General Fitz-John Porter, a loyalist of General McClellan, was to blame for his lack of success.

Pastry—
As Made by Mrs. Dahlgren

2 1/4 cups flour   1 1/2 tsp salt
3/4 cup lard   4 to 6 tbls cold water

Sift flour with salt. Cut in lard until mixture is granular. Sprinkle water over mixture. Blend lightly with fork. Add water sparingly until dough clings together but is not wet. Let stand 5 minutes before rolling. Makes two 9-inch crusts.

Baked pastry shells:

Roll pastry thin; place in pie pan or muffin pans. Trim 1/4 to 1/2 inch from edge. Double over edge of pastry and pinch with fingers to make an upright rim. Or shape pastry to outside of pans and trim close. Prick bottom and sides of pastry well with a fork to keep crust flat. Bake in very quick oven (450 degrees)

Ulrich Dahlgren (1842-1864)

HERITAGE: Son of an admiral in the Union Navy. Place of birth unknown.

RANK: Officer of unknown rank.

FOUGHT FOR: Union.

RELIGION: Christian.

EDUCATION: Unknown except that he was studying law when he joined the Union Army at beginning of the Civil War.

MARRIAGE: Unknown.

CHILDREN: Unknown.

CAREER HIGHLIGHTS & TIDBITS: Was General Franz Sigel's (1824-1902) Chief of Artillery during the Second Bull Run.
> Served on the staff of General George Meade
> Served on General Joseph Hooker's staff.
> Served on staff of General Ambrose Burnside.
> Was co-captain of the infamous Kilpatrick-Dahlgren raid.
> Killed on this raid near Richmond, Virginia in March of 1861.
> Incriminating papers found on his body described a planned assassination attempt on Jefferson Davis and his entire cabinet.
> Union leaders claimed these papers were a forgery.
> Current research suggests that the papers were authentic.

SAW ACTION AT: Second Bull Run, Gettysburg and Richmond as well as numerous other places.

LITTLE KNOWN FACTS: Severely wounded during the fighting at Gettysburg in July of 1863.
> Leg amputated.

Light Pastry—
Mrs. Farragut'sBest

1 cup flour

6 tbls shortening

1/2 tsp salt

3-4 tbls cold water

Stir flour and salt together in a wooden mixing bowl. Cut in shortening until the particles are the same size of small peas. Sprinkle cold water into flour mixture, 1 tbls at a time. Mix lightly with fork after each tbls until all flour is moistened. Mix dough with a fork until it sticks together and cleans the sides of bowl. Mixing beyond this point toughens pastry. Take pastry from the bowl, press into ball, and roll pastry out on lightly floured board.

David Glasgow Farragut (1801-1870)

HERITAGE: Born in Tennessee. Orphaned as youngster.

RANK: Admiral.

FOUGHT FOR: Union.

RELIGION: Christian (see quote below).

EDUCATION: Home schooled as a child by only the best of tutors.
Attended lectures at Yale while living in New Haven, Connecticut during the 1820's.
Attended lectures at the Smithsonian Institution while on a tour of duty in Washington, D.C.

CAREER HIGHLIGHTS & TIDBITS: First joined the Union Navy in 1810 when only nine years old.
Went to sea in 1811 on the frigate *U.S.S. Essex*.
Only 10 years old, he stayed under the watchful eye of his guardian, Commodore David Porter.
Porter gave this 12-year old midshipman his first shipboard command, a war prize captured in the Pacific Ocean.
Farragut sailed the vessel safely across the Pacific. Docked in Valparaiz, a Chilean seaport.
Served in the War of 1812 while 11 years old.
Became the Civil War's first admiral.
Destroyed the Confederate fleet in Mobile Bay on April 5, 1864.

QUOTABLE QUOTE: His son Lowell wrote this of his revered Christian father : *"He never felt so near his Master as he did in a storm, knowing that on his skill depended the safety of so many lives."*

LITTLE KNOWN FACT: Gideon Welles, Lincoln's Secretary of the Navy, had this to say: *"He would more willingly take great risks to obtain great results than any officer in either the Army or the Navy.*

Standard Golden Pastry—
As Made by Mrs. Benjamin

2 cups flour
1/4 tsp salt
1/2 cup shortening

1 egg, beaten
1 tbls vinegar
3 tbls cold water

Sift together flour and salt in wooden mixing bowl. Cut in shortening until the particles are the size of small peas. Blend beaten egg, vinegar, and water together. Sprinkle dry ingredients with this liquid mixture, a little at a time. Mix lightly until dough begins to stick together. When the mixture cleans the sides of the bowl, press pastry into a ball. You are ready to roll the pastry.

Double-crust pastries are usually filled and then baked according to specific direction of the filling recipe. Prior to baking, top curst may be brushed with milk or egg white for more even browning.

For a pre-baked single-crust pastry, prick the pastry with a fork to prevent puffing. Brush with milk or egg white if desired and bake in very quick oven (450 degrees) for 10 to 12 minutes.

The fillings for some single-crust pies such as egg custard and pecan are baked in the shell. This necessarily requires a longer cooking period than for pies prepared in pre-baked shells.

Judah Philip Benjamin (1811-1884)

HERITAGE: Foreign born to extremely poor Jewish parents.

POSITION: Confederate Statesman.

RELIGION: Jewish.

EDUCATION: Attended private academy in Charleston, South Carolina.
Attended Yale when 14 years old. Stayed for two years and then dropped out. Studied law on his own.

CAREER HIGHLIGHTS & TIDBITS: One of the strongest supporters of secession when Lincoln was elected President of the United States.
Became Secretary of War for the Confederate States of America in September 1861.
Attorney General under Jefferson Davis.
Blamed for the Confederacy's initial three defeats – Roanoke Island, Fort Henry, and Fort Donelson.
Lost favor when he remarked that Confederate soldiers were going shoeless because they traded for a bottle of whiskey.
Campaigned heavily in 1864 to educate slaves, draft them into the military and let them go into combat for the Confederacy.
Advocated that slaves who fought bravely were to be freed.
Never appeared to be concerned that he was the object of almost universal dislike among his peers.
Unsuccessful in running his sugar plantation.
Encountered financial difficulties, so he went into politics.
Served in the Louisiana legislature and the United States Senate.
Studied law in England for five months.
Admitted to the bar in 1866.

LITTLE KNOWN FACTS: Fled South with Confederate President Jefferson Davis at the end of the Civil War in 1865.
Deserted Presidential party in North Carolina and was able to escape to England.

Vinegar Pie?—
Yes! The Longstreet Family Enjoyed it Often

1 pastry shell, baked

3 egg yolks, beaten   2 cups water, boiling
1 cup sugar   1/4 cup vinegar
3 tbls flour   1 tsp lemon juice
1/3 tsp salt   3 egg whites

3 tbls sugar

Put egg yolks in wooden mixing bowl and beat until thick. Add sugar, flour, and salt. Mix thoroughly. Slowly add boiling water while stirring constantly. Stir in vinegar. Continue stirring mixture until thick and smooth. Lastly, stir in lemon juice. Pour into previously baked pastry shell. Set aside while beating egg whites and 3 tbls sugar in separate bowl until stiff. Cover pie with meringue. Bake in moderately slow oven (325 degrees) for 20 minutes.

James Longstreet (1821-1904)

HERITAGE: Born in South Carolina. Raised in Georgia and Alabama. Son of farmer.

RANK: General.

FOUGHT FOR: Confederacy.

RELIGION: Christian. Once said this: *"I am pleased to say I believe in God, the Father, and his only begotten Son, Jesus Christ, our Lord. It is my custom to read one or more chapters of my Bible daily for comfort, guidance, and instruction."*

MARRIAGE: Unknown.

EDUCATION: West Point graduate – class of 1842.
   Graduated near the bottom of his class.

CAREER HIGHLIGHTS TIDBITS: Considered by General Lee to be one of his most reliable commanders.
   Lee called him his *"Old War Horse"*.
   Seriously wounded at the Battle of the Wilderness in 1864.
   Unable to return to fighting for six months.
   Had earlier Fought in the Mexican War under Zachary Taylor.
   Was in charge of half of Lee's infantry in Summer of 1862.

QUOTABLE QUOTE: Once told his men: *"Throw your snowballs if you want to, as much as you please, but if one touches me, not a man in this brigade should have a furlough this winter. Remember that!"*

SAW ACTION AT: First Battle of Bull Run, Second Bull Run, Williamsburg, Seven Pines, Fredericksburg, Antietam, Manassas, Chickamauga, The Wilderness, Petersburg, Richmond, Knoxville, etc.

LITTLE KNOWN FACT: He and General Grant, and their wives, had developed a close, lasting friendship.
   They had served together at Jefferson barracks during the 1840's

14

Pies, Tarts, and Fillings
from Days Long Past

Coconut Pie—
As Made for the Mosby Family

¾ cup butter   2 tbls rosewater
1 1/2 cups sugar   2 1/2 cups coconut, grated
¼ cup white wine   1 tsp nutmeg
                5 egg whites, stiffly beaten

Cream butter and sugar in large wooden mixing bowl. When well blended, beat very light with wine and rosewater. Then add coconut and nutmeg with as little and as light stirring as possible. Finally fold in fluffy beaten egg whites with a few skillful strokes. Pour at once into open unbaked pie shells. Bake immediately in rather quick oven (400 degrees) for 25 to 30 minutes. Eat pies when cold with powdered sugar sifted over them.

John Singleton Mosby (1833-1916)

HERITAGE: Born and raised in Virginia.

RANK: Captain.

FOUGHT FOR: Confederacy.

RELIGION: Christian.

EDUCATION: Attended University of Virginia.
>Arrested and sailed for shooting another student.
>Released when it was discovered that the other student had "provoked him."
>Studied law while incarcerated and later became an attorney.

MARRIAGE: Unknown.

CAREER HIGHLIGHTS & TIDBITS: First volunteered as a private in the Confederate Army.
>So elusive was Mosby that he was referred to by General Grant as "The Gray Ghost."
>He firmly controlled the eastern part of Virginia.
>The area was called "Mosby's Confederacy."
>The spectacular and daring deeds of Mosby's Ranger's earned them an awesome reputation.

QUOTABLE QUOTE: *"Mosby has annoyed me considerably,"* despaired Union General Philip H. Sheridan.
>*"Hurrah for Mosby"* said General Robert E. Lee.

SAW ACTION AT: Many places – primarily took raids throughout Virginia with his band of "irregulars."

LITTLE KNOWN FACTS: After the Civil War ended, he became an attorney with the Department of Justice from 1904 to 1910.
>Several of Mosby's men were captured and hanged in Front Royal, Virginia, in September of 1864.

Pumpkin Pie
Mrs. Grant's Best

4 cups stewed pumpkin	1 tsp nutmeg
1 1/2 cups sugar	9 egg yolks, beaten
1 tsp mace	8 cups milk
1 tsp cinnamon	9 egg whites, beaten

or

4 cups stewed pumpkin	1 tsp cinnamon
1 cup sugar	7 egg yolks, beaten
1 tsp ginger	4 cups milk
1 tsp mace	7 egg whites, beaten

After you have stewed the pumpkin, press through a fine sieve. Blend in sugar and spices. Gradually stir in custard-like beaten egg whites. Pour into unbaked pie shells and bake without top crust in rather quick oven (450 degrees) for 10 minutes. Then reduce the heat in quick oven to moderate (350 degrees) and bake 20 to 25 minutes longer. Some people prefer to simply bake in rather quick oven (400 degrees) for 50 minutes. You can always tell if one of these pies is done by sticking a knife blade halfway between the middle and the outer edge. It should come out clean.

NOTE: Light brown sugar may be substituted for white sugar in either recipe. First recipe makes a superb culinary delight, but the second is also excellent. Squash may be used in place of pumpkin. In such cases, add 1 more egg for each pie made. These squash pies are really a taste treat.

Ulysses Simpson Grant (1822-1885)

HERITAGE: Born in Mt. Pleasant, Ohio. Father a tanner.

RANK: General.

FOUGHT FOR: Union.

RELIGION: Christian (see quote below).

EDUCATION: West Point graduate – class of 1843.
    Didn't especially stand out as a cadet.

MARRIAGE: Wed Julia Dent in 1848.

CAREER HIGHLIGHTS & TIDBITS: In 1865 Grant said this: *"Nations, like individuals, are punished for their transgressions. We got our punishment in the most sanguinary and expensive war of modern times."*
    An aide on Grant's staff, had this to offer about his commander: *"In the darkness of night, in the gloom of a tangled forest, after men's nerves had been racked by the strain of two day's desperate battle, the most immovable commander might have been shaken. But it was in just such emergencies that General Grant was always at his best."*

QUOTABLE QUOTE: *"I believe in the Holy Scriptures, and who lives by them will be benefited thereby. Men may differ as to the interpretation, which is human, but the Scriptures are man's best guide."*

SAW ACTION AT: Vicksburg, Missionary Ridge, Chattanooga, Shiloh, Petersburg, Fort Donelson, Fort Henry, The Wilderness, Spotsylvania, Five Forks, etc.

LITTLE KNOWN FACT: Was at one time a slave owner as were other Union military leaders including General Winfield Scot and General George Thomas. Even President Lincoln's wife came from a slaveholding family

Buttermilk Pie—
A Jeb Stuart Favorite

2/3 cup sugar
2 tbls flour
1/2 tbls butter, melted
1 cup buttermilk

1/8 tsp salt
4 tbls lemon juice
2 egg yolks, slightly beaten
2 egg whites

2 tbls sugar

Combine 2/3-cup sugar, flour, and melted butter in wooden mixing bowl and stir together. Add buttermilk, salt, lemon juice, and slightly beaten egg yolks. Blend thoroughly. Pour mixture into 8-inch pastry lined pie pan. Bake in quick oven (425 degrees) for about 40 minutes or until inserted knife blade comes out clean. When pie is finished, put two egg whites and 2 tablespoons sugar in a small bowl and beat until fluffy. Cover with this meringue and bake in moderately quick oven (325 degrees) for 20 minutes longer.

James Ewell Brown Stuart (1833-1864)

HERITAGE: Born on Laurel Hill Plantation, Patrick County, Virginia. Seventh of 10 children. Family was wealthy.

RANK: General.

FOUGHT FOR: Confederacy.

RELIGION: Christian. Quiet and not vocal about his religious beliefs. (see quote below)

EDUCATION: West Point graduate – class of 1854. He was 13th in a class of 46.
    Home-schooled as a child.

CAREER HIGHLIGHTS & TIDBITS: Never doubted that he was fighting for what he called the *"will of the Almighty."*
    Had a crush on General Lee's daughter.
    One of Lee's favorite cadets.
    Wanted to ask General Lee if he could *"court"* his daughter, but never did because a cadet simply did not ask the man in charge of West Point a question of this nature.
    Mortally wounded and his command defeated on May 11, 1864, during a fierce battle at Yellow Tavern, just north of Richmond.
    His death was a devastating blow to the Confederacy.
    A dashing young officer and brilliant military strategist.

QUOTABLE QUOTE: Stuart's last words before dying were: *"If it were God's will I should like to live longer and serve my country. If I must die, I should like to see my wife first, but if it is His will that I die now I am ready and willing to go if God and my country think that I have fulfilled by destiny and done my duty."*

SAW ACTION AT: Harper's Ferry, Bull Run, Chambersburg, Dumfries Raid, Chancellorsville, Gettysburg, Huddlesburg, etc.

LITTLE KNOWN FACT: His father-in-law was Virginia-born Union General Philip St. George Cooke, also a Cavalry leader.

Mince Pie
Eaten by the Early Family

1 1/2 pounds lean fresh beef	1 1/2 tbls cinnamon
1/2 pound beef suet, minced	1 1/2 tbls nutmeg
3 pounds apples, pared	1 1/2 tbls cloves
and chopped	3/4 tbls mace
9 cups raisins	3 quarts cider
4 cups currants	1 pint brandy

6 1/4 cups brown sugar

or

2 pounds lean fresh beef	2 tbls cinnamon
1 pound beef suet, minced	1 tbls nutmeg
5 pounds apples, pared	1 tbls cloves
and chopped	2 tbls mace
9 cups raisins	1 tbls allspice
4 cups currants	1 tbls salt
1 cup citron	1 cup golden sherry
6 1/4 cups brown sugar	1 pint brandy

This pie should be baked in very quick oven (450 degrees) for 10 minutes. Then reduce oven heat to moderate (350 degrees) and bake for 30 minutes longer. Some people prefer to simply bake it at 450 degrees for 35 minutes.

The meat used in either above recipe should be a good piece of lean beef. It is to be boiled the day before it is needed. The next day, when cold, chop meat, clean out all bits of gristle, and put in large wooden mixing bowl. Add finely minced raw suet and then apples. Then stir in various fruits, brown sugar, and spices in order given above. Lastly add liquids called for. Blend all these ingredients very thoroughly. Then cover bowl tightly and let mixture stand for 24 hours before making into pies.

Lay strips of pastry in a criss-cross pattern instead of using a top crust. Jubal Early had a weakness for mince pies of these types. His mother recommended not eating these pies at night before going to bed if you value your own sound slumber.

Jubal Anderson Early (1816-1894)

HERITAGE: Born in Franklin County, Virginia.

RANK: General.

FOUGHT FOR: Confederacy.

RELIGION: Christian. Always read passages from the *Bible* before going into battle.

EDUCATION: West Point graduate – class of 1837.

CAREER HIGHLIGHTS & TIDBITS: Was a nasty and bitter middle-age bachelor.

Nicknamed by his troops "old jubilee" as a sarcastic way of calling him a totally disliked, nasty, grouchy old man.

Had one of the finest military minds in the Confederate Army. Wounded during the fighting at Williamsburg.

Initially saw action in the Seminole War.

Led a cavalry force in an attempt to capture Washington for the Confederacy on July 9, 1864.

Union forces under General Wallace blocked his heroic efforts.

Relieved of his command after being routed by General Custer at Waynesboro in March of 1865.

Wrote his autobiography in 1912.

QUOTABLE QUOTE: He said of the Union Army in December of 1862: *"I not only wish them all dead, but I wish them all in Hell."*

SAW ACTION AT: First Bull Run, Peninsular Campaign, Second Bull Run, Williamsburg, Antietam, Fredericksburg, Cold Harbor, Chancellorsville, etc.

LITTLE KNOWN FACT: West Point classmates included General Joseph Hooker (Union), General John Sedgwick (Union), and General Braxton Bragg (confederacy).

Raspberry Cream Pie—
A Shaw Family Favorite

Raspberries to suit   Powdered sugar to suit

Line a pie pan with good crust. Put in a layer of fresh raspberries. Sprinkle with powdered sugar. Put in another layer of raspberries. Again sprinkle with powdered sugar. Continue doing this until pie shell is full. Cover with top crust, but do not pinch down edges. Bake immediately in quick oven (425 degrees) for 10 minutes. Then reduce oven heat to moderate (350 degrees) and bake 25 to 35 minutes longer. While pie is baking, start the following:

1/2 cup milk   2 egg whites
1/2 cup cream   1 tbls sugar
        1/2 tsp cornstarch wet in cold milk

Blend milk and cream in saucepan. Bring to boil. Then beat egg whites with sugar until stiff. Stir this into boiling milk and cream. Add cornstarch last to thicken. Boil three minutes. Take off stove and set aside to cool.

Remove pie from oven when done. Lift off top crust. When above mixture is cold, pour over raspberries in pie. Place top crust back on. Set pie aside to cool. Sprinkle sugar over the top crust before serving.

Robert Gould Shaw (1837-1863)

HERITAGE: Born and raised in Boston, Massachusetts.
   Son of prominent abolitionist family.

RANK: Captain in the 2nd Massachusetts.

FOUGHT FOR: Union.

RELIGION: Christian.

EDUCATION: Entered Harvard in 1856. Dropped out in 1859. No degree received.

CAREER HIGHLIGHTS & TIDBITS: A tall and handsome, debonair man.
   Extremely popular with the ladies in Boston society.
   Selected by Massachusetts Governor John Andrew for an important special assignment.
   He was to recruit free blacks from all over New England for a special regiment in the Union Army.
   Widely known as the 54th Massachusetts Colored Infantry.
   Left Boston to fight on May 28, 1863.
   First Battle on July 16, 1863 at James Island, South Carolina
   Held in contempt for leading "negro" troops into battle and for "championing their cause."
   He and around half of his black soldiers were killed along with other heavy Union losses.

LITTLE KNOWN FACTS: Confederate soldiers contemptuously tossed his body into a common grave with the bodies of dead black troops.
   His parents were pleased to hear this – they felt that is what their son would have wanted

Apple Custard Pie—
Made by Mrs. Butterfield

12 ripe tart apples	1 lemon, juice and grated rind
1 cup butter	nutmeg to suit
2 cups sugar	6 egg whites, beaten
6 egg yolks, beaten	

Pare, core, and finely grate apples. Set aside while you cream butter and sugar in a large wooden mixing bowl. Whip in custard-like beaten egg yolks, lemon juice, grated lemon rind, nutmeg, and grated apples. Lastly, stir in stiffly beaten egg whites. Stir these in very lightly. Pour into pie pans lined with unbaked crust. Cover top with crossbars of pastry dough. Bake in very quick oven (450 degrees) for 12 minutes. Then reduce heat to moderate (350 degrees). Bake for 25 to 30 minutes longer.

Daniel Butterfield (1831-1901)

HERITAGE: Born in New York.

RANK: General.

FOUGHT FOR: Union.

RELIGION: Christian.

EDUCATION: Unknown.

MARRIAGE: Unknown.

CHILDREN: Unknown.

CAREER HIGHLIGHTS & TIDBITS: Started out as a prominent New York merchant.
> Became a Brigadier General by September of 1861.
> Won the *Medal of Honor* for his heroism at Gaine's Mill.
> Chief of staff to General Joseph Hooker (1863-1864).
> Chief of Staff to General George Gordon Meade (1863-1864).
> Led a division in General Sherman's 1864 March to the Sea.
> Led the first Union regiment to reach Virginia.
> Served with distinction in the Eastern Theater.
> One of the most distinguished looking Generals in the war.
> Had extensive business interests at the end of the Civil War. Encompassed banks, railroads, and shipping endeavors.

SAW ACTION AT: Chancellorsville, Gettysburg, Missionary Ridge, The Atlanta Campaign, Mill CreekGap, New Hope Church, Pine Mountain, Resaca, etc.

LITTLE KNOWN FACTS: Composed the notes for the famous military *"Taps"* at age 31.
> It was written to be played at funerals and lights out.
> Written in 1862 at Virginia's most historic plantation – Berkeley.
> McClelland headquartered 140,000 of his men there at this time.

Lemon Pie—
A Stonewall Jackson Favorite

2 tbls butter   3 egg whites
3/4 cup sugar   3 tbls powdered sugar
3 egg yolks, beaten   rose water to suit
                1 lemon

Cream butter and sugar in large wooden mixing bowl. Blend in custard-like beaten egg yolks. Grate lemon rind and add it in. Then remove inner white rind from lemon. Quarter lemon and remove all seeds. Chop entire lemon up very fine. Stir this into mixture. Bake in an open unbaked pie shell. No top crust is needed. Bake in very quick oven (450 degrees) for 10 minutes. Then reduce oven heat to moderate (350 degrees) for 25 to 30 minutes longer.

Stonewall Jackson (1824-1863)

HERITAGE: Parents died in poverty when he was a child. Grew up as an orphan in Clarksburg, Virginia. Raised by uncle.

RANK: General.

FOUGHT FOR: Confederacy.

RELIGION: Christian – On his deathbed, he spoke to his wife: *"Please remember me in your prayers, but never forget to use the old petition, 'thy will be done'."*

EDUCATION: West Point graduate – class of 1846. Class included such future leaders as Confederate General A.P. Hill and Union General George McClellan.

MARRIAGE: First wife, Eleanor Jenkin, died (1854?). Remarried three years later to Mary Anna Morrison, daughter of a Presbyterian minister.

CAREER HIGHLIGHTS & TIDBITS: In September of 1862, Harper's Ferry surrendered to General Jackson. He stopped his horse in front of the 9th Vermont, removed his hat, and quietly said: *"Boys, don't feel bad. You couldn't help it. It was just as God willed it!"*

Colonel Sam Fulkerson of the 37th Virginia Infantry said this: *"Our men curse for the hard marching he makes them do, but still...have the most unbounded confidence in him. They say he can take them into harder places and get them out better than any other living man."*

QUOTABLE QUOTE: His final words before dying were: *"Let us cross over the river and rest in the shade of the trees."*

SAW ACTION AT: First Battle of Bull Run, Manassas, Shenandoah Valley Campaign, Front Royal, Kernstown, Winchester, Antietam, etc.

LITTLE KNOWN FACT: Commanded a cadet detachment that was present at the execution by hanging of John Brown

Chocolate Pie—
Mrs. Johnston's Best

1/2 pound baker's chocolate	4 egg whites, beaten
3 tbls milk	4 tbls sugar
1 tbls cornstarch, dissolved	1 tsp melted butter
in water	2 tbls vanilla
4 egg yolks, beaten	pinch of salt

1/2 tsp cinnamon

Grate chocolate into the milk and heat to boiling over the fire. Then add cornstarch and stir for 5 minutes until well thickened. Remove from the fire and pour into large wooden mixing bowl. While chocolate mixture is cooling, beat 2 egg whites with sugar until stiff. Then beat yolks to a custard-like consistency. · When chocolate is cold, stir in egg whites, yolks, melted butter, vanilla, salt, and cinnamon. Blend everything well and pour into unbaked pie shells. Bake immediately in a very quick oven (450 degrees) for 10 to 12 minutes. Then reduce oven heat to moderate (350 degrees) and bake for 20 to 30 minutes longer. When pies are done, cover with a meringue made by beating the other 2 egg whites with 2 tablespoons sugar and 1 teaspoon lemon juice. Continue beating until the meringue will stand-alone. Spread over the pie and place pie back in moderate oven (350 degrees) for 10 to 15 minutes or until the meringue is "set". Should the meringue brown too darkly, merely sift powdered sugar over it when cooled.

Albert Sidney Johnston (1803-1862)

HERITAGE: Born in Washington, Kentucky.

RANK: General.

FOUGHT FOR: Confederacy.

RELIGION: Christian. Attended Sunday school and church regularly as a child.

EDUCATION: West Point graduate – class of 1826.

CAREER HIGHLIGHTS & TIDBITS: Secretary of war for the Republic of Texas from 1838 to 1840.
Jefferson Davis once called him "the greatest soldier…then living."
Wounded in his leg at Shiloh on April 6, 1862, on the first day of the fighting.
Subsequently died from this injury.
His loss was called "irreparable" by Jefferson Davis.
Turned down offer by Lincoln to be General Winfield Scott's second-in-command.
Instead chose to become a full General in the Confederate cause.
Oversaw the retreat of Confederate forces from Nashville.

QUOTABLE QUOTE: *"I hoped and expected that I had others who would prove Generals, but I knew I had one, and that was Sidney Johnston,"* said Confederate President Jefferson Davis.

SAW ACTION AT: Shiloh.

LITTLE KNOWN FACT: Appointed to be the commander of the Texas Army. Resulted in a duel with another officer who believed that he should have been given the promotion instead of Johnston.

Custard Pie—
General Lee's Favorite

4 egg yolks   4 cups milk
4 tbls sugar   4 egg whites, beaten
vanilla to suit

Beat egg yolks with sugar until custard-like in consistency. Then blend with milk in large wooden mixing bowl. Add enough vanilla to suit personal taste. Then whip in egg whites, which should already have been beaten to a stiff froth. Mix well and pour into unbaked pie shells. Grate nutmeg over top and bake immediately in very quick oven (450 degrees) for 10 to 12 minutes. Then reduce the heat in oven to moderate (350 degrees) and bake for 25 to 30 minutes longer. Some people prefer to simply bake it at 400 degrees for 25 to 30 minutes.

Robert Edward Lee (1807-1870)

HERITAGE: Fourth son of Revolutionary War hero, Lighthouse Harry Lee. Born in Virginia, raised in Alexandria.

RANK: General.

FOUGHT FOR: Confederacy.

RELIGION: Christian – Professed to have a "personal relationship with the Lord Jesus Christ." Also see quote below.

EDUCATION: West Point graduate – class of 1829. Brilliant student – graduated second in his class.

MARRIAGE: Married Mary Anne Randolph Custis, great-granddaughter of Martha Dandridge Custis Washington.

CAREER HIGHLIGHTS & TIDBITS: Deeply religious man. No formal church affiliation. Didn't join Episcopal church until 1854.

One of two of the Civil War's greatest Christian Generals.
The other was Jonathan "Stonewall" Jackson.
Judged to be most promising officer when Civil War broke out. Offered field command of the Union Army by Lincoln. Rejected
Lincoln's offer. Resigned his military commission when Virginia seceded from the Union.
Prayed reverently before each battle asking only that the Lord's will be done. Never prayed for victory. After each victorious battle, God was given all the credit.

QUOTABLE QUOTE: *"God's will ought to be our aim and I am quite contented that His design should be accomplished and not mine."*

SAW ACTION AT: Seven Days Battles, Battle of Bull Run, Manassas, Antietam, Sharpsburg, Chancellorsville, Gettysburg, etc.

LITTLE KNOWN FACT: Indicted for treason in June of 1865 by U.S. Grand Jury in Norfolk, Virginia. Never brought to trial.

Mock Mincemeat Pie—
A Rhett Family Favorite

6 soda crackers, finely rolled
2 cups currants
1 cup brown sugar
1 1/2 cups melted butter
1 cup molasses
1/2 tbls cinnamon
1/2 tbls allspice

1 tsp nutmeg
1 tsp cloves
1 tsp salt
1 tsp black pepper
2 eggs, beaten light
2 cups cold water
1 cup sour cider

1/4 cup brandy

Blend the ingredients in order given above. This very old recipe is truly unique for it can fool the most avid mince pie eaters. It was often served during the summer months at my great-grandmother's boarding house. "Mince pie in the summer is a pleasant rarity." This was the remark of a hungry traveler as he passed his plate for a second generous triangle of pie. Mrs. Nelson smiled but said nothing until the guests had strolled out with their cigars. "I had to laugh," she remarked, "when they praised my 'mince pies.' They're better in summertime than the real thing." If anyone doubts the merits of this counterfeit mince pie, let them do as I did—try it!

This delightful pie is to be baked in very quick oven (450 degrees) for 10 minutes. Then reduce oven heat to moderate (350 degrees) and bake for 30 minutes longer. Some people prefer to simply bake it in rather quick oven (400 degrees) for 35 minutes.

Robert Barnwell Rhett (1800-1876)

HERITAGE: Born and raised in Beaufort, South Carolina. Family was aristocratic.

POSITION: Confederate politician, planter, lawyer.

RELIGION: Christian (see quote below).

EDUCATION: West Point graduate – class of 1837.

MARRIAGE: Unknown.

CHILDREN: Unknown.

CAREER HIGHLIGHTS & TIDBITS: Most often referred to as "The Father of Secession."
Drafted the South Carolina secession ordinance.
Slave owner.
Fire-eating secessionist.
Political views considered too extreme for the Confederate Presidency.
Jefferson Davis was instead selected.
Much animosity toward President Davis because of this fact.
Defeated in race for seat in the Confederate Congress.
Had previously worked tirelessly to get South Carolina to secede.
Chairman of the Committee that drafted the permanent *Confederate Constitution*.
Owner and editor of the *Charleston Mercury*.
Elected to Congress. Served 12 years from 1837 to 1849.
Served as U.S. Senator from 1850-1852.

QUOTABLE QUOTE: *"Jesus is Savior of all mankind. Need I explain further?"*

LITTLE KNOWN FACTS: Born as Robert Burnardo Smith.
Family changed their last name in 1837 from Smith to Rhett in order to honor a Revolutionary War ancestor

Open Rhubarb Pie—
Howell Cobb's Favorite

Skin rhubarb stalks with care. Cut into small pieces and put in saucepan with very little water. Stew slowly until soft. Sweeten while still hot. Do not cook sugar with fruit. It injures the flavor by making it taste like preserves. Have ready some freshly baked pie shells. Fill with hot rhubarb and they are ready to eat. You do not bake these pies after filling shell.

or

You may, after sweetening stewed rhubarb, stir in a lump of butter the size of a hickory nut for each pie. And also add in a well-beaten egg for each pie. Pour this blend into unbaked pastry shells, cover with crossbars of pastry, and immediately bake until lightly browned in very quick oven (450 degrees) for 12 minutes. Then reduce heat to moderate (350 degrees) and bake for 30 minutes longer. Some people prefer to simply bake it in rather quick oven (400 degrees) for 40 to 50 minutes.

Howell Cobb (1815-1868)

HERITAGE: Born on a plantation in Jefferson County, Georgia. Family wealthy and socially prominent.

RANK: General.

FOUGHT FOR: Confederacy.

RELIGION: Christian.

EDUCATION: Attended Franklin College, later to become the University of Georgia.

CAREER HIGHLIGHTS & TIDBITS: Became an ardent secessionist when Lincoln became President.

Had previously campaigned heavily to get Georgia not to secede and instead support the Union.

Chairmen of the Montgomery Convention of February of 1861. President of the Provisional Confederate Congress as well.

Organized the 16th Georgia unit for fighting in the Civil War.

Ultimately, had a distinguished military career despite not having any formal military training.

Governor of Georgia from 1851 to 1853.

Secretary of the Treasury under President James Buchanan from 1857 to 1860.

Strongly opposed the Radical Republican Reconstruction policies imposed on the Southern states after the Civil War.

SAW ACTION AT: Shiloh, Seven Pines, Seven Day's Battles, Second Bull Run, Antietam, etc.

LITTLE KNOWN FACT: His brother, an attorney and author, Thomas Reade Rootes Cobb (1823-1862) was killed during the fighting at Fredericksburg.

Apple Pie—
Benjamin Henry Grierson's Favorite

 Pare, core, and slice ripe, tart, winter apples. Line baking dish or pie pan with good crust. Put in layer of apples and sprinkle brown sugar thickly over them. Scatter half dozen whole cloves on this. Then lay on more apples, and so on, until entire pie shell is full. Cover with a top crust, pinch down edges and bake immediately in a very quick oven (450 degrees) for 15 minutes. Then reduce heat in oven to moderate (350 degrees) and bake for 30 minutes longer. Some people prefer to simply bake this pie in rather quick oven (400 degrees) for 50 minutes. Sift powdered sugar over the top before sending it to the table. Eat while hot or cold.

Benjamin Henry Grierson (1829-1911)

HERITAGE: Born and raised in Grennipin, Illinois.

RANK: General.

FOUGHT FOR: Union.

RELIGION: Christian.

MARRIAGE: Unknown.

CHILDREN: Unknown.

CAREER HIGHLIGHTS & TIDBITS: Despised horses, yet was made a major in the cavalry in 1861.
    A courageous, hard-riding cavalry officer.
    His brigade swept down from Mississippi to join with other Union units in Southern Louisiana.
    Virtually unopposed as most Confederate soldiers had been sent to fight in Tennessee.
    Became aide-de-camp to Union General Benjamin Prentiss.
    His cavalry became famous as Grierson's Brigade.
    His force of 1,700 men swept into Baton Rouge, Louisiana, on May 2, 1863.
    Rode for about 600 miles on this series of raids.
    Confiscated 1,000 horses and mules.
    Took 500 Confederate prisoners.
    Inflicted close to 100 casualties.
    Destroyed 50 miles of railroad lines.
    All of this at the cost of only 24 casualties from Grierson's Brigade.
    Later commanded the 10th Cavalry while fighting Indians on the Western frontier.

SAW ACTION AT: Vicksburg, several operations in Mississippi, Louisiana, and Tennessee, etc.

LITTLE KNOWN FACT: Was a music teacher in Illinois as a young man.

Molasses Pie—
As Made for the Forrest Family

3 egg yolks
1 1/2 cups molasses
2 tbls butter, melted
3/4 cup brown sugar
1/2 tsp nutmeg
1/2 cup cinnamon

1/2 tsp salt
1 tbls flour
1 tbls cornstarch
3 egg whites
1 cup pecans
sugar to suit

Put egg yolks in wooden mixing bowl and beat until thick. Stir in molasses and melted butter. Combine sugar, nutmeg, cinnamon, salt, flour, and cornstarch in separate bowl. Stir together and blend with first mixture. Set aside while egg whites are beaten until fluffy. Fold egg whites into previous mixture. Pour into pastry line pie pan. Bake in quick oven (425 degrees) for about 15 minutes. Take pie from oven and cover with generous layer of pecans. Sprinkle with sugar. Put back in oven and bake 15 minutes longer.

Nathan Bedford Forrest (1821-1877)

HERITAGE: Born in Tennessee. Father a blacksmith who settled on Tennessee frontier in 1806.

RANK: General.

FOUGHT FOR: Confederacy.

RELIGION: Christian. Raised in fundamental Christian home where the *Bible* was read nightly.

EDUCATION: Very little, if any, formal education.

MARRIAGE: Unknown.

CHILDREN: Unknown.

CAREER HIGHLIGHTS & TIDBITS: The most outstanding cavalry leader on either side of the Civil War.

Seriously wounded in 1862.

Recovered and went on to have a phenomenal military career.

Sometimes involved in controversy.

In April of 1864, according to some historians, his command participated in the infamous massacre of Negro troops at Fort Billow, Tennessee.

It is said they were killed while attempting to surrender.

Faced enemy fire more than 100 times.

Had from 27 to 39 horses shot out from under him.

QUOTABLE QUOTE: *"Follow Forest to the death if it costs 10,000 lives and breaks the [federal] treasury,"* exclaimed General Sherman. *"There will be no peace in Tennessee until Forrest is dead!"*

SAW ACTION AT: Fort Donelson; Murfreesboro; Chickamauga; Parker's Crossroad, Tennessee; Bryer's Crossroads; Tupelo; Selma; etc.

LITTLE KNOWN FACT: Once threatened General Bragg: *"You are a coward. I say to you that if ever you again interfere with me or cross my path again it will be at the point of your life."*

Appendix I

Food During the Civil War Period

Nothing is really much different today than it was to the housewife of the Civil War period regarding the variety of foods available to the average American family. It differed only in that there were none of what we know today as convenience foods – those little packages of cheese crackers, cream filled Twinkies and the huge assortment of candy bars found in every little local market. Nor could a family member rush down to a grocery store and pick up a few frozen dinners or a variety of canned fruits and vegetables. And they couldn't select a number of attractive packages of freeze-dried foods, take them home, simply add a little hot water and serve it to the family.

All of the foods enjoyed by people who lived during the Civil War were also available to the early Colonists. Oats were one of the first foods to be imported to New England on a British ship in 1602. Settlers in Plymouth began planting oats. They soon became a food staple on Colonial breakfast tables and for baking. Oats were also extensively used as cattle feed.

The first wheat was sown in 1611 Colonial Virginia. And in 1626, samples of wheat grown in the Dutch Colony at New Netherlands were exhibited in Holland. Wheat was ordered from England in 1629 to be used as seed. It is probable that wheat was sown in the Plymouth Colony prior to 1629, although there is no record of this. In 1718, the Western Company first introduced wheat into the valley of the Mississippi.

Most people today know little or nothing about the vast availability of food in the American Colonies. Almost everything our early American ancestors ate came from the land in which they lived. Colonists planted seeds they brought with them from England. Indians introduced the Colonists to:

potatoes	pumpkins
sweet potatoes	squash,
peanuts	wild rice

Indians also taught the settlers in the Colonies how to properly plant their gardens and grow their own crops. Every Colonist, with few exceptions, had their family garden where they raised:

sweet potatoes	onions
parsnips	rice
garlic	carrots
corn	turnips
potatoes	tomatoes

Tomatoes were known in the Colonies as *"love apples."* They were widely believed to be aphrodisiacs. Some Colonists were convinced tomatoes were poisonous and, therefore, quite dangerous to eat.

Sweet potatoes quickly became a popular favorite of the Colonists. They  were included in a great number of baking recipes. Here's an old one for **Sweet Potato Corn Bread** as made by Mary Leach. She became wife of Richard Dobbs Spaight, Sr. (1758-1802) of North Carolina, one of 39 men who signed the *Constitution*:

"2 sweet potatoes	*2 tsp cinnamon*
"2 sticks soft butter	*1 tsp baking soda*
"8 eggs, beaten	*2 cups cream*
"1 cup maple sugar	*4 cups cornmeal*

"Take a fork and prick holes in the sweet potatoes. Put them in the oven and bake at 350 degrees for about 45 minutes. Set aside to cool. When they are cooled, peel off the skin and throw it away. Put sweet potatoes in a large wooden mixing bowl and mash to a pulp. Stir in the butter. Beat the eggs thoroughly in a smaller bowl. Add brown sugar, cinnamon and baking soda and blend nicely. Stir this mixture into the mashed sweet potatoes. Lastly, add the cream and cornmeal. Stir until a smooth batter is obtained. Pour into two

*greased 9 x 9-inch baking pans. Bake in moderate oven (350 degrees)
for 50 minutes. The bread should be a golden brown when done."*

Incidentally, Margaret Brown, who became the wife of Thomas Stone (1743-1787), a Maryland signer of the *Declaration of Independence*, was a rather superstitious young woman. She believed, as many others in the Colonies did, that anything made with cornmeal should be eaten most often during the cold winter months. It was said to heat up the body. And she also would never fail to make a cross on top of her breads before slicing. This was to frighten Satan away from the family and keep him away from the home.

Fruit was readily available from local farms and orchards as well as from trees in the yards of the Colonists. Beacon Hill in Boston was the site of America's first apple orchard in 1625. Fruit trees were commonplace in the yards of Colonists, as were grape arbors. Wild berries were in abundance and easy to find. Therefore the Colonists had a nice supply of the following:

cherries	peaches
plums	pears
apples	apricots
cranberries	mulberries
strawberries	raspberries
gooseberries	huckleberries
blueberries	

A 1717 pamphlet, **"DISCOURSE CONCERNING THE DESIGN'D ESTABLISHMENT OF A NEW COLONY TO THE SOUTH OF CAROLINA IN THE MOST DELIGHTFUL COUNTRY OF THE UNIVERSE,"** had this to say about food in the Colonies:

> *"Vines, naturally flourishing upon the Hills, bear Grapes in most luxuriant Plenty. They have every Growth which we possess in England, and almost every Thing that England wants besides. The Orange and the Limon [lemon] thrive in the same common Orchard with the Apple, and the Pear-Tree, Plumbs [plums], Peaches, Apricots, and Nectarins [nectarines] Bear from Stones in three years growing."*

Domestic farm animals were raised on small farms and in the yards. These included sheep, pigs, cows and chickens. As a result, eggs, milk, cream and butter were plentiful and readily available for baking and the breakfast table. They, along with lard, quickly became household staples.

Butter made in the Colonies was always heavily salted. The woman of the house had to carefully rinse the salt from her butter before using it for baking.

Butter was sometimes in short supply in the Colonies. When the woman of the house wanted to bake and had no butter on hand, she simply substituted finely ground salt pork as her shortening. Amelia Simmons, in her 1796 **AMERICAN COOKERY,** told homemakers how to purchase butter as well as how it was to be stored. These pointers were long ago given to Amelia by Catherine Meade. Miss Meade became the wife of Thomas Fitzsimons (1741-1811), signer of the *Declaration of Independence* from Pennsylvania. Here is how Catherine's original instructions were worded:

"To have sweet butter in dog days, and thro' the vegetable seasons, send stone pots to honest, neat, and trusty dairy people, and procure it pack'd down in May, and let them be brought in the night, or cool rainy morning, covered with a clean cloth wet in cold water, and partake of no heat from the house, and set the pots in the coldest part of your cellar, or in the ice house. Some say that May butter thus preserved will go into the winter use, better than fall made butter."

Food, in some instances, was imported from England and the West Indies. Included were:

raisins......................pineapples
almonds.....................chocolate

In **REFRESHMENTS NOW AND THEN**, Patricia B. Mitchell offers this regarding chocolate in the Colonies:

"In the early 1700's, Rhode Island businessman Obadiah Brown established a 'chocklit' mill in which chocolate beans from the West Indies were ground. And in 1765 a chocolate factory financed by James Baker opened in Dorchester, Massachusetts. Thomas Jefferson praised 'the superiority of chocolate, both for health and nourishment.'"

A great variety of spices were also imported from the West Indies to add flavor to Colonial food preparations:

salt......................nutmeg
cinnamon (cassia).........pepper
marjoram..................mint
allspice ....caraway seeds
currants (raisins) ....mustard
coriander..................parsley
sassafras....................dill
mace.......................sage
thyme....................rosemary

Homemakers made their own vinegar. Liquid yeast and yeast cakes were made by the Colonists with grape leaves as well as potatoes. One method for making yeast from grape leaves was given to my Great-great grandmother, Huldah Radike Horton, by Hannah Jones. Hannah would afterwards become the wife of William Floyd (1734-1821) of New York, one of the 56 heroic men who signed the *Declaration of Independence.* Huldah used this yeast on a regular basis when making bread for her family. Here is how Hannah Floyd had carefully transcribed the "*receipt*" in her cooking ledger:

"Use eight or ten leaves for a quart of yeast; Boil them for ten minutes; Pour the hot liquor on the flour, the quantity of the latter being determined by whether the yeast is wanted thicke or thin; Use hop yeast to raise it to begin with, and afterwards that made of grape leaves. Dried leaves will be as good as fresh. If a dark film appears on the surface when rising, a little stirring will obviate it."

Following her fine yeast recipe, Mrs. Floyd then went on to offer this bit of information:

"Grape leaves make a yeast in some respects superior to hops, as the bread made from it rises sooner, and has not the peculiar taste which many object in that made from hops."

Since the Colonists didn't have refrigerators, root vegetables like potatoes and turnips were stored below ground in root cellars. Fruits were canned after making them into jams, jellies and apple butter. Cherries were often brandied.

Sugar and honey were available to the Colonists for use as a sweetener. In fact, a few short years after the American Revolution (in 1791), the first sugar refinery was opened in New Orleans, Louisiana. Prior to this, New England settlers initially imported all their sugar from Madeira and Holland. It was later imported it from the West Indies and Barbados.

According to Patricia Mitchell, this time in **PILGRIMS, PURITANS AND CAVALIERS**:

> *"The yellowish-looking sugar was formed in hard cone shapes up to two or three feet in length and weighing up to 55 pounds. The expensive cone, often packaged in blue paper, was covered with netting to keep flies away. Housewives sometimes strung smaller loaves from the ceiling in order to prevent animals and other pests from getting to them. A piece of tin was positioned on the string to prevent ants from climbing down from the ceiling."*

Mrs. Mitchell goes on to explain how Colonial homemakers used sugar:

> *"To use the sugar, chunks were knocked off with a hammer or cut with 'sugar snippers.' Next the homemaker had to pulverize the sugar by pounding it or grinding it with a mortar and pestle. Some women soaked the sugar in water to soften it. (The custom developed of suspending a sugarloaf over the tea table so that guests could bite off sugar to use to sweeten their tea!)."*

Maple trees were tapped to obtain sap. This sap was boiled down to make maple syrup and maple sugar. We owe the discovery of maple syrup to the American Indians. It is said that a squaw, short on water, boiled some sap instead and found the end result to be delightful.

Molasses was first imported in the late 1600s from the West Indies. It became a food staple in every home. The thick, dark liquid was poured over pancakes and eaten with other breakfast dishes. Molasses was also used for sweetening countless baking recipes including breads, cakes and cookies. And it didn't take long before it was being distilled to make rum for use as a flavoring agent in many baking recipes. Other drinks sometimes used to flavor a variety of baked goods in the Colonies were:

```
coffee...................beer
tea.....................ale
cyder (cider).........wine
```

Apparently, food never was in short supply in Colonial America. Read what George Percy had to say after he arrived in the Colonies in 1607. He recorded this observation:

"We found store of turkey nests and many egges. ... This countrey is a fruitful soile, bearing many goodly and fruitful trees as mulberries, cherries, walnuts and vines in great abundance."

Jamestown, Virginia, had America's first cow in 1611. **LEAH AND RACHEL** was a seventeenth century publication that told of the availability of meat and other foods in Colonial Virginia:

"Cattle and Hogs are every where, which yeeld beef, veal, milk, butter, cheese... These with the help of Orchards and Gardens...certainly cannot but be sufficient for a good diet... considering how plentifully they are."

Yes, apparently food *was not* in short supply in the Colonies, nor was it at the beginning of the War Between the States, the Civil War, or the War of Northern Aggression as it is commonly called by many unreconstructed Southerners. The problem of severe food shortages arose throughout the Confederacy when invading Union troops swarmed down from the Northern States. A "scorched earth" policy was undertaken by a little bantam rooster, General William Tecumseh Sherman. This military leader deliberately brought widespread starvation to the people of Georgia when he undertook his infamous *"March to the Sea."* He bragged to General Grant *"I can make Georgia Howl."* And his 60,000-man army then proceeded to do just that as they cut a devastating 60-mile swath of death and destruction across that State. His troops were ordered to burn or confiscate whatever food was found; steal all of the horses and cattle, and kill those animals they were unable to carry off. This was the official "scorched earth" policy carried out by Sherman. And this identical policy was also undertaken in other parts of the Confederacy by many other Union military leaders – and all with the consent of President Abraham Lincoln.

Appendix II

Old-Time Measurements and Today's Counterparts

Here's a list of old-time measurements used by homemakers as far back as the Colonial period and the ensuing War for American Independence. And later, a number of these same measurements were utilized in America during the Civil War, the War Between the States, or as it's commonly called by unreconstructed Southerners -- the War of Northern Aggression. The measurement used in the original writing of the recipe so many long years ago is first given. It is then followed by its modern day equivalent.

1 wineglass full = 4 tablespoonful; ½ gill; 2 ounces; ¼ cup.
4 wineglasses = 1 cup
1 gill = ½ cup or 8 tablespoonful
1 teacup = ¾ cup
2/3 teacup = ½ cup
1/3 teacup = ¼ cup
1 kitchen cup = 1 cup; 2 gills
1 coffee cup = 1 cup; 2 gills
1 tin cup = 1 cup; 2 gills
1 tumbler = 1 cup; ½ pint
1 gram =1/5 teaspoon
1 dram liquid = 1 teaspoon
1 dessert spoonful = 2 teaspoons
2 dessert spoonfuls = 1 tablespoon
1 saltspoonful = ¼ teaspoon; a pinch

4 saltspoonfuls = 1 teaspoon
Pinch of salt = 1/8 teaspoon
Handful salt or sugar = ¼ cup
Handful flour = ½ cup
Dash of pepper = 3 good shakes; 1/8 teaspoon
Lump of butter = 1 well rounded tablespoon
Butter the size of an egg = 2 tablespoons; ¼ cup; 2 ounces
Butter the size of a walnut = 1 tablespoon; 1 ounce
Pound of butter = 2 cups; 1 pint
Pound of flour (sifted) = 1 heaping quart; 4 heaping cups
Pound of graham flour = 4-1/2 cups
Pound of whole wheat flour = 4 cups
Pound of sugar = 2 cups; 1 pint
Pound of powdered sugar = 2-1/2 cups
Pound of milk = 2 cups; 1 pint
Pound of cornmeal (coarse) = 2-2/3 cups
              (fine) = 4 cups
Pound of ground suet = 4 cups
Pound of eggs = 8 large eggs (without shells);
           10 medium eggs (without shells)
           14 small eggs (without shells)
Quart of eggs = 16 large eggs (without shells)
          20 medium eggs (without shells)
          24 small eggs (without shells)
Cup of eggs =   4 large eggs
Pint of eggs =   2 cups;
          8 large eggs (without shells)
          10 medium eggs (without shells)
          12 small eggs (without shells)
I/2 pint eggs = 1 cup
          4 large eggs (without shells)
          5 medium eggs (without shells)
          6 small eggs (without shells)
4 old-fashioned teaspoonfuls = 1 modern tablespoon
40 drops of liquid = 1 old-fashioned teaspoonful
4 blades of mace =   1 teaspoon powdered mace

Oven Temperatures

Very Slow (275 degrees)……….. Moderately Quick (375 degrees)
Slow (300 degrees)……………... Rather Quick (400 to 425 degrees)
Moderately Slow (325 degrees)….Quick (425 degrees)
Moderate (350 degrees)…………. Very Quick (450 degrees)

Appendix III

About the Author

Robert W. Pelton has been writing and lecturing for more than 30 years on historical, biographical and other subjects. He has published hundreds of articles and numerous books.

Pelton has carefully mined hundreds of source for historical cooking and baking recipes from the early days of America. He has perused innumerable old cookbooks as well as yellowed and tattered handwritten receipt ledgers from both private and public archives and libraries. Through all this, he has been able to skillfully recreate these treasures of the past for use in kitchens of today.

Pelton speaks to groups all over the United States. Tom R. Murray offers this: "Mr. Pelton puts together rare combinations of intellectual energies as a writer and speaker that will captivate an audience."

Pelton may be contacted for convention speaking engagements or speaking before other groups at:

Freedom & Liberty Foundation
P.O. Box 12619
Knoxville, TN 37912-0619
Phone (toll free): 1-877-289-2665
Fax: 865-633-8398
E-mail: cookery@earthlink.net

Appendix IV

Historical Baking Recipe Notes

_____

_____

_____

_____

_____

_____

_____

_____

_____

_____

_____

Historical Baking Recipe Notes

_____

_____

_____

_____

_____

_____

_____

_____

_____

_____

_____

_____

Historical Baking Recipe Notes

_____
_____
_____
_____
_____
_____
_____
_____
_____
_____
_____
_____

Historical Baking Recipe Notes

_____

_____

_____

_____

_____

_____

_____

_____

_____

_____

_____

_____

INDEX

Another Title in the Pelton
Historical Cookbook Series

Civil War Period Cookery contains recipes favored by people who lived and loved and prayed during the period of the tragic War Between the States. Included are the favorite dishes of many men and women who fought for both the Union and the Confederacy. Here you will find such recipes as **Brown Sugar Cookies** eaten by General Ulysses S. Grant; a **Pork and Parsnip Stew** dish enjoyed by Medal of Honor winner, Mary Edwards Walker; and the **Molasses Pie** made by the mother of Nathan Bedford Forrest. Each unique historical recipe is followed by an enlightening biographical sketch. Profusely illustrated.

168 pp - 5-1/2 x 8-1/2 - $13.95 + $4.50 S&H
ISBN 0-7414-0971-2
Standard 40% Discount When Purchasing for Resale
Free Shipping on Orders of 20 or More Copies.

Available from Infinity Publishing, 1094 New DeHaven Street,
Suite 100, West Conshohocken, PA 19428
Toll free: 1-877-289-2665

Another Title in the Pelton
Historical Cookbook Series

    Historical Christmas Cookery is a collection of recipes enjoyed by Christian signers of the *Declaration of Independence* and heroes of the *Revolutionary War*. Included are the favorite dishes of many Christian men and women who wore both the Blue and the Gray during the *War Between the States*. Here will be found the recipe for Benjamin Franklin's **Mashed Turnip and Potato** dish; those **Sour Cream Cookies** so eagerly eaten by the great Jefferson Davis; Patrick Henry's special **French Flannel Cakes**; and the **Boiled Custard** made for Lincoln by his step-mother when he was a boy.. All of these men were known to be devout Christians. Each unique historical recipe is followed by an enlightening biographical sketch. Profusely illustrated.

215 pages – 5-1/2 x 8-1/2 -- $15.95 + $4.50 S&H
ISBN 0-7414-1088-5
Standard 40% Discount When Purchasing for Resale
Free Shipping on Orders of 20 or More Copies.

Available from Infinity Publishing, 1094 New DeHaven Street,
Suite 100, West Conshohocken, PA 19428
Toll free: 1-877-289-2665

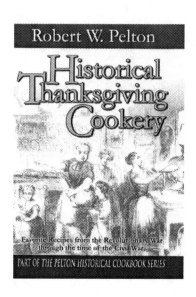

Another Title in the Pelton Historical Cookbook Series

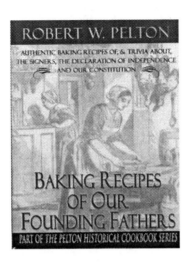

ROBERT W. PELTON

AUTHENTIC BAKING RECIPES OF, & TRIVIA ABOUT, THE SIGNERS, THE DECLARATION OF INDEPENDENCE AND OUR CONSTITUTION

BAKING RECIPES OF OUR FOUNDING FATHERS

PART OF THE PELTON HISTORICAL COOKBOOK SERIES

Baking Recipes of Our Founding Fathers is a collection of choice baked goodies enjoyed by all of the Signers of the *Declaration of Independence* and all of the Signers of our *Constitution*. It contains the favorite baking recipes from a number of the most heroic men in our glorious history. Included are recipes for those unusual yet tasty loaves of **Blood Bread** eaten by Alexander Hamilton; John Hancock's special **Currant-Walnut Loaf**; the **Custard-Crème Layer Cake** so often enjoyed by Samuel Adams; Benjamin Franklin's **Brandy Pound Cake** as it was made for him by his daughter, Sarah; and that **Sugarless Custard Corn Bread** as Martha Jefferson had it prepared for her husband, Thomas. An enlightening, attention-grabbing biographical sketch follows each recipe. Profusely illustrated.

280 pages -- 8 x 10-1/2 --$20.95 + $4.50 S&H
ISBN 0-7414-1053-4
**Standard 40% Discount when Purchasing for Resale
Free Shipping on Orders of 20 or More Copies.**

*Available from Infinity Publishing, 1094 New DeHaven Street, Suite 100, West Conshohocken, PA 19428
Toll free: 1-877-289-2665*

Printed in the United States
95285LV00008B/8/A